first edition

Developing Higher-Level Literacy in All Students

Building Reading, Reasoning, and Responding

Thomas G. Gunning

Professor Emeritus, Southern Connecticut State University
Adjunct Professor, Central Connecticut State University

PEARSON

Boston • New York • San Francisco
Mexico City • Montreal • Toronto • London • Madrid • Munich • Paris
Hong Kong • Singapore • Tokyo • Cape Town • Sydney

Executive Editor: Aurora Martínez Ramos
Editorial Assistant: Lynda Giles
Marketing Manager: Danae April
Production Editor: Paula Carroll
Editorial Production Service: Modern Graphics, Inc.
Composition Buyer: Linda Cox
Manufacturing Buyer: JoAnne Sweeney
Electronic Composition: Modern Graphics, Inc.
Cover Administrator: Elena Sidorova

For related titles and support materials, visit our online catalog at www.ablongman.com

Between the time website information is gathered and then published, it is not unusual for some sites to have closed. Also, the transcription of URLs can result in typographical errors. The publisher would appreciate notification where these errors occur so that they may be corrected in subsequent editions.

ISBN 10: 0-205-52220-3
ISBN 13: 978-0-205-52220-0

Library of Congress Cataloging-in-Publication Data

Gunning, Thomas G.
Developing higher-level literacy in all students : building reading, reasoning, and responding / Thomas G. Gunning.
   p. cm.
   Includes bibliographical references and index.
   ISBN 10: 0-205-52220-3
   ISBN 13: 978-0-205-52220-0
 1. Reading. 2. English language—Composition and exercises—Study and teaching.
 3. Critical thinking. I. Title.
LB1050.G82 2008
372.47'4—dc22

2007007667

Printed in the United States of America
10 9 8 7 6 5 4 3 2 1   11 10 09 08 07

*To my grandchildren, Alex and Paige Gunning
and Andrew Thomas and Timothy Jay Pizzuto,
and to all the students who assisted me by talking
to me about their literacy processes and
allowing me to test out ideas and materials.*

contents

chapter **4** *Using Strategies to Build Higher-Level*
Literacy Skills   **40**

chapter **10** *Using Writing to Improve Higher-Level Literacy Skills*   **159**

chapter **11** *Preparing Students for High-Stakes Tests*   **176** chapter **12** *Developing a Whole School Program*   *202*

While working as a consultant for a school that had just received a large grant to improve their literacy instruction, I assisted teachers as they implemented a new reading series. As part of the grant provision, teachers were required to assess students' progress on the end-of-theme (unit) tests that accompanied the reading series. In the past, students had been provided with activities that focused on lower-level skills. The tests accompanying the new literacy series included higher-level reading tasks. Despite doing fairly well in their oral discussions of stories, students were doing poorly on the end-of-theme tests. Based on an analysis of test results, observations, discussions with teachers, and working directly with students, I began constructing a program designed to develop higher-level thinking skills. I also visited other schools, talked to other consultants, and reviewed the research in this area. In addition, I examined students' performance on more than 200 released items from the National Assessment of Educational Progress (NAEP) in reading. This allowed me to validate on a national basis what I was seeing at the school where I was working. It also provided a broader picture of the problem. Based on my observations, talking with others, and analyzing the NAEP results, it is apparent that the majority of students in the United States have difficulty with higher-level reading and responding skills. In fact, this might be the most serious deficiency in the field of literacy.

The purpose of the text is to explore the problem and to suggest some practical solutions. Chapter 1 discusses in more detail the level of development of higher-level literacy skills in today's students as well as the demands of high-stakes tests. Chapter 2 provides a variety of suggestions for assessing and monitoring the development of higher-level literacy skills. Chapter 3 discusses general approaches for developing higher-level literacy; Chapters 4, 5, 6, and 7 explore approaches for developing specific strategies for developing higher-level literacy. Chapter 8 discusses approaches for integrating strategies. Chapter 9 explores the crucial role of talk in developing higher-level literacy and describes approaches that use talk to develop skills. Chapter 10 explains the key role that writing plays in developing higher-level reading, writing, reflecting, and responding. Chapter 11 discusses the difficulties that students have responding to higher-level items on high-stakes tasks and offers practical suggestions for building needed reading and responding strategies. Chapter 12 provides an example of an exemplary program and discusses components of a higher-level literacy program. Suggestions for assisting struggling readers and English language learners are also included.

This text is designed as a practical guide for classroom teachers. Teaching and assessment procedures are presented in step-by-step fashion so that teachers will have specific guidance in implementing them. Model lessons are included for key strategies and techniques. Model lessons are accompanied by practice sentences, paragraphs, and articles so that you will have the necessary materials for trying out lessons. Permission is granted to copy these materials for use with your students. The purpose of the lessons and accompanying practice materials is two-fold: to provide a concrete example of a technique and to provide you with the resources to try out the technique. Most lessons are written on third-grade or fourth-grade level so that they will be accessible to most students. If your students are reading beyond a third or fourth grade level, the lessons should still be appropriate. When introducing a comprehension strategy, it's best to do so with brief, easy materials so that students can focus on the strategy and not be hampered by difficulty with vocabulary or decoding. Of course, once they have grasped the skill, they should apply it to challenging material.

You may use the lessons as they are or adapt them. The practice lessons are starter lessons. You will need to provide additional lessons and additional reinforcement for virtually every strategy that you teach. As a rule of thumb, figure on 10 to 20 lessons for each key strategy.

Study Questions

You are encouraged to use this text as a vehicle for studying higher-level literacy. If possible, join with other professionals to form a study group. If that is not possible, you are urged to engage in self-study. Actually, if you can, do both. As you read each chapter, apply the information to your teaching situation. Ask yourself the following questions:

- What is the current status of my program in terms of the topic discussed?
- What's working?
- What's not working?
- What needs changing?
- What steps can I take to improve my program?

Specific study guide questions can be found at the end of each chapter. These questions embody information and suggestions contained in that chapter.

Although designed as a practical guide for teachers, the text can also be a resource for literacy coaches and administrators as they seek to improve the proficiencies of their students and help them meet the demands imposed by today's world and high-stakes tests.

Acknowledgments

I am indebted to Aurora Martínez Ramos, executive editor at Allyn and Bacon, whose suggestions encouraged me to reorganize and revise my original manuscript so that this text is far more practical and useful than it would have been. I am also grateful to Lynda Giles, editorial assistant at Allyn and Bacon, for her timely but gracious assistance. As always, I am indebted to Joan, my wife and lifelong best friend, for her encouragement and caring.

The following reviewers provided many perceptive comments and valuable suggestions: Polly Bill, Springer Middle School; Judith Goldbaum, Hanby Middle School; Susan Hampton, Virginia Middle School; and Sylvia Hoke, MacArthur (AR). They challenged me to reshape my original, highly theoretical manuscript into a more useful tool for teachers and other practitioners.

Higher-Level Literacy Skills Needed in Today's World and the World of the Future

Both in school and out, the level of literacy required for effective functioning has skyrocketed. The literal comprehension that earned passing grades in past years is no longer adequate. Today's reading programs present and assess a wide variety of basic and higher-level skills. Many of the high-stakes tests administered by the states include questions that ask students to summarize, make inferences, draw conclusions, compare texts, and identify and explain the impact of techniques used by writers, as well as assess the credibility of the piece. In the outside world students must cope with an unprecedented amount of information, the Internet being a case in point. Locating information on the Internet requires sophisticated search skills. It also requires the ability to assess the credibility of information and to synthesize information from a variety of sources. Speaking of today's literacy demands, a group of distinguished literacy and content area educators commented:

> In years past, literacy was limited to the ability to read and understand a simple document and write one's name on a contract. Literacy demands in today's workplace have accelerated. High school graduates are required to interpret a wide range of reference materials: journal articles, memoranda, and other documents that may contain technical information, including intricate charts and graphs. Increasingly, they are expected to judge the credibility of sources, evaluate arguments, develop and defend their own conclusions, and convey complex

information in ways that will either advance scholarship in a discipline or contribute to workplace productivity—skills well beyond the reach of poor readers. (International Reading Association, 2006, p. 1)

Status of Higher-Level Thinking Proficiency

Faced with basic literal questions, students in the United States do fairly well. In fact, our fourth graders rank with the five top nations in reading proficiency (Mullis, Martin, Gonzalez & Kennedy, 2003). However, when required to answer questions that tap higher-level thinking skills, students do poorly. A recent assessment of nearly 20,000 fifth graders provides insight into the comprehension of today's elementary school students. Overall, 97 percent of fifth graders were proficient in sentence comprehension, 87 percent in making literal inferences, and 70 percent in making and supporting inferences. However, only 44 percent were proficient in making connections or evaluating the author's craft. And just 7 percent were able to identify the author's purpose or give evidence for and against a position (Princiotta, Flanagan & Germino-Hausken, 2006). As the results indicate, fifth graders do well with lower-level comprehension, but performance falls when they are faced with higher-level tasks. Results from the NAEP reading assessment show a similar pattern for fourth and eighth graders (Perie, Grigg & Donahue, 2005). Weakness in higher-level thinking skills has implications beyond the classroom. For instance, what is your reaction upon reading the following excerpt from a popular website entitled *The Pacific Northwest Tree Octopus*?

> The Pacific Northwest tree octopus (Octopus paxarbolis) can be found in the temperate rainforests of the Olympic Peninsula on the west coast of North America. Their habitat lies on the Eastern side of the Olympic mountain range, adjacent to Hood Canal. These solitary cephalopods reach an average size (measured from arm-tip to mantle-tip) of 30–33 cm. Unlike most other cephalopods, tree octopuses are amphibious, spending only their early life and the period of their mating season in their ancestral aquatic environment. Because of the moistness of the rainforests and specialized skin adaptations, they are able to keep from becoming desiccated for prolonged periods of time, but given the chance they would prefer resting in pooled water. (Zapatopia, 2006)

Are you chuckling to yourself? Do you feel more than a little skeptical about the existence of an octopus that inhabits trees? When a class of seventh graders went to the site and read the article, all but one believed the information to be accurate (Leu, 2006). Most continued to believe in the existence of the tree octopus even after being informed that the site was a hoax. The incident dramatizes the importance of teaching higher-level thinking skills, in this case critical thinking. In a related study researchers determined that only 4 percent of middle school students reported always checking the accuracy of the information they read online at school (New Literacies Research Team, 2006). Only 2 percent of students always check the accuracy of the information they read online outside of school. In general, students failed to evaluate the accuracy or credibility of information provided on the Internet.

Tests Might Mask Abilities

On the other hand, it might be that higher-level tests students are taking sometimes mask rather than reveal their abilities. While working as a consultant in an urban school, I experienced what I would term an epiphany. I was observing a class during a test-taking session. Students were taking an end-of-theme test that was part of the newly purchased basal anthology reading program. The test assessed skills taught during the unit. One of the students began crying. She was one of the last to finish her end-of-theme test. When I asked her what was wrong, she replied, "I don't know how to do this." The question that puzzled her was a constructed query that asked, "Could this story have happened in real life the way it is told here?" (Valencia, 2001, p. 10). I asked her to read the question to see if maybe she didn't understand the question. She read it smoothly. Thinking that maybe she didn't understand the story or the story was written on too high a level for her, I asked her to read a few lines. She read those smoothly. I then talked to her about the story. The story, *Who Took the Farmer's Hat?* (Nodset, 1963), was about a farmer whose hat blew off. I asked her if that could happen in real life. She replied that it could. We then discussed the part in which the farmer asks the squirrel if he had seen his hat. The student said that couldn't happen because animals can't talk. She said that the story was a fantasy. I suggested that she write down what she had just explained. However, her answer stated, "The story couldn't happen in real life. It is a fantasy."

The discussion with the student suggested that her comprehension of the selection was adequate as was her reasoning about the selection. However, she apparently didn't understand the question or didn't realize that she knew the answer. Even after stating the answer, she had difficulty formulating a written response. She failed to state why the story was a fantasy. In retrospect, I should have asked her to explain why it was a fantasy so that she might realize that she needed to prove that it could not have happened in real life.

Interviews with other students revealed similar difficulties (Gunning, 2005b). Although some students did evidence faulty comprehension, many could respond orally but had difficulty composing a written response. Ironically, college freshmen evidence a similar problem. Calder and Carlson (2002) found that the oral responses of many of the middle-level students were superior to their written answers. They inferred that "for them, deep understandings seemed to evaporate when they tried to wrestle their thoughts to paper. This told us that we had work to do if we wanted to distinguish between assessing understanding and assessing students' ability to communicate their understanding" (p. 2).

Discussions with Students

In an attempt to probe students' thinking and responding processes, I also took part in discussions and teaching sessions with small groups of students. Although a few students had serious comprehension difficulties, in most instances, when students were given prompts and probes, they were able to respond correctly. The potential was there. It just hadn't been developed.

Overall, the students demonstrated an encouraging ability to read and comprehend on a higher level. However, it was obvious that to live up to their potential, they needed a systematic, high-intensity program designed to foster a fuller range of literacy skills, and that particular emphasis needed to be placed on higher-level skills.

Analysis of Literacy Programs

An examination of major literacy programs revealed that they do include a range of both basic and higher-level skills. However, the instructional and practice components are simply not sufficient, especially for students who are struggling. Teachers estimated that their students needed twice as many practice activities as were provided. However, teacher practices were also at fault. During classroom discussions, teacher questions tended to be low level. Even when higher-level questions were posed, teachers generally failed to supply prompts or other forms of support that would have assisted the learners to provide fuller or more accurate responses. There was a tendency to simply move onto the next student. In addition, discussions were teacher-to-student and rarely student-to-student. There was a very limited use of discussion groups. To get a broader, more complete look at students' thinking and responding skills, I analyzed several sets of completed comprehension tests. I also analyzed responses from NAEP and state-level tests, where these were available.

Analysis of Responses

An analysis of sample responses to more than 200 open-ended questions revealed that students had the most difficulty explaining why (Gunning, 2005b). They failed to provide reasons, causes, examples, and explanations. They failed to support opinions or didn't provide sufficient support. Asked to give three examples, they often gave one or two. They failed to make inferences. Asked to explain what kind of a person a character was, they described an action but did not infer a character trait based on that action. A number of responses were superficial. Asked to compare characters, they responded that both were girls but did not explain any personal traits. Often they responded with personal opinions or personal information not related to the text. They also used wrong information and misinterpreted details in the selections. However, most of the responses failed to receive full credit because the students didn't fully answer questions, provide necessary explanations, or give adequate support from the text. Again, as with the students in the schools in which I had worked, one gets the impression that frequently the answer is in the students' heads, but they have difficulty putting the information together and formulating an acceptable response. Given systematic instruction in effective reading, reasoning, and responding strategies, most students in grades three and above should be able to respond to higher-level literacy tasks.

Demands of Today's Proficiency Tests

Today's proficiency tests require higher-level skills as well as more basic ones. Recently the Florida Center for Reading Research (Torgesen, 2004) undertook a study to find out what kinds of reading, language, and cognitive skills were needed to pass the FCAT, the state's demanding proficiency test. The investigators concluded that

> We must also engage all students in deeply thoughtful interactions with print so that critical, inferential, and analytic skills continue to develop. . . . It's at least as much about building content knowledge, vocabulary, and thinking skills as it about helping children learn to read accurately and fluently. (p. 17)

The Nature of Higher-Level Thinking Skills

The first order of business in initiating a program of developing higher-level skills is to get a sense of the kinds of higher-level tasks students will be expected to perform. As a practical matter, with the emphasis on high-stakes tests, a starting point would be to look at the tests that students will be required to take. Although tests vary from state to state, many are modeled on the National Assessment of Educational Progress (NAEP).

NAEP Framework   In its current framework, NAEP assesses four aspects of reading: forming a general understanding, developing interpretation, making reader/text connections, and examining content and structure. These four aspects are assessed within three contexts or types of reading: literary text, informational text, and practical text. The NAEP framework is now being replaced. The 2009 framework will emphasize the cognitive demands made by reading (National Assessment Governing Board, 2005). The current framework will be replaced by one that encompasses three key cognitive skills: locate and recall, integrate and interpret, and critique and evaluate. This text will use the 2009 framework but will note features of the current framework. With its emphasis on cognitive demands made by reading tasks, the 2009 framework is easier to use as a basis for understanding the comprehension processes students are using or not using, and also to plan instruction (Salinger, Kamil, Kapinus & Afflerbach, 2005). Actually, there is a great deal of overlap between the two frameworks.

Cognitive Dimensions of Reading

Locate and Recall

The skill of locating and recalling consists of comprehending main ideas and details, and basic story elements, such as, setting, characters, and plot. Except for main ideas, it deals with literal, explicitly stated text. Summarizing and locating information are also included. Locating information, which is sometimes known as "lookbacks," entails going back over a selection to find supporting details or other information. Locate and Recall is similar to the current framework's Forming a General Understanding.

Integrate and Interpret

The skill of integrating and interpreting consists of establishing relationships among ideas. However, in many instances, some of those ideas will be outside the text. Integrate and Interpret typically requires elaboration. In an elaboration the reader makes a connection between the text and background knowledge. Integrate and Interpret includes inferring, asking questions, creating images, drawing a conclusion, and comparing and contrasting information or characters. Integrate and Interpret is similar to the current framework's Developing Interpretation. Most of the current framework's Reader/Text Connections fits into the Integrate and Interpret category.

Critique and Evaluate

The skill of critiquing and evaluating requires taking a critical look at the text and evaluating the fairness of the author's message or the literary quality of a selection. The reader looks at the author's craft and effectiveness of literacy devices. For informational text, logic, coherence, completeness, accuracy, objectivity, and credibility are considered. Critique and Evaluate includes what was traditionally known as "critical reading." When reading critically students go beyond merely forming an opinion. They construct an evaluation based on internal or external standards or both. Critique and Evaluate is similar to the current framework's Examining Content and Structure.

Other Strategies

Additional strategies include Preparing and Monitoring. These areas aren't usually directly assessed, but are an essential part of higher-level comprehension. Preparational strategies are all those things, such as previewing, activating background knowledge, and setting goals and purposes that the readers use to get ready to read a selection. (Readers also predict, but prediction, which is an inferential skill, is included under Integrate and Interpret.) Monitoring includes regulating one's reading according to the demands of the task, checking one's reading to make sure it makes sense, and repairing one's reading when it isn't making sense, by rereading, using illustrations, looking up words in the glossary, or taking other steps to construct an appropriate meaning. Monitoring is an integral part of all levels of comprehension. Key skills/strategies are listed in Table 1.1.

These skills are universal and should be taught regardless of the demands made by the specific tests that your students will be required to take. Students who have mastered the skills listed above should do well on virtually any reading test that they will be required to take. However, in your instruction and activities, include the wording of the questions and the format that students will be meeting on the high-stakes tests that they will be taking. Examine the standards or goals that are the basis for your literacy curriculum. If some of the key skills are missing, you might want to augment the goals or standards. If you don't have a set of goals, these skills might form the basis for formulating a series of goals or standards for your students.

Study Questions

- What are the key comprehension skills?
- Which of these skills are included in my literacy program?
- Which of these skills are not covered?
- What are the higher-level literacy demands being made upon my students?
- What skills/strategies might I need to include to meet the demands made upon my students?

Table 1.1 ● Key Skills/Strategies

Cognitive Dimension	Skills/Strategies	Supporting Skills
Preparing	Previewing	
	Activating prior knowledge	
	Setting purpose/goals	
Locate and Recall	Locating details	Locate supporting or other information.
	Determining main idea/supporting details	Use details to generate main idea.
		Support main idea by citing details.
	Summarizing	
Integrate and Interpret	Inferring/concluding	Generalize and draw conclusions based on facts, details, and examples.
		Support inferences & conclusions.
	Predicting	Base predictions on text & background. Support predictions.
	Imaging	
	Questioning	Learn to formulate questions.
	Comparing/contrasting	Select essential elements for comparisons.
	Connecting	Justify/explain connections.
Critique and Evaluate	Identifying author's purpose	
	Judging effectiveness of literary techniques	Support judgments.
	Distinguishing between facts & opinions	Support opinions based on information in the selection.
Monitoring	Regulating one's reading	Reflect on processes one uses.
	Checking to see that reading makes sense	Demand meaning from reading.
	Repairing reading by rereading etc.	Learn fix-up strategies.

Assessing Higher-Level Skills Development

A ssessment provides the information needed to plan an effective program of developing higher-level reading and responding skills. Suggested steps for assessing higher-level skills development include the following:

Step 1: Analyze the demands of tests that your students are required to take, and compare the demands of the tests with the skills and strategies that are taught. Add skills if necessary. Integrate the teaching of needed skills into your curriculum. Some states assess a dozen or more skills. That's too many to cover in a year's time. Set priorities. Decide on a half-dozen skills that you judge are most essential. Teach these thoroughly. To obtain maximum coverage for skills, set up a program for all the grades. If some skills have been taught in lower grades, you might only need to review them.

Step 2: Determine students' overall reading levels. Determining students' reading levels so a match can be made between the level of materials and the students' reading levels is absolutely essential. Although most high-stakes tests are written on grade level or above, all students should be taught and provided with practice materials that are on their instructional levels. There are two main reasons for this. If the material is so difficult that they can't understand it because there were too many missed words or too many unknown concepts, then they won't be able to apply higher-level thinking skills to the materials. Secondly, if the material is so difficult that they expend a large amount of mental capacity decoding the materials and perhaps constructing some basic understanding of it, there won't be enough mental capacity available for them to apply higher-level strategies (Meichenbaum & Biemiller, 1998). For struggling readers, it might be necessary to provide materials that are one or two or more levels below their grade level. Obviously, every effort will be made to bring students up to grade level, but the best way to do so will be to start where they are and head upwards. Students do best on comprehension tasks when they know at least 98 percent of the words (Daane, Campbell, Grigg, Goodman & Oranje, 2005).

To determine students' reading levels, use an individual placement test, such as an informal reading inventory or running record. If it is not feasible to administer an individual placement test, administer a group placement assessment. Group placement assessments include the Degrees of Reading Power (Touchstone Associates), STAR (Renaissance Learning), or the Scholastic Reading Inventory. You can create your own inventory by using passages from the DIBELS. The DIBELS <http://dibels .uoregon.edu/ > has graded passages beginning at mid-first grade and extending up to sixth grade. To use DIBELS as a placement assessment, administer it as you would an informal reading inventory. Select and have available articles from mid-first to sixth grade, which is the full range of the DIBELS. As students read orally, note their errors or miscues just as on an informal reading inventory. To assess comprehension, you will need to use a retelling or construct questions for the selections.

Step 3: Assess students' comprehension skills. In order to plan an effective program, you need to build on the skills that students already possess. You also need to develop skills that they lack. Students' comprehension skills might be assessed in a variety of ways. NAEP has available a number of passages and questions for grades four, eight, and twelve that have been released and that might be used to assess comprehension. Questions are presented in such a way that they can be omitted, re-arranged, or rewritten. Questions might also be added. Most states also have sample passages and questions that can be used for assessment purposes. In addition, there are a number of test prep programs. Passages from these might be used to assess students' comprehension. One of the more promising systems for assessing students' ability to handle high-stakes tests is 4Sight (Success for All Foundation). 4Sight is a benchmark assessment tool designed to help teachers predict students' reading achievement five times a year. 4Sight assessments are one-hour tests that have the same formats and coverage as state reading assessments. They yield overall scores that predict students' scores on state assessments and also provide scores on key subtests: interpreting text, drawing conclusions, determining purpose of text, and so on. The tests are accompanied by scoring rubrics.

Most reading programs have an assessment component. All of today's major basal/anthology programs provide end-of-unit or end-of-theme tests that assess higher-level skills. These tests are geared to the skills presented in the unit being tested, so not all essential skills are assessed at one time. However, students' responses to open-ended items provide a sense of how well they are able to construct answers.

Appendix A contains the Survey of Higher-Level Reading and Responding Skills. The purpose of the Survey is to gain insight into students' ability to apply key comprehension and response skills. The Survey is designed to show which elements of a skill the student has mastered and which are posing difficulties. For instance, students might be able to select the main idea when given four options but might not be able to construct a main idea statement. Students might be able to draw a conclusion but might have difficulty supporting it. Or a student might be able to provide an oral response but might have difficulty getting her thoughts down on paper. As you examine students' work, note what went well. Also note areas of need. Plan instruction to shore up the areas of need. As a result of being in a group that examined students' work, Franzen (Williams, 1999), a teacher in Chicago, examines students' work to see what is going well and what isn't. "I look at the kinds of mistakes my students make. I figure out where they went wrong, and I ask myself, 'What do I need to do differently so they get it?' "

Diagnostic Conversations

Paper and pencil tests are an efficient way to get an overall sense of students' comprehension abilities and needs. However, they don't provide insight into the processes that students are using. For this, a diagnostic conversation is needed. The anecdote about the second grader, who was crying because she didn't know what to do, is an example of a diagnostic conversation. An examination of that student's written response would have simply indicated that she was unable to respond. A teacher examining her answer would most likely have concluded that she hadn't understood the passage. However, a brief conversation revealed that she had the necessary comprehension skills but was having difficulty with the responding skills. Teaching the comprehension skills would not have resulted in an improvement in performance. What was needed was instruction in how to interpret the question, how to formulate an answer, and how to explain or support a response.

Think-Alouds

Think-alouds can be a part of a diagnostic conversation. In a think-aloud, students explain how they go about reading a passage, how they derive a main idea, how they draw a conclusion and use context clues for difficult words, or what steps they take when a passage is confusing. Think-alouds might be informal or formal. They frequently are one on one, but might involve a small group or a whole class. Asking a question such as "What do you do before you begin reading a passage?" "What was going on in your mind as you read?" "What led you to that conclusion" invites students to talk about their thinking and comprehending processes so that you can see what is going well and what needs teaching. Informal think-aloud questions can be asked as part of a small-group or whole-class discussion.

For a more systematic think-aloud, select a challenging passage of at least 200 words (Monti & Cicchetti, 1993). Select a passage that is on the student's

● ....

12

instructional level (95 to 98 percent word recognition and reasonable fluency). Mark off stopping sections. This might be at the end of a paragraph or section. Before students read, observe them to see what they do. Note if they preview the text. Also ask the before-reading prompt questions as in Table 2.1. At each stopping point, ask during-reading questions. At the end of the entire selection, ask the after-reading questions.

As students think aloud, record their responses. Note which of the following activities they engaged in:

- Previewed before reading
- Activated background knowledge
- Made predictions
- Revised predictions or conclusions based on new information
- Made inferences or drew conclusions
- Made judgments
- Visualized or created images
- Summarized or paraphrased
- Constructed questions
- Made connections
- Reasoned about reading
- Monitored for meaning
- Noted difficult words
- Reread difficult sections or confusing passages
- Used illustrations as an aid
- Used context or other decoding skills

Analyze student's responses. Note which strategies were used. Ask yourself: What strategies is the student using? How effectively is she using the strategies? Is she monitoring for meaning? Based on the student's performance, what kind of instruction would seem to be most beneficial?

If students have not previously engaged in thinking aloud, they may be reluctant to do so or may tell you what they think you want to know. To get students used to the idea, model the process. Tell them to take time every once in a while to think about what they are doing. This will get them used to noticing their thinking and, if done before you conduct a think-aloud, it should enhance the richness of the think-aloud.

Observation

During discussions of read-alouds and selections that students have read, note the quality of their responses. Probe responses, both those that are right on the money and those that are off the mark, to gain insight into students' thought processes. Ask follow-up

Table 2.1 ● Think-Aloud Prompts

Type of Prompt	Think-Aloud Prompt	Features to Note
Before reading (Note whether student engages in any prereading activities, such as surveying the text.)	What do you think this selection might be about? What makes you think so?	Does the student survey before reading? Does the student predict? Are predictions based on survey? Does the student activate background knowledge? What is the extent of the student's background knowledge?
During reading (Note whether student is apparently rereading portions or using text features such as illustrations.)	What was going on in your mind as you read the selection? What were you thinking about? What is this selection mainly about? Were there any parts that were hard to understand? What did you do when you came across parts that were hard to understand? Were there any hard words? What did you do when you came across hard words? What do you think will happen next in the section? What makes you think so?	Does the student ask questions? Does the student use imaging? Does the student paraphrase or summarize? Does the student make inferences? Does the student evaluate or judge the information? Does the student use text features, such as headings and illustrations? Does the student reread or use other fix-up strategies when a passage is puzzling? Does the student make ongoing predictions?
After reading	What was this selection mainly about?	Does the student include most of the main points in the summary? The student should be able to include 60 to 70% of the main ideas in the summary. If the summary is incomplete, you can encourage the student to tell you more.
Connections	How does the information in this passage fit in with what you already know? Is there anything in this passage that made you think of something that you read about or heard about? Is there anything in this passage that reminds you of something that has happened in your life?	Does the student make connections?

questions, such as "What makes you say that?" or "What led you to that conclusion?" or "How did you figure that out?" If appropriate, prompt to see if the student is able to use lookbacks as a strategy. "What might you do to help you answer that question? Can you go back over the story?" Prompts should be tailored to fit the questions being asked and the students' needs. Note the number of prompts that are required in order to help students provide a fuller response or a more accurate one. Students who require one or two surface prompts might need just a little review. Those who need a series of extensive prompts might need intensive instruction. Be particularly observant of the ways in which students respond to higher-level questions. "Those discussions and responses permit teachers to observe readers' thinking habits and skills, the extent of their background knowledge, and the ways that they use that background when they read. They enable teachers to identify obstacles to clearer and more sophisticated thinking, and ultimately make it possible to adjust instruction to meet the needs of students" (Applegate, Quinn & Applegate, 2006, pp. 48–49).

Note, too, the progress that students make as a result of instruction and practice. If all or most of the students fail to improve, then you need to examine the program. If one or two fail to improve, you need to seek the reasons for their difficulty. Perhaps, they need added instruction or practice or maybe the materials they are reading are on too high a level.

Using Rubrics

Rubrics are descriptive sets of guidelines used to assess the relative quality of a task or piece of work (note the rubrics in Appendix B). Rubrics are used to assess written pieces of work, open-ended questions, and even portfolios. However, rubrics can be used to assess virtually any learning task, including class presentations and quality of small-group discussions. Rubrics can serve a double function. If teachers use rubrics to check students' work, they are better able to detect areas of strength and weakness. Using the rubric, teachers are better able to build on students' strengths and remedy their deficiencies. Rubrics also provide students with a better idea of what they are being asked to do. And if rubrics are developed cooperatively with students, students gain a sense of ownership of the rubrics.

Monitoring Progress

The key steps to bringing about significant improvement in students' learning include emphasizing elements, such as systematic instruction in higher-level skills and reading challenging materials (ones that are substantial enough to boost students' learning), effective staff development, adequate implementation, and setting of goals (Joyce & Showers, 2002). Along with setting goals, decide how you will monitor students' progress toward meeting those goals. (If you don't have goals for higher-level literacy skills, consult the standards or goals issued by your state or local school district or school, or use the key skills listed on pages 6 to 8 as a starting point.).

Monitoring progress and providing feedback and corrective instruction, if necessary, are essential. Students need to know how they are doing. And if they are struggling, they need a helping hand. As the teacher, you need to know if students are making progress and whether they need more instruction or more practice or both. Higher-level literacy skills are complex and so are difficult to assess. Informal methods of monitoring, such as observation and discussion, are helpful, as are samples of students' work, and paper and pencil tests of the type provided by reading programs. However, you may also find it helpful to construct tests in which you assess the skills that you have targeted. Since some skills, such as summarizing, are continuously developing, you may want to assess them on a continuous basis. Assessments might be cumulative. Assess key skills previously taught as well as skills currently being taught.

A number of other assessments can be used to monitor comprehension. Informal reading inventories, running records, the Development Reading Assessment, all of which are individual tests, might be administered periodically. A number of group tests can be administered multiple times. These include Degrees of Reading Power (DRP), STAR (Renaissance Learning), Scholastic Reading Inventory, and Mazes (aimsweb.com). All of these use modified cloze, which requires filling in the blanks when given a choice of words. The Scholastic Reading Inventory and DRP are paper-and-pencil tests. However, a computerized version of the DRP is also available. Star and Mazes are computerized. Other computerized assessment that might be used for continuous monitoring include:

- **easyCBM.com.** easyCBM.com, which has been created by the Center for Educational Assessment Accountability at the University of Oregon, has 20 passages each at grades two, three, and four. Passage comprehension is assessed with 20 multiple-choice questions. easyCBM.com is free. The assessment is administered and marked online. One disadvantage is that students must scroll through the test's passages to read them. This means that it is more difficult to look back at the passages.
- **Measures of Academic Progress (MAP).** The MAP tests consist of sentences or brief paragraphs and have a multiple-choice format. They can be given in grades 2 through 10 and can be administered four times a year to monitor progress. MAP tests, which are used as Idaho's high-stakes test, also can be used to indicate a student's reading level. MAP and STAR are adaptive tests. Based on the students' responses, these tests adapt. If a student is getting all the

questions correct, then he is moved up to a higher level. If the student is getting all or most of the items wrong, the test moves to a lower level.

To set up a monitoring system, plan backwards. Based on students' current command of higher-level skills and your program's goals or standards, decide what students should know and be able to do at the end of the year. If you are planning for a fifth-grade class, picture in your mind what you want your fifth graders to know and to be able to do when they enter sixth grade. This should, of course, include school and district standards or goals, but should also include your vision for your students. In backwards planning, you start with the end-of-year goals and then plan whatever activities and instruction might be needed to reach the goals. As part of your monitoring plan, decide where students need to be at certain points during the year so that they will reach the goals that have been set. You might administer a progress monitoring assessment four times a year, every six weeks, or monthly. A sample monitoring chart is presented in Table 2.2.

As they read and write, students use multiple strategies. As a practical matter, as you teach strategies, you might want to focus on one strategy. However, also review strategies previously taught and provide students with opportunities to apply multiple strategies.

Study Group Questions

- What is my plan for assessing my students' reading levels and higher-level literacy?
- What are my students' placement (reading) levels?
- What skills are my students required to know? What skills are assessed on tests they are required to take?
- Based on the administration of the Survey of Higher-Level Reading and Responding Skills or other assessment measures, what are my students' strengths and weakness?
- What skills do they need to be taught? What is my yearlong plan for teaching and monitoring these skills?

Table 2.2 ● Comprehension Progress Monitoring Chart

Percent Correct							
100							
90							
80							
70							
60							
50							
40							
30							
20							
10							
0							
Skill Focus	Preparing/ Monitoring Predicting/ Connecting	Main Idea/ Details	Inferring/ Concluding	Comparing/ Contrasting	Imaging	Evaluating/ Critiquing	Integrating

chapter 3

General Approaches for Developing Higher-Level Literacy

Fostering higher-level thinking skills means making thinking skills the foundation of the curriculum and an integral part of the school's environment. Although it is essential to teach higher-level thinking skills systematically and in depth, there are a number of general activities that will build higher-level skills. These include creating a culture of understanding, developing higher-level talk, developing the language of thinking, using read-alouds and listening, using graphic organizers, encouraging wide reading, building background, maximizing academic learning time, teaching students to think about thinking, and differentiating instruction, especially in terms of matching materials and instruction with achievement and ability. These elements should pervade any curriculum but especially one that seeks to raise the level of students' thinking.

Creating a Culture of Understanding

The first step in developing higher-level skills is to create a culture of comprehension. This should begin in prekindergarten or kindergarten and continue right through twelfth grade. In a culture of understanding, the teacher stresses that understanding is key (Collins, K., 2005). Teachers make sure that everyone understands everything that is going on in the classroom. Teachers take pains to make sure directions and instruction are clear. They also teach students to seek understanding. Students are taught that if they don't understand directions, they should seek help. Students are instructed to demand meaning from what they read and hear.

Understanding becomes part of the community's routines. Students learn to speak, listen, and write in such a way that understanding is fostered. Students get in the habit of asking for clarification or asking to have instructions or explanations repeated. During instruction, you might stop periodically and ask students to give you a thumbs-up if everything is clear or a thumbs-down if it is not. This helps the children who are too shy or too polite to ask for clarification or added explanation. When universal understanding is the foundation, improved thinking and communication are sure to follow.

As part of fostering understanding, make sure students experience what it feels like to read a selection with comprehension. If below-level readers are constantly reading text that is a bit too difficult or even far too hard, they might not know what it feels like to understand a selection. Novice readers might be so involved in decoding words that that don't realize that they should be seeking meaning. Model how you feel when you are understanding (Collins, 2004).

If students are falling behind, provide opportunities for them to catch up. Also teach students to be advocates for their learning. This means knowing how to seek help when confusion reigns. For English-language learners (ELL), it means teaching them how to ask to have directions repeated or requesting that a speaker talk more slowly.

Developing Higher-Level Talk

In their study of exemplary teachers, researchers discovered that a key characteristic was the nature of their classroom talk (Allington, Johnston & Day, 2002). Teachers talked to their students on a personal level to find out about their interests, their activities, and their concerns. In their instructional talk, they encouraged students to go beyond the surface and to think deeply about topics. Results of the teachers' talks were significant. The teachers "produced students who demonstrated dramatic improvements in their literate conversations, evidence of internalizing the thinking that was routinely demonstrated" (p. 465). "Much, if not most, of the learning was fostered by the routine engagement in powerful classroom conversations" (p. 466).

Developing the Language of Thinking

Along with general language development, build the language of thinking. The language of thinking simply specifies in a precise way what kinds of cognitive activities or operations are to be carried out. Instead of asking students to think carefully before responding to the question: "What kind of a person is the main character? Explain your answer," ask them to analyze the main character's actions, and based on her actions, make a judgment about the main character. Instead of asking students to "think carefully," specify the kind of thinking that you want them to do. As Costa and Marzano (2001) admonish, thinking covers a variety of processes. Ask students to compare, contrast, analyze, infer, predict, or engage in whatever other thinking process is appropriate (see Table 3.1). Also demonstrate the process; show how you would compare, contrast, or predict, and so forth. Think aloud as you demonstrate the process, so that students gain insight into cognitive processes. A primary advantage of using the language of thinking is that it replaces vague language.

Using the language of thinking takes some practice—old speech habits die hard—but takes no more time. In fact, because more precise language is being used, there is probably a saving of time. The language of thinking can and should be used in all content areas and also in classroom management. Teaching the language of thinking is not another add-on topic.

Using Thinking and Language to Develop Self-Management Skills

Developing self-management skills can be an occasion for fostering thinking. Instead of telling students what behavior to cease or avoid, help them to analyze the situation and decide how to correct it. Use questions that encourage appropriate behavior (Costa & Marzano, 2001). Instead of telling Sean to put his baseball cards away, say, "Sean, you seem to be distracted by your baseball cards. What can you do so that you won't be distracted by them and you'll get your work done?" Instead of saying, "Class, be quiet," say, "It's so noisy that a number of students can't hear what is being said. What do we need to do about that? What rule do we need to follow?" "When you forget to bring your pencils, it takes away from our learning time. What can we do about this?"

Much of the school day is taken up with giving directions. Use the occasion to provide instructions that teach students how to figure out what they should do (Costa & Marzano, 2001). "Center time will be over in two minutes. What do you need to do so that I know you did your center work? What do you need to do so that the center will be ready for the next group using it?"

The Role of Read-Alouds and Listening in Building Higher-Level Skills

Because it bypasses decoding skills, reading orally to students is an excellent way to build background as well as higher-level skills. Oral reading is an effective technique from preschool through high school. Through a preliminary discussion, dramatic reading, and on-the-spot explanation of difficult concepts or passages, text that

Table 3.1 ● Thinking Terms

Thinking Terms	Common Word or Phrase
analyze	think about
compare	tell how they are alike
contrast	tell how they are different
describe	tell about
define	tell what the word means
infer	read between the lines
conclude	think about and reach a decision
predict	guess
similar	almost the same
similarity	being almost the same or alike
summarize	tell about
support	prove

normally would be too difficult for students is made accessible. As part of the oral reading, you might introduce imaging in which students try to picture the main character, or you might call attention to the importance of setting, or you might stop periodically and demonstrate how you summarize a portion of the text before moving on. Or you might want to emphasize the author's use of alliteration or onomatopoeia. One word of caution: don't overdo it. If you stop too often, students will lose the thread of the story or explanation. Lengthy discussions should be delayed until after the selection has been read. However, if you wish to demonstrate a skill or concept, you might read aloud or share read a brief selection specifically selected for that purpose.

The Role of Graphic Organizers in Fostering Higher-Level Literacy

Visualization is a powerful but often neglected way of thinking. One way of visualizing information is through the use of graphic organizers. As Whitley (2005) comments, visual organizers are "a better representation of how we store knowledge in the brain" (p. 10). Graphic organizers help students separate what's important from what might be interesting but is not essential (Ellis, 2004). Because they highlight key information, graphic organizers also reduce processing demands, so that students can learn higher-level content and more easily use higher-level thinking skills (Ellis, 2004). Perhaps most important of all, constructing graphic organizers involves using a variety of key thinking strategies. As Ellis (2004) explains,

> What is important to understand is the powerful nature of all the processes that occur both *before* and *after* the information is put into the boxes. Before the information is put into boxes, students have to engage in powerful information processing and higher order thinking skills such as using cues to recognize important information, making decisions about what is important or essential, consolidating information and identifying main ideas and supporting details, making decisions about the best way to structure the informa-tion. . . . (p. 2)

After graphic organizers have been constructed, they can be used as the basis for discussing a piece of writing, and they can also used as study sheets. Students who use graphic organizers often improve their grade averages because they have processed information more systematically and they have highlighted the most important information. Graphic organizers also lend themselves to cooperative learning and discussion. Pairs or small groups can work together on a graphic organizer, especially one that has many parts.

Systematic Use of Graphic Organizers

Many schools introduce a common set of comprehension strategies and a common terminology for referring to strategies and prompting their use. However, except for using webs and Venn diagrams, many don't have an agreed-upon system for using graphic organizers. It is possible for students to encounter dozens of different organizers or the same organizers explained in slightly different ways. Presented below are Key Graphic Organizers, as adapted from Hyerle's (2001) Thinking Maps. The Key Graphic Organizers display major ways of organizing and thinking about information. The patterns of thinking and their accompanying organizers are presented in approximate order of complexity.

Descriptive Organization   This category includes highlighting key features and also classifying and categorizing. Key graphic organizers are webs and semantic maps as in Figures 3.1 and 3.2. The web simply presents descriptive features. The map is more complex because it classifies and categorizes. At the earliest levels, maps can be very basic and very simple. At more advanced levels, they can be expanded to include a number of features.

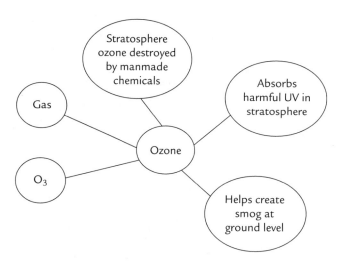

Figure 3.1 ● Descriptive Map: Ozone

Sequential Organization   Webs and maps are used for main idea-details or object-modifiers kinds of structures. For events that are in chronological order, use a timeline as in Figure 3.3 or sequence map as in Figure 3.4. A sequence map or timeline simply shows events in chronological order. (The sequence map in Figure 3.4 could have been constructed as a timeline.) The events in a sequence map occur after each other but not necessarily because of each other.

Process Organization   For steps in a process, use a process or chain map as in Figure 3.5. In a process or chain map, one step leads to the next and may depend upon the previous step. Note that the process map in Figure 3.5 has a cause-effect element. Chain or process maps incorporate relationships among steps that are not present in chronological maps or timelines. Chain or process maps help students see how each step is related to the next. Cyclical maps are a kind of process map used to show processes that are circular, such as the food chain or water cycle as in Figure 3.6.

Hierarchical Organizers   Hierarchical organizers show relationships between general and specific categories and display how broader categories subsume more narrow ones. Students must classify and categorize to create a hierarchical organizer. Hierarchical organizers are a cognitive step beyond simple maps because they show relationships among general and specific items. For a hierarchical organization, use a tree diagram as in Figure 3.7. A common example of a tree diagram is the family tree.

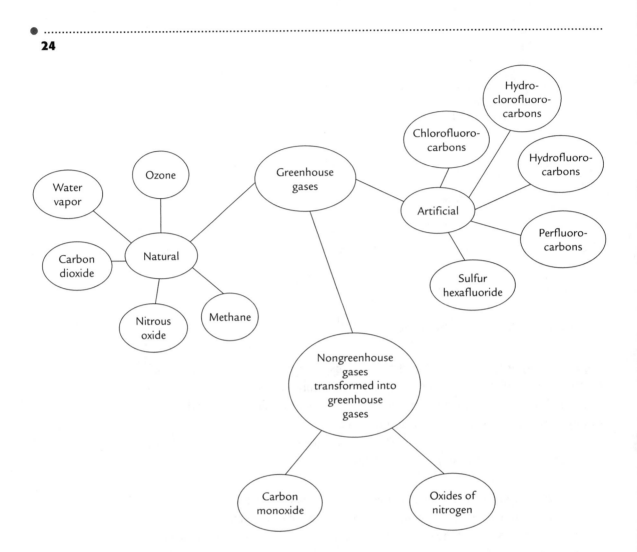

Figure 3.2 ● Classification Map: Greenhouse Gases

Comparing and Contrasting In comparing and contrasting, students are required to identify and organize similarities and differences. Venn diagrams are frequently used to display comparisons and contrasts. In a Venn diagram, two overlapping circles are drawn. Similarities are listed where the circles overlap. Differences are listed where there is no overlap as in Figure 3.8. Although relatively easy to construct, Venn diagrams have several shortcomings. Characteristics of items being compared are not grouped or categorized. Only two or three items can be compared. In most situations, a frame matrix or a compare-contrast map works better. A frame matrix map is recommended because it presents a side-by-side comparison and allows comparison of a virtually unlimited number of elements. A frame matrix has two components: a *frame*, which lists essential categories of information—such as location, area, population, average income—and the *matrix*. The matrix consists of the elements being compared. Two or more elements may be compared (see Table 3.2).

To construct a frame matrix, decide on the important categories of information for a topic. Then note how each category might be subdivided. Possible frame matrix elements for a chapter or a book on weather disasters might include "main characteristics," "causes," "damage," how they're forecast, "signs of," "protection

Highlights of Revolutionary War

1775	April 18	Paul Revere's Ride
1775	April 19	Lexington & Concord
1775	June 16	Bunker Hill
1776	July 4	Declaration of Independence
1776	July–August	Battle of New York
1776	December 26	Battle of Trenton
1777	January 3	Battle of Princeton
1777	September 10	Battle of Brandywine
1777	October 13	Battle of Saratoga
1777–1778	Winter	Valley Forge
1778	June 28	Battle of Monmouth
1779	September 23	*Bonne Homme Richard* vs. *Serapis*
1780	August 16	Battle of Camden
1781	January 17	Battle of Cowpens
1781	October 19	Battle of Yorktown

Figure 3.3 ● Time Line: Highlights of Revolutionary War

Figure 3.4 ● Sequence Map: Lewis & Clark Expedition

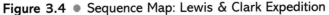

against," "examples of." A frame matrix helps students see relationships. Students can see at a glance what entities are being compared and what the major categories of information are. Making comparisons is facilitated because categories being compared are lined up side by side. A shortcoming of the frame matrix is that differences and similarities are not highlighted as well as they are in the Venn diagram.

To foster drawing conclusions about the elements displayed in a frame matrix, students might complete a column that asks them to supply a conclusion for each

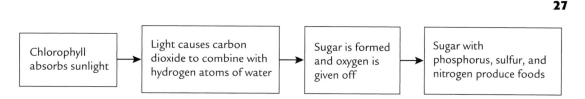

Figure 3.5 ● Process Map Photosynthesis

row as in Table 3.2 (Ellis, 2004). Students might also compose conclusions or summaries for other graphic organizers. This would give them the opportunity to interpret the information in the graphic organizers.

Cause-Effect   For cause-effect, use a cause-effect map, which can be expanded to indicate numerous causes as in Figure 3.9. It can also be used to show a chain of causes and effects.

Once students have a grasp of the fundamental graphic organizers, they can decide which one to use to organize their thinking. Being asked to decide upon the graphic organizer to be used gets students involved in reflecting on the pattern of the text and how this might be represented. It also gets them to use thinking-skill terminology, such as *comparing, contrasting, describing*. Having students fill in the blanks of prepared graphic organizers is easier for the students but fails to develop a flexible, in-depth application of thinking skills.

As a bonus, graphic organizers provide an excellent scaffold for English-language learners. Because graphic organizers require less language, they provide ELL with an opportunity to organize and demonstrate their learning.

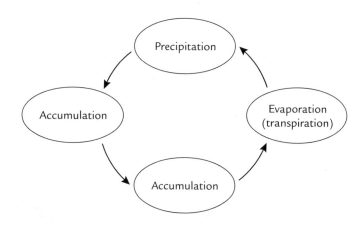

Figure 3.6 ● Cyclical Map: Water Cycle

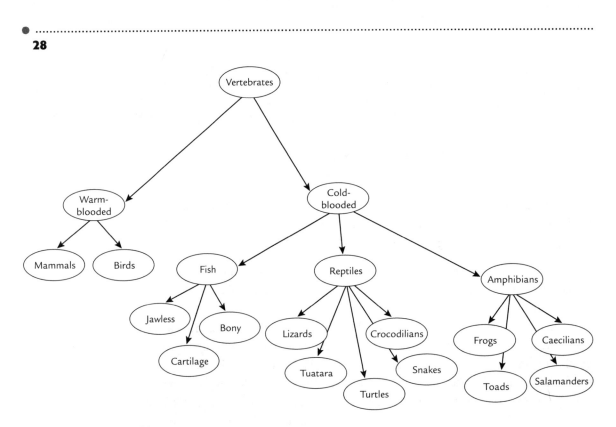

Figure 3.7 ● Tree Diagram

Using a Coherent System of Graphic Organizers

Whether using the graphic organizers recommended in this text or Hyerle's or another system, the important thing is to use a coherent system that everyone agrees upon so that the learning community is using a system that all understand and that is reinforced to the point that students can select and apply an organizer with relative ease. The design of the graphic organizers stays the same across grades and content area. However, the basic design can be expanded as needed.

Using Graphic Organizers to Foster Discussion and Writing

The graphic organizers may also be integrated with discussion. Using their graphic organizers, students can reflect on the cognitive processes they used to create them. Using a simple attributes map, one group of students observed and listed the main characteristics of granite and gneiss rocks (Hyerle, 2004). They then used a graphic organizer similar to a frame to compare and contrast granite and gneiss rocks. After

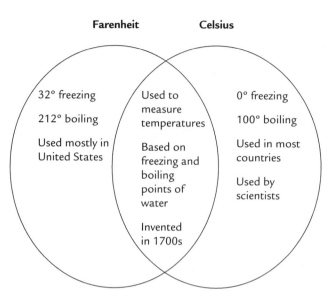

Farenheit | Celsius

32° freezing

212° boiling

Used mostly in United States

Used to measure temperatures

Based on freezing and boiling points of water

Invented in 1700s

0° freezing

100° boiling

Used in most countries

Used by scientists

Figure 3.8 ● Venn Diagram

studying all twelve kinds of rocks, students used a tree map to display the interrelations among the rocks.

Graphic organizers can also be used to help students develop writing skills. Students can be shown how to put their graphic organizers into a verbal explanation or to make a statement or draw a conclusion based on the information in the organizer. In a frame matrix, for example, a column asking for conclusions might be

Table 3.2 ● Frame Matrix: Largest Cities in the United States

	Location (state)	Population	Area (square miles)	Income per Person	Conclusion
New York	New York	8,104,079	303	40,899	Has the highest income. Is most crowded.
Los Angeles	California	3,845,541	469	33,347	Has the lowest income.
Chicago	Illinois	2,862,244	227	35,464	
Houston	Texas	2,012,626	579	34,578	Has the largest area. Is the least crowded.
Philadelphia	Pennsylvania	1,470,151	135	37,059	Has the smallest area.

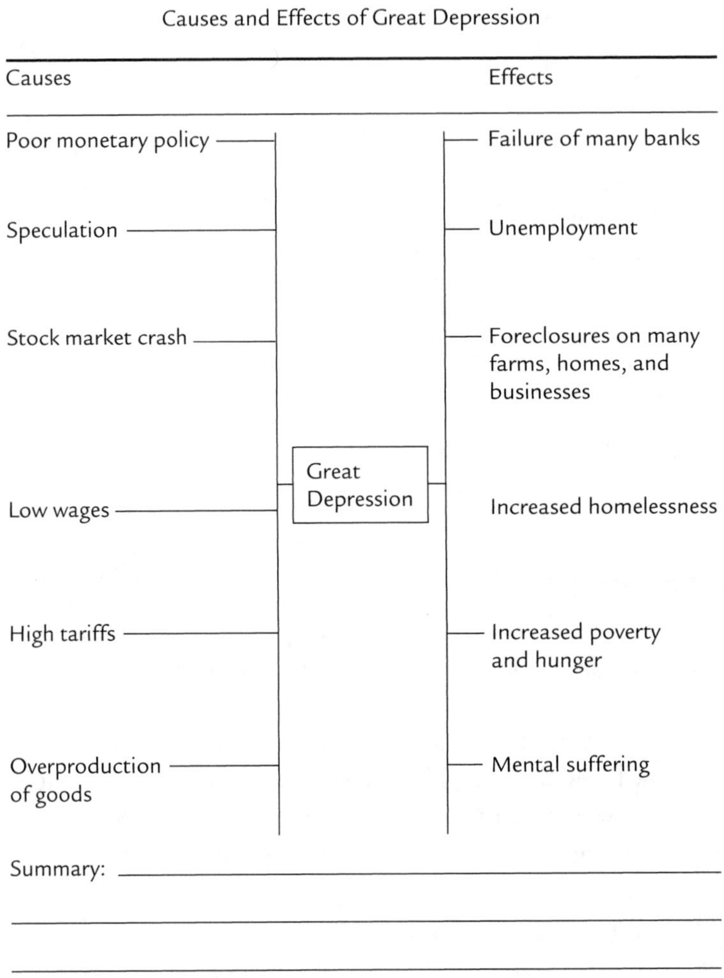

Causes and Effects of Great Depression

Causes	Effects
Poor monetary policy	Failure of many banks
Speculation	Unemployment
Stock market crash	Foreclosures on many farms, homes, and businesses
Low wages	Increased homelessness
High tariffs	Increased poverty and hunger
Overproduction of goods	Mental suffering

Great Depression

Summary: _____

_____

_____

Figure 3.9 ● Cause-Effect Map

added. For each item being compared, the students would write a brief conclusion. In blanks placed under a graphic organizer, students might summarize data or draw conclusions about it (Ellis, 2004).

Intensive Teaching and Extensive Practice

As with any complex technique, thinking maps and other graphic organizers require a commitment of time and energy. As Ellis (2004) notes, students need from fifteen to twenty experiences with a structure before they can acquire an effective command of it. Along with teaching students how to construct graphic organizers, also discuss with them which graphic organizer works best when a particular topic is displayed. For instance, help them to see that a map is usually best when a concept and its attributes are being organized, but a frame is best when comparing or contrasting. As opportunities present themselves to organize information, have students discuss and decide which organizer to use. Emphasize the use of graphic organizers as both a way of organizing information that has been read, heard, or viewed and also a way of preparing for writing. Post a chart similar to the one in Table 3.3 that highlights key graphic organizers.

Fostering Wide Reading

Nothing is better at building higher-level thinking skills than wide reading. On the basis of a number of research studies, Cunningham and Stanovich (1998) concluded that reading fosters cognitive development. "All of our studies have demonstrated that reading yields significant dividends for everyone—not just for the 'smart kids' or the more able readers. Even the child with limited reading and comprehension skills will build vocabulary and cognitive structures through reading. . . . Those who read a lot will enhance their verbal intelligence; that is, reading will make them smarter" (p. 7). They recommend providing "all children regardless of their achievement levels, with as many reading experiences as possible. Indeed, this becomes doubly imperative for precisely those children whose verbal abilities are most in need of bolstering, for it is the very act of reading that can build those capacities" (pp. 6–7).

Maximizing the Benefit

Although simply reading more will build background and reasoning skills, discussions of outside reading will multiply the benefit. Set aside a few minutes each day for students to talk over their outside reading. They might want to form book discussion groups in which four or five students read and discuss the same book or read and discuss books by the same author or read and discuss books on the same topic. You might just have pairs of students meet and talk over what they read the previous night.

A more formal procedure is to use an approach known as "buddy buzz." In buddy buzz, students gather in pairs or groups of three or four and discuss their books (Fountas & Pinnell, 2001). To enhance the effectiveness of the buzz, students are given a prompt beforehand. The prompt might simply request that they attach stick-on notes to two passages that they would like to share. Or they could mark two passages that were funny, sad, exciting, particularly well written or confusing, or

Table 3.3 ● Key Graphic Organizers

Organizer	Thinking Skill	Example
Descriptive Map (Web)	Locate and assemble main idea and details	
Classification Map (Semantic Map)	Categorize and classify	
Sequence Map	Arrange in chronological order	
Process Map (Chain or Flow Map)	Arrange in step-by-step fashion	
Cyclical Map	Arrange in circular fashion to show a process	
Tree Diagram	Categorize and classify in hierarchical fashion	
Frame Matrix (or Venn Diagram)	Compare and contrast	
Cause-Effect Map	Locate or infer causes and/or effects	

that contain useful or unbelievable information. During the buzz, they read the passages that have been marked and explain why they chose them. They also ask each other questions. Before engaging in buddy buzz, students are taught to listen attentively, ask questions after each presentation, and take turns. Although they are taught to be respectful of each other, they also learn how to provide support for their statements and how to politely voice opposing opinions.

Talking about books fosters thinking in a way that no other technique can. As Calkins (2001) explains, "It is by talking about books that children learn to conduct a dialogue in their minds, to think about books even when they read alone" (p. 75).

Reading to Deepen Understanding

The more students know about a topic, the more deeply they can think about it. As part of your read-aloud, read books that are on a theme or topic being studied in class, whether it be trees, World War I, or energy. Also have available in the classroom, school, and local library, books, periodicals, and other materials on the topic. A good source of information about books available on just about any topic is Titlewave <www.titlewave.com>. TITLEWAVE has two parts: Library TITLE-WAVE and Curriculum TITLEWAVE. Using Library TITLEWAVE, you can locate books, ebooks, and audiovisual titles on virtually any topic. You can search by topic, author, title, reading level, or grade level. A synopsis of the book and readability level are provided along with reviews. Curriculum TITLEWAVE offers lists of recommended books. Included are

- Lists of books that support language arts, science, social studies, and science standards on both the state and national level.
- Lists of books that support commercial programs in the content areas.
- Lists of books that support commercial basal/anthology and other literacy programs.
- Lists of books for guided reading.
- Popular bibliographies in a variety of areas.

Building Background Knowledge

Background knowledge is a key component of thinking. "Having extensive knowledge enables us to make generalizations about the subject, to decide what's important, and to make judgments, and to apply knowledge. As Beyer (2001) notes, "Unfortunately, many educators continue to view skills of all kinds as performances only, ignoring the fact that skills involve certain kinds of knowledge as well" (p. 37). Background knowledge provides the foundation for future learning. The more we know, the more we are prepared to learn. Having knowledge provides a foundation for understanding and adding new information to what we already know. Background knowledge is also a critical element in achievement. According to Marzano (2004), almost half of what we learn depends upon what we already know.

Background knowledge is determined by two key factors: "the number and frequency of our academically oriented experiences" and "our ability to process and store information" (Marzano, 2004, p. 4). The quality of children's schooling and the quality of their home experiences are crucial. It isn't just the number of experiences; it's the quality of those experiences. What children learn from a trip to the zoo depends to a great extent upon how much explanation they receive. If parents name the animals, read explanatory signs to or with their children, and discuss the animals, perhaps comparing and contrasting animals and explaining why there are different environments in the zoo, the children will learn a great deal more than if the conversation centers more on how funny the monkeys are and how fierce the tigers look. However, children's interest and curiosity and their ability to process information are also factors. As Sternberg (1985) comments, "What seems to be critical is not sheer amount of experience but rather what one has been able to learn from and do with experience" (p. 307).

The relationship between knowledge and processing ability is reciprocal. Increased knowledge gives us more to think about. Having more to think about improves our thinking. It also moves us to higher levels of thinking. Having a greater depth of knowledge leads to a deeper level of understanding, so that we are better able to draw conclusions and apply our knowledge.

The Critical Role of Content Area Literacy

Content area instruction is an essential background builder. Content area instruction provides students with a systematic introduction to key concepts in the physical and social sciences. In an attempt to boost scores on high-stakes tests, some schools have deemphasized content area instruction and reduced the amount of time devoted to social studies and science. Apart from its role in building key science and socials studies concepts, background, and vocabulary, content area instruction develops literacy and thinking skills.

Importance of Academic Learning Time

Although time on task is a key ingredient in learning, the nature of the task plays a major role. If the task is too easy or too difficult or not educationally valid, the time is wasted. A better gauge is academic learning time. Academic learning time (ALT) is the amount of time a student spends attending to relevant academic tasks while performing those tasks with a high rate of success (Caldwell, Huitt & Graeber, 1982; Berliner, 1984). "For engaged time to be really useful, the student must be participating in useful activities at a high rate of success. Neither succeeding at worthless activities nor failing at worthwhile tasks will lead to improved performance.

Improvement requires success at worthwhile activities" (Vockell, 2004). Students who complete learning tasks with 90 percent accuracy benefit more than students who completed the same tasks with 50 percent accuracy.

To increase academic learning time, provide instruction and activities that are worthwhile but which are in the student's zone of proximal development. Monitor progress and provide appropriate feedback. An effective technique for determining if students are engaged in academic learning is to ask: "What are you thinking about (the topic under discussion or target task)?" (Peterson & Swing, 1992). Students who report that they are paying attention, understand what is being taught, and/or can describe the strategies they are using do better than those who can't. Even students who report that they are not understanding the topic or task but can point out why they don't understand do better than those who report a lack of understanding but can't explain why.

Metacognition: Thinking about Thinking

Through metacognition, which is the ability to reflect on one's thinking, students take control of their learning. As cognitive psychologist Laura Resnick (1999) explains:

> Today, metacognition and self-regulatory capabilities are widely recognized as a key aspect of what it takes to be a good learner. Moreover, there is little argument that metacognitive strategies are both learnable and teachable. But effective strategy instruction depends on certain conditions. For example, students need to know how and why the strategies work. They need to understand that their mastery of the strategies is a developmental process and that sustained effort will produce increasing competence. They need scaffolding at first—in the form of modeling, direct teaching, and prompting—and then that scaffolding needs to be gradually removed so that students assume responsibility for using the strategies appropriately.

Students are best able to reflect on their thinking and their learning processes when the tasks they are performing are on the appropriate level of challenge. As Meichenbaum and Biemiller (1998) explain,

> Students typically learn metacognitive skills while they are involved in learning something else. If they are to do this successfully, it is extremely important that the learners have overlearned the prerequisite content knowledge for the subject matter topic being studied. If that prerequisite knowledge has not been mastered to a sufficient level of automaticity, then the working memory of the learner will be overwhelmed by the subject matter; and the result will be no time for metacognitive reflection. For example, when children who have largely mastered the prerequisite skills try to solve a word problem in arithmetic, they can afford to talk to themselves about what they are doing, because their working memory is not totally occupied with other demands. That is, well

prepared children will have time for metacognitive practice. On the other hand, when children who are missing some of these prerequisite skills try to solve the same problem, their working memory is likely to be totally occupied with a frantic need to find the basic skills and facts needed to solve the problem. If this is the case, they not only have solved the problem less effectively; but they also have little or no time for practicing or developing metacognitive skills. (p. 83)

To foster metacognition, have students place stick-on notes on confusing passages or obstacles to understanding. You can assess the amount of difficulty students are having by noting the number of stick-on notes that they used.

Lessons from Experts

All of us are experts in a number of areas. You might be an expert in playing chess or basketball. You might be an expert teacher or writer. Or perhaps you have expertise in cooking or auto repair. Select the area in which you have the most expertise. Then trace your development from novice to expert. How did you learn to be an expert? Who helped you? Did you put in a lot of practice time? What was your degree of motivation? Did difficult tasks become easy over time? Have you made modifications in your skills? Have you gone beyond what you were taught to explore new areas? Do you help others? (Meichenbaum & Biemiller, 1998). The major goal of this text is to develop expertise in high-level literacy skills in virtually all children. By reflecting on how we and others became experts, we can apply this knowledge to the students we teach, especially those who are struggling or who are at risk.

Experts differ from novices in knowledge, strategy use, and motivation. Experts have a depth of knowledge that is well organized and therefore easy to retrieve and apply. Experts see the big picture. When difficulties arise, experts have strategies for dealing with them. Experts plan their writing. They engage in knowledge transformation. They add to, alter, synthesize, personalize, or, in some other way, transform knowledge. Novices engage in "knowledge telling," which means that they simply write what they know (Bereiter & Scardamalia, 1982). Experts are more aware of their thought processes. This enables them to plan and monitor their work. They are also highly motivated. They put in the necessary practice time and persist when the going gets tough.

In school, expert readers and writers display the same kinds of characteristics as experts in chess, gymnastics, and other areas. Low-achieving students tend to be inefficient strategy users, have limited knowledge, engage in learning activities without really understanding them, and are more reliant on their teacher for help. Given these characteristics, low achievers participate less in class discussions and so miss the opportunity to talk about what they know and relate prior knowledge to new knowledge (Good & Brophy, 1994). Achieving students are called on more frequently than nonachieving students and are given more prompts. Low achievers have less opportunity to talk over what they know. This is true even in small-group discussions. They are also off task more often, about 50 to 60 percent of the time, whereas achieving students are off task only about 15 percent of the time. On-task behavior does increase when low achievers are given materials on their level (Anderson, 1990).

Since much instruction is geared to average students, above-average students learn the material with ease, whereas low achievers don't quite master it. They go on to the next topic or skill with insufficient mastery of past learning. Not having mastered topics, low achievers are deprived of the opportunity to acquire the in-depth knowledge that higher-level thinking skills demand. As Meichembaum and Biemiller (1998) point out, low achievers are capable of learning higher-level skills. However, instruction must match the ability of the students.

Differentiating Instruction

Requiring all children to achieve at the same level causes problems. "We believe that each child should be treated 'the same,' in the sense of having opportunities to learn new skills, strategies, and concepts that build on existing knowledge and skills, and at having opportunities to build expertise and self-direction on tasks at which they're competent and can exercise their competence with others. All students need the opportunities that the top 30 percent are given. Teachers often give able students tasks that are easy or challenging, while giving less-able students tasks that are too difficult for them" (Meichenbaum & Biemiller, 1998, p. 92). When provided with tasks at their level and in which they engaged in cross-aged tutoring, less self-directed children engaged in highly self-directed behavior (Meichenbaum & Biemiller, 1998). Meichenbaum & Biemiller estimate that 70 to 90 percent of students could reach or exceed mastery if given enough time and an appropriate range of mastery tasks. One goal of teaching is to provide opportunities for students to reflect on their skills and provide consultation for other students. In other words all students should be given the opportunity to function like experts. This builds metacognitive awareness.

As students explain how and why they performed a task, they become more aware of their cognitive processes. Explaining a process requires that they analyze the process, which leads to a deeper understanding of the process. Often when students ask for help and explain why they are having difficulty, they spontaneously come up with a solution. "As students put what they know and don't know into words or into diagrams, they often generate solutions" (Meichenbaum & Biemiller, 1998, p. 38).

> Understanding is more likely to occur when a student is required to explain, elaborate, or defend his position to others; the burden of explanation is often the push needed to make him or her evaluate, integrate, and elaborate knowledge in new ways. (Brown & Campione, 1996, p. 306)

Differentiating instruction fosters achievement and motivation and also helps develop metacognition. When students are working at the appropriate level of challenge, they are able to think about the processes they are using.

Matching Materials and Instruction with Achievement and Ability

Students must have materials that are on the appropriate level. As noted earlier, if the material is so difficult that students expend a large amount of mental capacity decoding the materials and perhaps constructing some basic understanding of it, their cognitive capacities will be overloaded and there will be insufficient mental capacity available for them to apply higher-level strategies (Meichenbaum & Biemiller, 1998). As a rule of thumb, students should know at least 95 percent of the words in a selection that they read with the teacher's help. Their comprehension should be 70 percent. The 95–70 percent criteria is instructional level, which means that students can read successfully if they know at least 95 words out of a 100 because they will be getting instructional help, such as being taught difficult vocabulary or unfamiliar concepts before they read. If students are going to read on their own, they should know at least 98–99 percent of the words and have 80–90 percent comprehension. This is their independent level. When reading on their own, they should be reading materials that are on their independent level. When higher-level strategies are being introduced, students should be given materials that are on their independent level. That way they can focus all their cognitive resources on becoming familiar with the new strategy. Once they have a basic grasp of the strategy, they can apply it to materials on their instructional level. Unfortunately, in all too many instances, at-risk readers are faced with the dual task of learning a new strategy and coping with material that is very difficult for them.

Study Group Questions

Chapter 3 covers a lot of ground. You might want to set priorities and focus on the most essential areas. To set priorities, you might ask: Which area(s) are most urgent for my class? How might I improve my students' performance in that area or areas? In coming chapters, you will be asked to apply the principles and procedures explored in this chapter. As part of strategy instruction, for instance, you will need to make sure that students are being taught on the appropriate level. Students will also be using graphic organizers as a part of applying strategies, and they will be applying strategies to content areas and outside reading. Throughout, building a culture of understanding and developing background knowledge and language will be important elements in your program. Specific questions and areas include the following:

- How would I describe the culture of understanding in my class? How might I go about improving the culture of understanding?
- What is the status of higher-level talk in my class? How can I improve higher-level talk?
- How do I use graphic organizers? How might I implement a system of graphic organizers?
- How much outside reading do my students do? How can I increase voluntary reading? What can I do to maximize the benefit of outside reading?
- How can I more effectively build background knowledge?
- What role does content area literacy play in my program?
- What is the extent of academic learning time in my class? How can I increase academic learning time?
- How can I develop metacognitive awareness?
- To what extent is instruction differentiated? Does differentiation need improvement in my class? If so, how might I go about improving it? How can I differentiate instruction?

chapter 4

Using Strategies to Build Higher-Level Literacy Skills

Comprehension strategies are guides (usually verbal) for planning tasks that foster understanding (Meichenbaum & Biemiller, 1998). The task includes the goal, steps taken to achieve the goal, monitoring of progress, and evaluation of one's efforts (Meichenbaum and Biemiller, 1998). There are three phases: acquisition, consolidation, and consultation. In the acquisition phase, the learner is reliant on the teacher's direction. In the consolidation phase, performance is becoming more automatic. In the consultation phases, learners can apply the strategy to other situations and explain the strategy to others. Unfortunately, both the consolidation and consultation stages are often neglected so that students end up with an incomplete grasp of strategies and are unable to apply them on their own. Students should probably spend no more than 25 percent of their time in acquisition. The rest of the time should be spent in consolidation and consultation (Meichenbaum & Biemiller, 1998). The consolidation phase takes the largest proportion of time. This is the phase during which students practice the skill. However, feedback and assistance should be provided. The assistance given should be such that it moves the student toward independence. There are two kinds of consolidation tasks: those that provide repeated practice and those that are practiced in the context of reading and writing. Repeated reading is an example of repeated practice. Guided reading, in which students read stories or articles under the teacher's direction, is an example of contextual practice. Practice activities should be such that students experience a high degree of success: from 80 to 90 percent. Feedback should be provided, and students should monitor and reflect on their progress.

Consolidated learning should be accompanied by instruction and assistance as needed. Objectives should be defined. The objective might be greater accuracy or increased reading speed or more elaborated responses. Difficulties that students might have completing consolidation tasks need to be anticipated. Task goals should be explained. Students should understand why they are being asked to read a selection rapidly when the goal is to increase reading rate but are asked to slow down when the goal is accuracy of responses. Teachers should also display cognitive empathy. Errors should be viewed as inevitable and as opportunities for learning. Students should know when and how to get assistance. Students should also reflect on their progress. Emphasis should be placed on student progress rather than meeting a certain standard. Unfortunately, the current climate emphasizes standards but neglects affirming progress.

Reflecting and Sharing

Students must not only acquire and consolidate knowledge; they also need to reflect on it and share. They need to understand what they did, how they did it, and why they did it, so that they can do it again. Because it involves reflecting, the consultation phase refines and integrates students' learning and leads to mastery. Students can consult in three ways:

- *Assisting or tutoring other students.* As with other skills, students need to be taught how to be good helpers or tutors.
- *Collaborating with other students.* Students collaborate best when their abilities or knowledge are approximately equal.
- *Self-consulting by reflecting on their learning or solving problems.* Writing, because it incorporates a mental representation of learning, is an excellent way for students to reflect on their performance (Meichenbaum & Biemiller, 1998). Mental representation may take a variety of forms: it can be a think-aloud, a

presentation, a log entry, a graphic organizer, a report, or a skit (Meichenbaum & Biemiller, 1998).

Approaches to Teaching Reading, Reasoning, and Responding Strategies

The two major approaches to developing strategies are the inductive and the deductive. In an inductive approach, students analyze a strategy task and decide what steps might be taken to apply the strategy or complete the task. In a deductive approach, students are told what strategy to apply. Strategies are most often taught deductively. The steps are then explained and/or demonstrated.

Taking a Deductive Approach

The teacher provides students with a list of procedures to use when applying the strategy. Students then engage in guided practice and, eventually, in independent practice and application. Here are the steps in a deductive approach.

Step 1: Introducing the Strategy   The teacher describes the strategy, gives examples of it, tells why it is important, and explains how it will help students to become better readers.

Step 2: Presenting the Strategy   The teacher demonstrates the strategy. The demonstration is usually accompanied by a think-aloud in which the teacher explains what is going on in her mind as she applies the strategy in the demonstration lesson. The teacher provides students with a list of procedures to use when applying the strategy. The teacher also tells where and when the strategy is used.

Step 3: Guided Practice   Guided practice can take a number of forms. Two effective forms are scaffolded practice and cued practice. In scaffolded practice, a procedural checklist, a series of prompts, or a graphic organizer is used to assist students in applying the strategy (Beyer, 2001b). A procedural checklist, which is the most explicit of the scaffolds, is a list of steps to use in completing the strategy (see the steps for constructing the main idea on p. 55). Prompts are a series of questions that guide students through the process of using the strategy: What does the heading suggest that the main ideas might be? What are all or most of the sentences talking about? Graphic organizers use diagrams or other visual hints and may also use checklists or questions (see Figure 5.2). The advantage of a scaffold is that it " enables students to concentrate on carrying out the steps in a procedure for executing a skill without simultaneously trying to recall which steps to use next" (Beyer, 2001a, p. 398).

After students have a fairly good grasp of a strategy and need only occasional reminders, cues might be used. Cues differ from scaffolds because they provide brief reminders but do not "tell us all that we are to do or say" (Beyer, 2001b, p. 421). To cue students we might simply mention the name of a strategy to be used, or the students might use a mnemonic. Cues might be placed on charts or on bookmarks. A cueing card might contain actions for students to consider as they read a selection: Preview, Question, Visualize, Infer, Monitor, Summarize, Connect. As you implement suggestions in this text with your students, you might use cueing cards.

The guidance in guided practice for a strategy can vary in intensity and explicitness. The guidance might begin as being very structured and gradually turn over more responsibility to students. Boyles (2004) calls this initial guidance "structured practice." In structured practice activities, the teacher does most of the work but students help out. In less-structured guided practice the students do the work, but the teacher provides assistance.

Although strategies might be taught to the whole class, Boyles (2004) recommends that guided practice be completed in small groups of four to six at the earlier grades and up to eight in the upper grades. The size of the group should be such that all members feel free to participate. The advantage of small group instruction is that students can be grouped according to reading ability, and instruction can be pinpointed to their level of development. The level and intensity of instruction and the amount of explanation and assistance can be geared to the students' progress. In addition, their progress can be monitored. Best of all, in a small group they can become more active learners. It's hard to daydream or hide out when you are in small group.

Step 4: Independent Practice   Students practice the skill on their own, but the results of the practice are discussed in small groups or the whole class and/or checked by the teacher.

Step 5: Application   Strategy learning is contextual. Unfortunately, its application tends to be limited to the context or subject in which it was learned. In order to foster transfer, students must apply the skill to other contexts or other content areas. Since students have already been introduced to the skill, a brief review should suffice. However, as part of the review, model the use of the strategy in the new context and provide opportunities for guided practice, if necessary, before students apply the skill independently. As part of the consultative phase, students should reflect on their use of the strategy and might also work with partners or small groups to apply the strategy.

Taking an Inductive Approach

In an inductive approach, students compose steps for strategy implementation based on their analysis of what works for them. The inductive approach can be especially effective for older students who possess strategies but who may not be using them efficiently or effectively or who may not realize that there are ways in which they could adapt or adopt strategies. An inductive approach can also be diagnostic, as both students and the teacher discover how much students know about a strategy and how well they apply it. In an inductive approach, the teacher previews a strategy, such as inferring, evaluating, summarizing, or predicting, and then directs the students to apply the strategy to a task, such as reading a piece of text (Beyer, 2001). After applying the strategy, the students discuss with a partner how they went about applying the strategy. Students are then asked to explain to the whole class how they applied the strategy. The teacher records the processes described by students. The class discusses students' responses. Based on students' responses, a series of steps for applying the strategy is elicited. As a double-check, students' apply the strategy using the steps listed. Students share with each other and with the whole class how well they were able to apply the strategy. In particular they discuss any steps that might not be clear, need to be added, or aren't needed. With the students' input the teacher edits the description of the strategy and the steps involved in its application.

The inductive approach has several advantages. Because they are composing the strategy, students are more actively involved and have a better understanding of the strategy. The strategy steps would be more reality based. They would be based on the processes that students actually use. An inductive approach is a good way to introduce teachers to strategy instruction. It helps them to become aware of the strategies they use and how they implement them. Here is how a strategy might be taught inductively.

Step 1: Introducing the Strategy   The strategy and its benefits are explained. Students are asked to tell about times when they applied the strategy. A paragraph or longer piece is presented, and students apply the strategy to it. As students apply the strategy, the teacher notes how well they are able to use it and what steps they seem to be taking.

Step 2: Sharing with a Partner   Have students share their efforts with each other. Have them tell in particular how they went about applying the strategy. Listen in on conversations to gain insight into the processes students used.

Step 3: Eliciting Strategy Steps Discuss the group's use of the strategy. If students were using a summarizing strategy, you might elicit a group summary. Then ask them to tell what steps they used in applying the strategy. Revise the steps as needed. List and post the revised steps. Guided and independent practice and application are the same as those noted for a deductive approach.

Need for Sustained Instruction

Instruction needs to be sustained. For instance, one group of students who were being taught strategies for making inferences didn't begin to show progress until after four weeks of instruction (Dewitz, Carr & Patberg, 1987). However, the progress was substantial. Harris and Graham (1996) estimate that it takes four to nine teaching and practice sessions before students are able to use a strategy independently.

Instruction also has to be thorough. Often instruction in a skill consists of testing that skill. "Much so-called teaching of thinking skills consists largely of giving students practice in answering old test questions, a procedure that probably focuses students' attention more on question-answering techniques than on the specific cognitive skills that are the intended outcome of such activities" (Beyer, 2001. p. 39).

Study Group Questions

- What are the two main approaches to teaching higher-level strategies?
- How do I go about teaching strategies? How might I improve my instruction of strategies?
- How might I go about developing students' ability to reflect on their strategy use?

chapter 5

Developing Specific Strategies and Skills

This chapter is the core of the book. It applies key concepts explored in previous chapters by focusing on comprehension skills and strategies in three key cognitive areas: locate and recall, integrate and interpret, and critique and evaluate.

Locate and Recall (Forming a General Understanding)

Locate and Recall encompasses comprehending main ideas, comprehending essential details, and summarizing. For fiction, the reader is asked to construct a theme rather than a main idea. Typical questions might include:

> Give three reasons from the article why Philo Farnsworth should be considered the main inventor of television.
> What is this article (or section) mainly about? Use information from the article to support your answer.
> Summarize the article.

Locating and Comprehending Details

Although this text explores higher-level literacy, locating and comprehending details form the foundation for higher-level understanding. The main reason students lose credit on higher-level questions is that they fail to base their responses on essential details or they fail to include the details needed to support their responses. Locate and recall are strategic partners. When we fail to recall information, we then go back to the text to locate it. In reading this strategy is commonly referred to as a "look-back." Recently, I served on a committee that was reviewing high-stakes tests. As part of the review, we read the tests and answered the accompanying questions. For most questions, I found myself going back to the passage to locate information so that I could select an answer or compose a response. Being able to locate information is an essential everyday reading skill. For test taking, whether the test is multiple-choice or constructed response, lookback might be the most important strategy of all. It is hard to see how any student who lacks lookback skills can pass a high-stakes test. Indeed, the number one shortcoming in students' responses to constructed responses high-stakes tests is the failure to support responses (Gunning, 2006a). Supporting a response frequently requires going back to the selection and locating supporting details. When memory fails them or they aren't sure of a response, students need to learn how to go back to a passage to locate a detail to answer a question, verify information, and/or obtain support for a position. On the easiest level, students will simply be locating directly stated information. On a higher level they will be generalizing a main idea or making inferences and drawing conclusions from information they have located.

Despite the importance of the lookback strategy, observations and discussions indicate that many students do not go back to the passage. In fact, some seem unaware that they could go back to the passage. One student expressed the belief that it was cheating to do so. The lookback strategy should be explained, modeled, and practiced so that it becomes virtually automatic. To introduce lookbacks, explain to students that we can't remember everything we read, but we can go back and check facts or find details, if we can't recall them. Do a think-aloud with a sample multiple-choice test. Explain as you come to challenging questions that you are not sure which is the correct answer, so you go over the test passage and locate information that will help you. Show how you quickly skim over the passage to find the pertinent information. Provide students with a lengthy fact-packed passage, such as the one below, and ask lots of questions about it. As a class, read the passage and then respond to the questions. Help students as they go back over the passage to locate information.

Ears and Hearing

Our ears are very speedy. Our ears pick up sounds faster than our fingers pick up vibrations or our eyes pick up sights. But one ear is just a tiny bit faster than the other. Can you tell which one? Sounds travel through the air. The ear closer to the sound picks it up first. Hearing a sound at slightly different times makes it possible to tell where the sound is coming from.

Loud sounds can harm our ears. Sounds are measured in decibels. A decibel is a measure of how loud a sound is. It's like inches, but instead of measuring how long something is, you are measuring how loud it is. Sounds are measured on a scale of 0 to 145. Soft breathing is 10 decibels, the rustling of leaves is 20 decibels, a nearby jet engine is 140. Sounds above 85 decibels can be harmful. Here is the decibel count for some common sounds:

Decibels of Common Sounds

Sounds	Decibels
Breathing	10
Leaves rustling	20
Whisper	30
Refrigerator humming	40
Conversation	50–65
Hair dryer	70
Traffic	80
Chain saw	100
Thunder nearby	120
Jet engine nearby	140

If we want our ears to keep on hearing, then we have to take care of them. Stay away from loud sounds. If you have to be around them, wear earplugs or earmuffs. Take care of your ears, and they'll take care of your hearing.

Possible questions that might be asked include:

- How fast are our ears at picking up sounds?
- Why don't both ears hear sounds at the same time?
- How are sounds measured?
- How loud is a breath?
- How loud is a refrigerator?
- How loud is traffic?
- Which is louder, thunder or a jet engine?
- At what point on the decibel scale do sounds begin to harm our hearing?

As students answer these questions, direct them to go back to the article to find details if they don't recall the needed information. Also have them read from the article to verify their answers. Provide additional practice with this skill. It would be tedious if students had to answer a long list of questions as they did in this exercise, but do include opportunities for them to apply this skill. Students don't have to have total mastery of the lookback strategy before moving on. However, this is a cumulative foundational skill that students need for literal comprehension but will also need as they move into higher levels of comprehension and are required to find support to back up conclusions or make critical judgments as they read. Continue to review and instruct students in the use of this strategy throughout the school year.

Embed instruction in ongoing class activities. During discussions, direct students to use lookbacks when they can't answer questions. Also ask them to read passages to support a point they are making, especially if the point is controversial. Pose questions such as "Can you read the passage that tells us when the first TV was invented?" "Can you read the passages that support your position that Philo Farnsworth deserves the most credit for inventing TV?" When students are completing assignments or taking tests, remind them of the importance of looking back.

Along with reinforcing the lookback strategy in discussions, also provide instruction and practice in applying this skill in writing. As students become accustomed to going back to the passage to verify information or locate a key detail, introduce the skill of using information from a passage to construct a response. Being able to discuss a skill is a prerequisite for being able to use the skill for writing but is no guarantee that students will be able to do so. Have students compose written responses for some of the questions. As a part of instruction, introduce words that they most likely will have to use in composing their responses. For "why" questions, students are likely to need to use the words "because" and "therefore." You might begin with items in which they simply have to complete the sentence and gradually have them compose responses on their own.

Why should we stay away from loud noises?

We should stay away from noises that are more than 85 decibels because _____

_____.

Why don't both ears hear a sound at exactly the same time?

Both ears don't hear a sound at exactly the same time because _____

_____.

Once students have demonstrated adequate literal comprehension, move into main ideas. As you develop students' ability to comprehend and generate main ideas, you will naturally be applying and expanding their ability to comprehend details and use the lookback strategy.

Main Idea

The main idea of a passage is what the passage is all about. It encompasses all of the details in a passage. Students sometimes believe that the main idea is the most interesting detail or most important detail rather than the one that includes all the others. Constructing the main idea requires the ability to classify and categorize. To derive a main idea, the reader must detect similarities among the details in a paragraph and then must choose the sentence that categorizes or tells about all the others (if the main idea is stated) or construct a category statement that encompasses all the details in a passage (if the main idea is not stated). Because deriving a main idea requires seeing similarities in ideas and determining what that similarity is, have students engage in classifying activities. Younger students can classify objects and then easy words, such as *wagon, ball, teddy bear, doll house* (toys). Older students classify more advanced words: *football, basketball, soccer, ice hockey* (sports). (Observe students' ability to classify. If students can already classify, move on to the next task.) Once students are able to classify objects and words, have them classify sentences. Make up your own exercises or take them from a carefully structured paragraph that contains a main idea sentence and at least three supporting details. Rearrange the sentences in list form, with the main idea sentence appearing in the middle of the list or last. Have students identify the main idea sentence or topic sentence. Ask students to support their selections by showing how each of the other sentences supports the main idea sentence. Sample exercises are presented below:

> Some robots weigh just a few pounds.
> Other robots weigh thousands of pounds.
> Robots come in many shapes and sizes.
> Most robots look like metal arms.
> Some robots look like people.

> Most robots work in factories.
> Other robots have been built to cut sheep's wool, help make cookies, or pick up soil from other planets.
> Robots have been built to do a number of different jobs.
> Robots have also been built to drop off and pick up mail in offices.
> Robots have been built to serve food in restaurants (Gunning, 2006d).

> Cats are quiet.
> Cats don't bark.
> Cats clean themselves.
> Cats don't eat much,
> Cats are fun to watch and play with.
> Cats make good pets.
> Cats are affectionate animals.

To provide additional reinforcement, give students a main idea and have them fill in the details. Emphasize that each detail should support the main idea.

Dogs make good pets.
Soccer is an exciting sport.
Computers have made life easier.
Cell phones have made it easier for people to communicate.
Saturday is my favorite day of the week.

To help students see that the main idea functions as a kind of container in which details are placed or an umbrella under which details fall, cut up brief paragraphs that contain a topic sentence. Have students place the topic sentence at the top of a column and the supporting details under the topic sentence. This manipulative activity helps students better see the relationship between the main idea and its supporting details.

Selecting Main Ideas in Paragraphs   After students achieve proficiency classifying sentences in a list, have them select the main idea in brief, well-constructed paragraphs similar to those listed below. One strategy for deriving a main idea is to seek out the topic sentence, which is generally, but not always, the first sentence. Of course, the reader can't tell if a particular sentence is the topic sentence until she has read all or most of the paragraph. Model how you determine whether the first sentence seems to be stating a main idea, and how you note, as you read the paragraph, whether the details are supporting the hypothesized main idea. If some sentences are not supporting the main idea, then you seek another main idea sentence. Show how the main idea might be found in a middle or even an ending sentence. Place paragraphs on cards or sheets that have the answer on the back. That way the exercise can be self-correcting. Use the following or similar practice paragraphs.

> Robots make good workers. They never get tired. They can work 24 hours a day, seven days a week, 52 weeks a year. And they never get bored. They can do the same job over and over again. They can put car parts together and paint cars faster and better than people can. And they won't get sick from paint fumes or burn themselves with a welding torch (Gunning, 2006d).

> Robots can do dangerous jobs. Robots can pick up bombs. And Robots can handle dangerous chemicals. Robots can go into burning buildings. A robot by the name of Dante II went into a volcano where it took samples of very hot gases (Gunning, 2006d).

Applying the Skills   Maintain a file of paragraphs from periodicals or other sources that contain main idea sentences. Duplicate and distribute these to students. Also have students apply the skill by locating main idea sentences in science and social studies textbooks and trade books. Explain that not all paragraphs have at topic sentence. Only about one in four do (Baumann, 1986). Discuss students' paragraphs and the topic sentences. Encourage students to justify their choices by noting the details that support the main idea.

Using Writing to Reinforce Main Ideas Have younger students write an all-about book (Calkins & Pessah, 2003). Students select a topic—frogs, clouds, elephants, basketball, games, flowers—and write "all about" it. They use as models picture books that tell "all about" weather, lions, trucks, or another topic. After selecting a topic, they compose a table of contents. The table of contents breaks down the topic into subtopics. A book on taking care of a pet cat might include Feeding My Cat, Playing with My Cat, Getting a Bed for My Cat, Taking My Cat to the Vet. Students then develop each subtopic. Developing subtopics is similar to classifying. Students need to determine under which subtopic information will fall. To facilitate the process, students devote a separate page to each subtopic. As part of the revising process, students go back over their writing to make sure that the details they have written are placed on the right page. As students learn to develop a main idea and stick to a topic, they are using and expanding skill in classifying and categorizing. As they move up through the grades, they develop these basic skills in greater depth and complexity. As the teacher reminds the students,

> Today, writers, will you get out your books right now, and while you are on the rug, will you start rereading them? Remember, first reread the chapter title. Then reread what is under the title, asking, "Does this go here?" You will have to cross things out like I did, and to move things too. This work will be really important for you to do for the rest of your life, whenever you write in chapters or in categories. (p. 110)

At more advanced levels, students compose headings or subtitles (Portalupi & Fletcher, 2004). Subtitles are presented as being similar to titles, except that instead of telling what the whole selection is about, they only indicate the content of an individual section. Subtitles should first be presented as a reading skill. Once students become used to seeing and using subtitles in their reading, they can discuss ways of using them in their nonfiction writing. Emphasize that subtitles aid the reader. However, they can also help the writer. Subtitles can help writers organize their presentations. If the writer draws up an outline or other plan beforehand, the major points in the plan might become subtitles. You might want to explain to students that subtitles can be written as a piece is being written or after the piece has been written.

Implied Main Idea In most pieces of writing main ideas are implied rather than directly stated. To introduce the concept of implied main ideas, first demonstrate the difference between a stated and implied main idea by giving the main idea of a topic and then discussing it as in Set 1 below. Contrast that with jumping into a topic without telling students what the main idea is as in Set 2 below. Discuss which set of sentences is easier to understand and why.

Set 1

Here are some new books for our class library.
Here is a book on taking care of pets.
Here is a book on Mars.
Here is a book on César Chavez.
Here is a book of riddles and jokes.

Set 2

Here is a book on taking care of pets.
Here is a book on Mars.
Here is a book on César Chavez.
Here is a book of riddles and jokes.

To show students how main ideas are constructed when they are not directly stated, place paragraphs on the board or overhead, such as the following, in which the main idea is implied. Model for students how you construct a main idea by putting the details of a paragraph together and using the details to construct a main idea. To double-check, once you have hypothesized a main idea, show how you go back over the paragraph to make sure that the details support the main idea. Start with paragraphs where this is easy to do and gradually advance to paragraphs that are more complex. One device for obtaining suitable paragraphs is to remove the main idea sentence from already constructed paragraphs and have students construct a main idea sentence for them. In preparation for presenting main idea and related skills, start a file of materials that might be used to illustrate key concepts or to provide practice. You might obtain paragraphs from children's periodicals, old workbooks, children's informational books, and local newspapers.

> (The coyote is loved and hated at the same time.) Some people say that the coyote is a helpful creature. It does kill off rats and other harmful animals. But other people hate the coyote. To them, it's a clever killer. Ranchers and farmers say that coyotes kill thousands of their cows and sheep each year. To some people, the howl of the coyote is a welcome sound. To others, it's a sound that makes their blood boil (Gunning, 2006d).

> (The polar bear is a clever hunter.) On land the polar bear slowly sneaks up on its prey. If the prey looks around, the polar bear becomes very still. When it is very

Locate and Recall (Forming a General Understanding)

close, the polar bear charges its prey. At sea the polar bear waits on the ice next to an opening in the ice where whales or seals come up to breathe. With its heavy white paws, it covers its dark eyes and dark nose, so that its prey won't spot it. When the prey comes up for air, the polar bear swiftly attacks.

To prepare students for constructing main idea sentences, have them complete the following or similar exercises in which they select from three or four options the one that states the main idea of the paragraph. Be sure to discuss their choices. Emphasize the need to validate choices by supplying supporting details. (Formats such as this are a staple of multiple-choice items on high-stakes tests. However, the wording might vary. Check the wording used in your states' high-stakes tests, and use that in the examples you provide students.)

Large animals send signals by barking, growling, or howling. Small animals make sounds, too. Crickets make their noises by beating their wings together. Some grasshoppers rub their back legs against their wings. They look like violin players. But the termite may have the strangest way of making noise. It beats its head against its wooden home.

Which sentence below best tells what this paragraph is about?

 a. Animals make sounds in many different ways.
 b. Animals send signals by barking, growling, or howling.
 c. Termites have a strange way of making noise.
 d. Crickets make noise by beating their wings together (Gunning, 2006d).

One kind of catfish is called the glass catfish. Its body is like a thin piece of glass. You can look through its skin and see its insides. Another kind of catfish is called the upside-down catfish. This strange fish often swims on its back. But the strangest catfish of all is the walking catfish. The walking catfish can "walk" on land by using its tail and fins to push itself along the ground.

 a. One kind of catfish swims upside down.
 b. There are some mighty strange creatures in the catfish family.
 c. The walking catfish is the strangest catfish of all.
 d. The glass catfish has a very thin body (Gunning, 2006d).

Constructing the Main Idea Expert readers tend to use either a whole-to-part strategy or part-to-whole strategy to construct a main idea. With the whole-to-part strategy, students use the title, headings, and graphics and apparent topic sentence to draft or hypothesize the main idea and check their hypothesis by seeing if the details support it. Using a part-to-whole strategy, they get the main idea by noting key details, and constructing a main idea statement about the relationship among them (Afflerbach, 1990; Afflerbach & Johnston, 1986). If a title and/or heading is available, students might use the following steps to select a stated main idea or construct a main idea if it is not stated:

1. Use the title or heading to make a hypothesis (careful guess) as to what the main idea is.
2. Read each sentence and see whether it supports the hypothesis. If not, revise the hypothesis.
3. If you can't make a hypothesis as to what the main idea is, see what all or most of the sentences have in common or are talking about.
4. Select a sentence or make a sentence that tells what all the sentences are about. (Post these steps or an adaptation of them.) (Gunning, 2005a, p. 284)

Have students practice constructing main ideas with brief paragraphs such as the following. Remind them to use titles to help them predict what the main idea might be.

Working Together

When it's time for eggs to be laid, the male and female hornbills build a mud wall across an opening in a tree. Hornbills are large birds that have long bills. The female hornbill works from the inside of the tree. The male works from the outside. They leave a small hole in the wall so that the female can breathe. The mud hardens. Now the female hornbill has a safe place to lay her eggs and raise her young. The male hornbill gathers food for his mate and passes it to her through the small opening. When the eggs hatch, the father gathers food for the young birds, too. In time he grows thin and weak. But as the young hornbills grow stronger, the mother breaks through the wall and helps out (Gunning, 2006d).

Helping Each Other

The tickbird spends much of its time on the back of a rhino. It eats bugs off the rhino's back. In return for a free ride and a free meal, the tickbird acts as a lookout. The rhino has poor eyesight. So the tickbird watches for danger. And if a dangerous animal appears, the tickbird gives out a warning cry (Gunning, 2006d).

The following article has a title and headings that indicate main ideas. Using the selection below or another brief selection, demonstrate how the title and headings might be used to create a hypothesis as to what the main idea is. Show how the selection is read with the hypothesis in mind and is changed if need be. Model how you might select from the passage the main idea sentence.

One-Room Schoolhouses

In the early 1800s, most schools had only one large room and one teacher who taught all subjects to all pupils. Pupils were grouped according to what they knew. There were no grades. As soon as students learned to add and subtract, they could go on to long division. The students were not held back while others caught up. If some students took extra time to learn their addition or subtraction, that was all right. Those students could just stay in the addition and subtraction group. There was no rush. Actually, groups were so small that students got more of the teacher's attention.

Teaching All Subjects to All Ages

How could one teacher teach all subjects to children of a number of different ages? It wasn't easy. The first subject of the day was reading. The first group of students was called up to the recitation bench. The recitation bench was the place where students sat when they were reciting or telling answers to questions or telling what they had learned. Taking their seats on the bench they talked over the story they read, or they might read it aloud. They were then given an assignment to do and sent back to their seats. Then the next group was called up. While others were reciting, the children at their desks might read a story, write some practice words or sentences on their slates, or memorize a poem or some facts. Depending on how well they spelled, children were given different lists to practice with and learn to spell. The children were also grouped for math. When younger children were finished their work, they might listen to the older children reciting. That way they got in some extra learning.

Students Help Each Other

Since the teacher couldn't be everywhere at once, students helped each other. When the older children were finished their reciting, they might help the younger children with their math or their reading. Teaching others helped both the student who was teaching and the student who was being helped. When explaining a math problem or hard word to another pupil, students found that it became clearer in their own minds (Gunning, 2006d).

Titles   Titles generally play a two-part role. They announce the main idea or subject of a piece, and they may also be designed to attract readers or viewers. Discuss with students how titles can help them get the main idea or provide a sense of what a story night be about. Discuss titles that you found especially intriguing and have students name their favorite titles. Model the process of constructing a title for a story or piece that you have written. Read brief stories to students, and have them select titles. Discuss their choices. After students have read and discussed a selection, have the class make up another title for the piece.

When constructing a main idea for a text that has no title or heading, follow these steps:

1. Read the paragraph.
2. As you read, note what the paragraph is all about. This will be the main idea.
3. Check to see if the sentences support the main idea. If not, try again.

Demonstrate the process of constructing a main idea when there is no title or heading or when the title or heading fails to provide an adequate clue. You might use the following or similar paragraphs.

> Did you know that bats have thumbs? Bats' thumbs have large hooks. Some bats use them for climbing. Other bats hang by their thumbs. And some kinds of bats even use their thumbs to walk. When sneaking up on other animals, the vampire bat hops along on its feet and thumbs (Gunning, 2006d).

> If you are afraid of bats, don't go near Carlsbad Caverns in New Mexico, especially at night in the summertime. When the summer sky grows dark, thousands and thousands of bats come flying out of the caves to find insects for food. There are so many bats that it takes four hours before all of them are out of the caves. No one has ever counted the Carlsbad bats. But scientists say there may be five or six million of them (Gunning, 2006d).

When asked to select or construct main ideas, students have a tendency to choose or provide a sentence that expresses essential or very interesting information, but that is not general enough to include all the ideas in the paragraph (Williams, 1986). Model how you go about selecting main ideas that include all the ideas in a paragraph. It might also be helpful if the task is broken down into a series of prompts that guide students' thought processes as they select main ideas. Ask them what the paragraph is about. If they supply a general topic, such as pets, ask them to tell what the paragraph as a whole has to says about pets (older pets need special care). Then have them check to see that the details support the main idea (need special diet, need more checkups, might need medicine, need more rest).

Applying Main Idea Strategies to Longer Text As students gain in proficiency, have them derive main ideas from paragraphs in content area selections that they are reading

Locate and Recall (Forming a General Understanding)

and from selections in their literacy program or classroom periodicals. Gradually, move into longer selections as the one on page 56, ones that have multiple paragraphs. Model how you use titles and subheads to hypothesize what the main idea is. Show students how to preview a selection by examining titles and headings so that they have a good sense of what the main ideas are.

Using Text Structure   To further develop students' understanding of the structure of written language, have them note some of the principal ways in which main ideas can be supported. Some main ideas are supported with details; others are supported with causes, effects, examples, or reasons. More complex structures are those in which the main idea is the statement of a problem and is supported by an explanation of the problem, or there is a comparison-contrast structure. Being able to identify the structure fosters comprehension and retention by providing students with a structure for organizing and mentally storing information.

When teaching expository text, try using the CORE model (*C*onnect, *O*rganize, *R*eflect, *E*xtend) (Dymock, 2005). In the Connect step the teacher helps the students build on the known by connecting what they know about the topic to be investigated. In the Organize step, the teacher helps the students to see how the information in the text is structured. Each major text structure is explicitly taught. Students learn to diagram or display text according to its organization. In the Reflect step, students think over how the text was organized and how knowing the organization of the text helps them to better understand it. The teacher might ask: What was the structure of the text that we read today? What would be a good way to diagram it? In the Extend step, students expand their learning. Having used a semantic map to diagram information from a main idea-details story, they might gather additional information and add to the map. Having created a frame for bears, they might compose one for foxes. Here are examples of the major organizational patterns. You might use these to demonstrate to students how ideas might be organized and also how the CORE model might be implemented. Here is how CORE might be applied to a paragraph that is developed with reasons:

Main Idea/Reasons   "I forgot. I can't remember." Do you catch yourself saying either of these two sentences from time to time? Most of us do. There are several reasons why we forget things. At times we forget because we aren't paying close attention. We only half hear what is said. At other times our memories fail us because some clues are missing. We see a familiar person playing tennis. But we just can't remember who the person is. The next day we see the same person in a police uniform. Now we remember. It's the officer who directs traffic in front of school. Our memories need the extra clue of the uniform even though we see the officer almost every day (Gunning, 2006d).

Connect: Have you ever had a problem because you forgot something important? What do you do if you have something important to remember? What might you do to keep from forgetting something important?

Organize: How is the information organized? Which sentence gives the main idea? How is the main idea developed?

Reflect: How does knowing how the information is organized help us to understand and remember it? How might we show this information in a graphic organizer? Which organizer might we use? (This assumes that Key Organizers are displayed.)

Extension: What are some things we can do to help us remember? (Students read a selection about improving retention of information.)

You might use the following paragraphs to illustrate other kinds of structure or to provide additional practice with CORE.

Main Idea/Details

The whale shark was named for its size. It is a shark, but it is as big as a whale. A whale shark is about 30 feet long. That is as long as two large cars parked in a row. Some whale sharks have grown to be 60 feet long. Whale sharks can weigh as much as 72,000 pounds. That is about how much 20 large cars would weigh. The only sea creatures bigger than the whale shark are the large whales (Gunning, 2006d).

Main Idea/Examples

P. T. Barnum had a way with the truth. He stretched it as far as it would go. In the 1800s, P. T. made a bundle of money with a show that starred Joice Heth. She was supposed to be a 161-year-old slave who had helped raise George Washington. At first, a lot of people went to see the show. Then the crowds dropped off. So Barnum secretly passed the word that Joice Heth was a fake. He said that she was really a rubber dummy. People became interested again. They wanted to decide for themselves whether or not Joice Heth was real. The crowds returned to the show. P. T. Barnum would stretch the truth any way he could just so long as his truth stretching brought people to his show (Gunning, 2006d).

Sequence/Details

The archerfish has an unusual way of catching bugs. Believe it or not, it spits at them. Here's what happens. A grasshopper is resting on a leaf near the water. The archerfish spots the bug. Quickly, it forms a drop of water in its mouth. Then it

Locate and Recall (Forming a General Understanding)

rises to the surface, aims, and shoots. The drop of water smacks the grasshopper and knocks it off the leaf. The grasshopper falls into the open mouth of the archer-fish. Dinner is served (Gunning, 2006d).

Cause/Effect/Details

When oil is spilled in the ocean, it can be very harmful. Sea birds are the first to be hurt. The oil soaks into their feathers. The birds can no longer float. Many drown because they can't rest in the water. Others just keep flying until they drop from the air. Oil also kills fish, clams, and other sea animals. Even whales are harmed by spilled oil. Oil kills the tiny sea plants and animals that whales eat. People are hurt by spilled oil, too. There are fewer fish to catch for food. And beaches can become too dirty to use. There is a saying that it's no use crying over spilled milk. But maybe we should cry a little when oil is spilled (Gunning, 2006d).

Comparison/Contrast/Details

Have you are heard of an animal called the dugong? Dugongs are large sea animals. They can grow to be 10 feet long (3 meters) and weigh up to 400 kilograms. Dugongs are sometimes known as "sea cows." Like cows they spend much of their time eating. Only the grass they eat is under the sea. Dugongs are mammals. This means that they need to breathe air. They can only stay under water for a few minutes. Dugongs live for 70 years or more. They are one of the longest-living mammals on earth. They live just about as long as people.

Manatees are cousins to dugongs. Manatees are also large sea creatures. They can be 12 feet long and weigh 1,500 pounds or more. Like dugongs, they eat sea plants. They feed on the plants that grow at the bottom of streams, rivers, and canals. Manatees eat a lot. They eat up to 200 pounds of plants a day. Manatees are mammals so they must breathe air. They can only stay under water for two or three minutes. Manatees grow up a little faster than dugongs and don't live quite as long. They only live for about 60 years (Gunning, 2006d).

Processing Main Ideas and Details

Before reading, expert readers engage in several activities. They preview and activate prior knowledge and schema. Based on their preview and schema activation, they get a sense of the information the selection contains. This allows them to set purposes in the form of questions to be answered. They make use of titles and headings to get a sense of the main information that the selection will present. They turn headings into questions and read to answer the questions. As they read, they may find that they are not able to answer their questions. They slow down or reread. At the end of each section, they see if they can summarize what they have read. If they can't, they reread. If they have a specific question in mind but are unable to answer it, they scan the selection until they find the bit of information needed to answer the question. They consciously or automatically use the structure of the piece to help them grasp and organize essential details. As an expert reader, model the process for your students.

Determining Importance of Information

Being able to determine which details in a selection are important is an essential skill. Otherwise, the reader gets lost in a forest of details. Comprehending main ideas and determining the importance of information are closely related skills. Main ideas are summary statements of the details in a selection, or, to put it another way, details spell out the main idea. Main ideas are also used to determine which details are important and to organize details. For instance, once they know that the main idea of an article is how to grow tomatoes, readers can focus on the steps in the process, since these will be the most essential details. Knowledge of text structure is also an aid to understanding and retaining main ideas. Realizing that the structure is sequential, the reader notes the order in which the steps are presented. The adept reader also makes use of signal words and relational terms (Afflerbach & Johnston, 1986). Phrases such as "follow the directions" or "the following steps" alert the adept reader to a sequential, process organization. Phrases such as "three essential factors" or the "main reasons" signal a main idea/supporting detail structure. Words and phrases such as *first, next*, and *last, most important of all, finally*, and *on the other hand* guide readers as they attempt to put the details together into a coherent whole. Readers have to ask themselves which details support or explain a selection's main idea or, if the article is especially rich in details, which are the most important. If an article cites a dozen jobs that robots can undertake, readers might decide which five are most important. Text structure also signals relative importance (Afflerbach & Johnston, 1986). With a problem-solution structure, the strategic reader will seek out the problem and solution and ignore extraneous descriptions or examples.

To develop students' ability to determine relative importance of information, have them categorize details from an article as being relevant or irrelevant or as being essential or nonessential. Discuss relevance in terms of the purpose set for reading. Ask: "Do the details help answer the question that has been established?" Discuss why some details are relevant and some are irrelevant. Also discuss how the details function. They might be a step in a process, an example, a cause or effect, or a supporting detail (Buddy, 2005).

Asking Why

Simply asking why increases comprehension and retention of factual information. (Menke & Pressley, 1994). Asking why helps to make the information more meaningful. Asking why requires the reader to connect the new information with background knowledge (Benson-Castagna, 2005). This strategy is simple to apply. After reading that African elephants have larger ears than Asian elephants, the reader asks why that might be so. The strategy has three steps:

1. Identify the main point in the text or an essential detail.
2. Ask why about the fact or turn the fact into a why question.
3. List possible reasons. The possible reasons can come from the text, background knowledge, or both (Benson-Castagna, 2005).

You might use the box in Table 5.1 to frame a statement and a why response.

Themes

Fictional pieces don't have main ideas. Main idea instruction is more appropriate for nonfiction than for fiction. Fiction has a theme rather than a main idea. Identifying a theme can be subtler and more complex than noting a main idea. Theme is the underlying meaning of the story, a universal truth, a significant statement the story is making about society, human nature, or the human condition (Stauffer, 1999). The theme is not the same as a lesson or moral. Analysis of changes in characters can often provide insight into a particular theme. In young people's books, the theme frequently concerns the process of growing up. "The theme may be concerned with overcoming jealousy or fear, adjusting to a physical handicap, or accepting a stepparent" (Sutherland, 1997, p. 31).

Developing the concept of theme is a two-part process. In the first part students draw generalizations or themes from the text; in the second part they seek support for

Table 5.1 ● Why Chart

Main Idea or Key Detail	Why?
African elephants have larger ears than Asian elephants.	It is hotter in Africa, African elephants use their larger ears to cool off.

these generalizations or themes (Norton, 1989). Readers are seeking the answers to two questions: "What is the author trying to tell us that would make a difference in our lives? How do we know the author is telling us _____?" (Norton, 1989, p. 431).

Identifying lessons and themes can be a difficult task. When asked to identify a lesson or theme, students might retell the story. Remind them to think about what the author is trying to say in the story. What is she trying to get across? Students might also provide a very minor lesson to be learned. In a story about two children who saved a dog from drowning in an icy pond, some students responded that the lesson was not to walk on thin ice. Although it is true that people and animals shouldn't walk on thin ice, the overall story showed how two children by working together and helping each other saved the dog. A more appropriate lesson would be the value of cooperative effort. In your instruction, emphasize the selection of over-all lessons and themes. Through prompting, lead students beyond the minor lesson of not walking on ice to the overall lesson or theme of the piece. In Maryland's high-stakes test students are required to make a connection in addition to summariz-ing the selection (Krehbiel, 2005). However, they couldn't make just any connec-tion; they had to make a connection with the selection's theme. After reading about King Midas, a connection such as knowing someone who has a gold necklace wouldn't be adequate. The personal connection would need to be one in which the students made a connection between how King Midas learns to value the people around him and nature, and a person whom the student knows who values the im-portant things in life or an experience that the student had which helped her or him to see what is important in life.

To introduce the concept of theme, read a short story or picture book to stu-dents. Read a selection that is brief but that has a well-developed theme. Before reading the selection, set a purpose. Have students listen to discover what important things the author is trying to tell readers about life. Discuss with students possible themes. List the possible themes. Read the selection again. This time have students listen to the story in order to find support for the themes. List the evidence on the chalkboard under the theme. One way of getting at the theme is to use a story ele-ments map (Beck, Omanson & McKeown, 1982). A story elements map lists the key components of a story: problem or conflict and the major events or plot and theme. One way of creating a story elements map is to begin by noting the problem or the conflict. Then list the major events leading up to the resolution. It is also helpful to note changes in the main character. At that point, use that information to compose the story's theme or lesson.

Younger students might be asked to provide the lesson being taught in a story. Aesop's fables, trickster tales, or other traditional tales are good places to begin with the lessons conveyed by stories. However, themes shouldn't be equated with lessons or messages. While good literature provides insight into our humanity, it doesn't necessarily teach us a lesson.

Techniques for Developing Themes   Develop a theme that students can readily relate to. Once you have established the theme you wish to develop, activate students' experiential background that relates to the theme. For instance, if the theme is "to have friends, you have to be a friend," have students talk over times that they have been helpful to a friend or let the friend have the first choice of activities. Then have students read the story to find situations in which the main character was or was not acting like a friend. Discuss the story and the main character's actions in terms of whether she or he was being a friend. In the text *Swimmy* (Lionni, 1963), for instance, students might talk about how they have treated people who are different. In the after-reading discussion, they might respond to the question: "Did the red fish treat Swimmy the way we often treat people who are different?" (Applegate, 2004). In the discussion students use the text to support their views.

Working with older students, Kelly Gallagher (2005) encourages them to keep a theme notebook. After constructing themes based on *To Kill a Mockingbird* (Lee, 1961), students choose one theme and then keep a record of movies, TV shows, stories, poems, or real-life incidents that incorporate the theme. For instance, having discussed the theme, "standing up for what you believe in takes courage," students note other examples of the theme. This helps them to understand what a theme is and to understand the universality of some themes. It also provides deeper connections and understanding. As students note other examples of the theme, they should provide support or explanation to show that the inclusion is a manifestation of the target theme. Gallagher also insists that students state their themes in sentences, so that they are expressions of themes rather than labels for topics. *Courage* is not a theme. "Courage is sometimes found in unexpected places" is.

Summarizing

Summarizing is probably the most difficult comprehension strategy to teach and learn. However, it is worth the effort that is put into teaching and learning it. According to research (Pressley, Johnson, Symons, McGoldrick & Kurita, 1989), summarizing is the most useful strategy. Summarizing is rooted in retelling. In fact, summarizing can be thought of as a refined, selective retelling.

Retelling   Retellings come in different forms (see Table 5.2). A start-to-finish retelling starts at the beginning and flows through to the end. This is the easiest of the retellings (Collins, 2004). A gist retelling is a kind of a summary of the events or

Table 5.2 ● Types of Retellings

Type of Retelling	Content	Organization	Language
Start-to-finish	All the events/ details	Chronological	First, next, last, finally, suddenly, in the end
Gist	Most important events/details	Main idea/ supporting details/story structure	Most important, main
Point-by-point	Most important events/details	Order of importance/chronological	First, next, last, finally
Point of View	Viewpoint with support	Position/supporting details	Evaluative statement: "This book was the scariest I have ever read."

the ideas. In a gist retelling, the student highlights the most important elements. A point-by-point retelling goes through the main ideas or events in a logical or chronological order. A point of view retelling includes judgment and will probably emphasize the positive or negative depending upon the teller's point of view. It might also include the teller's evaluative commentary. As part of teaching students how to retell, instruct them in the language they might use in their retelling. This is helpful to all students, but is especially beneficial for ELL. For a standard or chronological retelling, teach students time or sequence words: *first, next, then, last, finally, suddenly, in the end* (Collins, 2004). For a summary retelling, Collins (2004) provides her students with words that lead to it: "This story is about . . ." In a point-of-view retelling, students might begin with an evaluative statement: "This book was one of the funniest I have ever read." The retelling might also be guided by a story map so that the teller focuses on the key elements: "The story took place 100 years ago in an imaginary land known as Krinklewood . . ."

Narratives with a start-to-finish retelling have a familiar time-sequence organization and so are typically easier to retell and summarize. The student simply begins with first incident and proceeds to the last incident. For young students this might not be as easy as it seems. They might have difficulty with the sequence and might omit key incidents or, on the other hand, include an overabundance of nonessential happenings. To prepare students to compose more effective summaries, develop their ability to construct more effective retellings. Because retelling is such a natural, pervasive activity, it is often overlooked instructionally, except to remind students to include the most important information. An approach known as developmental retelling helps develop needed retelling skills.

Developmental Retelling   Being egocentric, young students often assume that listeners know what they know. They may have difficulty taking the perspective of someone who has no knowledge of a series of events or a story, so they might omit some essential details. If the teacher is the person who has requested the retelling and the students believe that the teacher is familiar with the story, the students might be inclined to give a very brief overview of the events and leave out crucial explanations or identifications. The students might simply say that Pam and Dan were looking for Anna without explaining that Pam and Dan had started a pet sitting business and Anna was a pet cat who had slipped away. The teacher needs to explain that the students are to retell the story as though they were telling it to someone who was absent the day the story was read.

When Benson and Cummins (2002) set out to help teachers improve their students' retellings, they quickly discovered that they needed a systematic approach built on the way students develop increasingly complex skills. They identified four stages: pretelling, guided retelling, story map or graphic organizer retelling, and written retelling.

Pretelling   Students explain the steps in a commonplace activity. They explain how to wrap a present, play a computer game, tie shoes, make no-cook pudding, write a story, dribble a basketball, or any other common activity. Pretelling requires students to reverse the process of carrying out the task. The students must be able to think back to the first step and then order each of the steps. To demonstrate the process, explain each step and think aloud as you make a booklet or other item. Then holding up the finished product, go through each step in order. Write the steps on the chalkboard and use the words *first, second, third, last* to signal the order of each step. Working in pairs, have students pretell the activity and create their own booklets. Provide added instruction and practice as needed. You might integrate the pretelling activities with classroom routines, such as selecting and checking out independent reading books, working at centers, or lining up for lunch.

Guided Retelling   Illustrations and props are used to guide students' retelling. At the easiest levels, use illustrations to retell a selection. Initially, pick brief books in which all the key events are clearly illustrated. Books such as, *Have You Seen My Cat?* (Carle, 1987), *The Chick and the Duckling* (Ginsburg, 1972), and *The Turnip* (Ziefert, 1996) would be especially appropriate for young students. When retelling, students should use only the illustrations and not the words.

Using Props   When students no longer need the kind of full support provided by illustrations, they graduate to using props. Props can be real objects, such as a lacrosse stick, ball, and helmet or maybe toy replicas or even pictures. In guided retelling using illustrations, all the key events are depicted. In guided retelling using props, not every event is represented by a prop. In *Too Many Tamales* (Soto, 1993), props might include a fake diamond ring, one or more tamales, a bowl for mixing ingredient for tamales and a pan for placing the tamales. For *Stone Soup* (McGovern, 1968), props might include a stone, a pot, and plastic foods. Demonstrate and explain how you might use props in a retelling and provide students with guided practice as they attempt using props. Stress the importance of selecting props that highlight key events or processes. Stress that students need not have a prop for every event or process, but emphasize the importance of putting the props in order. Handmade puppets can, of course, be used as props. Create a prop box in which you store props that might be used in retellings. You might also arrange to acquire props for some of the books so that these can be used for demonstration or practice. In addition to providing guidance, props reassure shy speakers by giving them concrete reminders. Props also add interest to presentations. As an added benefit, props are helpful to students learning the language.

Using Story Maps and Other Graphic Organizers   Ultimately, students complete story maps and other graphic organizers to assist them with their retellings. The graphic organizers become a way of selecting and organizing materials for the retelling. Although story maps are a good way to highlight the key elements in a story, they should be used flexibly when providing assistance with a retelling. A retelling format in which the student always gave the setting, names of characters, problem, plot, and solution would be tiresome. Sometimes the setting is not important. More often, a retelling would start with a description of the main characters and the story problem, and then would proceed through the plot to the resolution of the story problem. Sometimes the setting is crucial, as in a story about time travel. Retellings based on a story map would need to be flexible and dictated by the nature of the story.

For expository text, graphic organizers would be used to plan and structure the retelling. The type of graphic organizer used would be determined by the structure of the written piece. A key skill in learning to retell would be the ability to determine what kind of organizer would best convey essential information about a selection.

Discovering Why Summaries Are Important Students learn best when they make connections between what they are learning and their own experiences. Students might not realize that they have been composing summaries much of their lives. To introduce the concept of summarizing, explain how you use summaries. Explain that if you see the principal and the principal asks how your day went, you don't give every single detail, but tell the principal only the most important information, and if someone asks you about a book you are reading, you only tell the most important things. Explain that this is summarizing. Ask students if they have done any of the following:

- Told someone at home what you did at school.
- Told about a trip that you took.
- Told the main parts of a story that you read.
- Told the main parts of a movie that you saw or a game that you watched.

Explain to students that if they have done any of the above, then they have summarized. Tell students that in addition to summarizing orally, we also summarize in writing. For example, they might be asked on a test to tell briefly what a story or article was about or to tell what happened to the main character. Or maybe they wrote a summary of a book that they read. Explain, too, that they have read summaries. Locate and discuss the summaries provided at the end of textbook chapters and the blurbs on book jackets or recommended annotated reading lists. Explain to students that summarizing is the most important reading and writing skill that they will learn.

Discovering the Characteristics of a Good Summary Before students can summarize effectively, they need to know what a good summary is like. Provide examples of well-crafted summaries and the original. Help students discover what makes an effective summary. Ask: "What do you notice about the summaries?"

- What is in the first sentence of each summary?
- What comes next?
- What kinds of details does the summary include?
- How does the summary end?

To provide practice in recognizing the key elements of a summary, have students select from three or four options the best summary as in the example below. Discuss students' choices. Have them explain their selections. Discuss why one of the summaries was better than the others. Once students have a basic understanding of what a good summary is, and have had practice with oral summaries, help them develop the ability to compose summaries.

How Dogs Help Disabled People

Dogs can help disabled people in many ways. A guide dog becomes the eyes for a blind person. It helps its owner get from place to place. A hearing ear dog alerts its owner when it hears certain sounds. A mobility assist dog becomes its owner's helping hands. It helps its owner by picking up objects and bringing them to its owner. It picks up objects that the owner has dropped or can't reach. It can also pull its owner's wheelchair, carry things in a backpack, and open and close doors. It can even help its owner get dressed. Dogs that assist disabled people are known as service dogs.

Circle the letter of the best summary.

a. Dogs can help disabled people in many ways. Dogs that assist disabled people are known as service dogs.

b. Service dogs can help disabled people in many ways. Guide dogs help the blind. Hearing ear dogs help the deaf. Mobility assist dogs help people who can't get around or do things for themselves.

c. Service dogs can help disabled people in many ways. Guide dogs help the blind. Hearing ear dogs help the deaf. Mobility assist dogs help people who can't get around or do things for themselves. A mobility assist dog becomes its owner's helping hands. It helps its owner in many ways. It helps its owner by picking up objects and bringing them to its owner. It picks up objects that the owner has dropped or can't reach. It can also pull its owner's wheelchair, carries things in a backpack, and open and close doors. It can even help its owner get dressed.

d. Dogs can help disabled people in many ways. Dogs that assist disabled people are known as service dogs. One kind of service dog is the guide dog. A guide dog becomes the eyes for a blind person. It helps its owner get from place to place (Gunning, 2006d).

Preparing Students for Written Summaries To prepare students for written summaries, have them summarize orally. Actually, summarizing is a pervasive part of everyday life. Students summarize their day when they arrive home from school or play and their parents ask them what they were doing, or if they tell about a book they read or a frightening or humorous experience that they had. These informal summaries, especially when delivered by younger students, tend to be all-inclusive. No detail, no matter how small, is omitted. In class summaries, emphasize the importance of stressing the most important details. Include summarizing questions in your discussions of selections read. Model oral summarizing by summarizing lessons and accounts of books or stories that you have read.

To foster improved oral summarizing, formulate questions that help students provide summaries: What did James do to improve his playing? What are the steps in making cheese? What are the five main effects of global warming?

Introducing Written Summaries   Model the process of writing a summary. Explain why you are composing a summary and how you might go about it. Think aloud as you compose your summary so students can gain some insight into the processes involved. The summary could be one that is especially planned for demonstration purposes, or it might be one that you were going to compose anyway. For instance, you might compose a summary of a lesson or a day's events or an article that you have read to the class.

As you compose summaries invite the class to join in. If you regularly compose summaries, this could be an ongoing activity. From time to time, compose group summaries with the class. Gradually work into scaffolded individual summaries.

Scaffolding Summaries   In scaffolding students' responses, you supply prompts or frames that help them compose a response. You proceed from providing maximum support to gradually lessening support until the students reach a point where they can work independently. Frames can be used to organize both oral and written responses. Frames are just what their name suggests. They provide a written framework for a response. Frames can be narrative or expository. Frames can be used to help students summarize a whole story or just segments of it. Frames can be used to compare characters or summarize a plot. For expository text, frames can take a problem-solution, main idea–details, cause-effect or virtually any other format.

In a frame, you provide a template. The students compose the summary by filling in the template. The template can vary in the amount of assistance it supplies. The sample frame below provides a medium amount of support.

Read the following article. After reading it, finish writing the summary. Include only the most important information. Leave out any unnecessary words.

Service Dogs at Work

Many service dogs wear special vests. Some vests have patches on them. The patch tells what kind of work the dog is doing. The patch might say, "Hearing Dog" or "Search Dog." The vest and the patch inform people that the dog is working. Most people don't know what to do when they see a service dog. If you notice a service dog at work, the best thing to do is to do nothing. Don't talk to the dog. Don't call it. Don't feed it. Don't pet it. The dog is working. It is helping its owner, so don't distract it. Taking the dog's attention away from its work just makes its job harder.

Many service dogs wear special vests to let people know _____

_____ .

If you a see service dog at work, _____

_____ .

Now compare your answer with the sample answer.

Sample Answer

Many service dogs wear special vests to let people know they are working. If you see a service dog at work, don't distract it (Gunning, 2006d).

Discuss students' summaries with them. Emphasize that their summaries don't have to have exactly the same wording, but the ideas should be the same or similar.

Using Graphic Organizers to Summarize Story maps and graphic organizers can be used to help students compose summaries. Being easier to compose than a written summary, a graphic organizer can be used to summarize the information. Students might then use the graphic organizer as a planner for their summary. Because they limit the amount of writing, graphic organizers help develop the concept of emphasizing essential information and condensing. Using the following or a similar paragraph, enlist the class's help as you create a graphic organizer summary (see Figure 5.1).

Keeping Your Eyes on the Zebra's Ears

A zebra's ears are worth watching. They tell you how the zebra is feeling. If a zebra's ears are standing straight up, it's a sign that the zebra is feeling calm. If the zebra's ears are pointed forward, then danger may be near. Ears pointed forward mean that a zebra is afraid. If a zebra's ears are pointed backward, you better hope that there a fence between you and the striped creature. Ears flattened backward are a sign of anger. The zebra may be getting ready to attack (Gunning, 2006d).

Because of space limitations, graphic organizers encourage selecting the most essential details and condensing. After cooperatively using graphic organizers to summarize, have students complete partially finished organizers. As students become proficient, have them create organizers on their own, but supply help as needed.

Figure 5.1 ● Graphic Organizer Summary

Using Questions to Develop a Summary   A series of questions can also be used to help students develop summaries. The following questions might be used to prompt the writing of a story summary:

- Who is the main character? What is her or his problem?
- What are the main things that happened because of the problem?
- How was the problem finally solved?

For informational text, the following prompting questions might be used to elicit a summary:

- What is the main point of this article?
- What main details does the author use to support the main idea?

Summarizing with Somebody Wanted But So   Somebody Wanted But So is a framework designed to help students summarize a narrative piece (Beers, 2003). The frame consists of four columns, one for each word (see Table 5.3). Under the *Somebody* column, the main character's name is placed. Under the *Wanted* column, students tell what the main character wanted or wanted to do. This would most often be a statement of the main's character's goal. The *But* column contains a statement of the conflict or the problem that the main character encounters. The *So* column contains the resolution of

Table 5.3 ● Somebody-Wanted-But-So Summary

Somebody	Wanted	But	So
Bessie Coleman	To learn to fly	She couldn't find anyone in the United States to teach her	She saved her money and traveled to France to learn.

the problem, or the outcome of the main character's efforts to achieve a goal. For some selections, students will be able to sum up the whole story with one set of statements. For more complex selections, students will need to add to the basic frame. Students add a *Then* and fill in another set of Somebody Wanted But So statements. If there is more than one main character, students can write more than one set of statements.

Summarizing Expository Text Summarizing expository text offers somewhat of a greater challenge because students typically have less experience both reading and writing expository text. Expository text is generally more complex. In order to summarize expository text, students must first determine the main idea. After that it's a question of including the details that support the main idea. One way of approaching summarizing is to use the same structure to summarize as the author used to write the article.

Condensing Summarizing is a difficult skill because in addition to requiring the reader to present the key information, it also demands that information be condensed. This is a difficult task, one that requires a fair amount of instruction and practice along with continued guidance. With younger students, stress the content of summaries.

A key element in composing a summary is having a grasp of the content. If students struggled to read an article, they will have difficulty summarizing. They may not have understood the article well enough to select what is important. If their understanding is fragile, chances are they will have difficulty putting the information into their own words.

Reinforcing the Concept of an Effective Summary To remind students of the elements of an effective summary, post steps for creating a summary. Also post a model summary and compose a rubric for a summary. For best results, the whole school should agree on what goes into an effective summary, and all teachers should teach it as it applies to their area. While discussing examples of their students' work, fifth grade teachers in Montgomery County, Maryland, agreed that their students had not grasped the concept of writing a summary. The teachers also discovered that they weren't doing a good job teaching summarizing because they didn't agree on what a good summary was (Krehbiel, 2005). So that they could get a feel for the task, teachers read a test selection and composed a summary. Having composed and reflected on the task of composing a summary, the teachers decided that in order to plan an effective program, they would first have to create a rubric that spelled out what an effective summary was at each of the target grade levels. Once the teachers had established a clear definition of what an effective summary was and rubrics for each grade level, then they were in a better position to plan instruction. They could see where they were going and what they had to do to get there.

Although it took time to explore summaries and hammer out rubrics, in the long run it saved time. Planning took less time because teachers had a clearer sense of what kind of instruction was needed. Teachers also shared instructional ideas. Having rubrics at various levels gave the teachers a kind of scope and sequence to follow. In addition, teachers could use rubrics for lower grades to assess the summaries of struggling students and the rubrics of upper grades to assess the work of advanced students. Teachers also enlisted the efforts of all staff members. The special teachers and support staff included instruction in summaries in their classes. Listed below in Figure 5.2 are the steps for writing a summary. Presented in Table 5.4 is a graphic organizer that might be used to help students get the essential information for a summary. Listed in Table 5.5 is a rubric for assessing a summary. You might want to use this as a starting point for developing a rubric with your class or co-workers. Also presented is a model summary. For best results, compose a checklist for writing a summary and a rubric for assessing the summary with students. Encourage students to use the checklist as they write their summaries and the rubric after they have written their summaries as a device for revising their summaries. With your class, you might try out the rubric with sample summaries, some of which need improvement. Compose these samples yourself or use summaries from past years. Don't embarrass students by using current students' work.

Figure 5.2 ● Steps for Writing a Summary

1. Determine the main idea.
2. Write the main idea.
3. Write the most important details that support the main idea.
4. Shorten the summary. Combine ideas. Get rid of ideas that are not important. Get rid of unnecessary words.
5. Read over the summary. Make sure that it has the main idea and key details. Make sure that it is clear.

Table 5.4 • Summary Graphic Organizer

What is the main idea?	What are the key supporting details?

Providing a Model Summary   Develop a model summary with students or use the following paragraph and its summary. Discuss what makes an effective summary. Students might practice using their rubric on the summary to see if maybe there might be some room for improvement.

Model Summary: How Bats Use Their Ears

A bat uses its ears to find its way. Even in the darkest places, a bat has no trouble getting around. As it flies, it makes noises. Some of the bat noises are clicks. Others are screeching sounds. Many are so high that people can't hear them. The bat noises move out in waves. When they hit something, they bounce back. The bat picks up the sounds with its ears. By carefully using its ears, a bat can tell where things are. The longer it takes the sound waves to bounce back, the farther the object is. Using sound waves, bats can even find small bugs flying at high speeds. In one test, bats were able to catch more than a hundred bugs in just one minute (Gunning, 2006d).

Summary

A bat uses its ears to find its way. It makes sounds and then listens for the sounds as they bounce off objects and return. They can tell where the object is by how long the sound waves take to return.

Calling Attention to Everyday Summaries   Call attention to summaries. Orally summarize lessons and discussions in the content areas. If possible, record key summaries, and talk about what you are doing as you compose your summary. This has a double benefit. Students review the topic, and they see how a summary is composed. This is even more beneficial if you involve students in the writing of the summary. Structure the summary by including questions similar to the following:

Table 5.5 ● Rubric for Assessing a Summary

	Advanced	Basic	Developing
Main idea	States main idea clearly and concisely.	States main idea.	Main idea is not stated or is mixed in with details.
Essential details	States all of the important details.	States most of the important details.	States a few important details. Contains unimportant details.
Organization	Ideas or events are told in order.	Ideas may not be in best order.	Lacks organization.
Condenses ideas	Details are combined where possible.	Some details are combined.	Details are not combined.
Condenses language	Does not have unnecessary words.	Some words could be omitted.	A number of words could be omitted.
Clearly written	Summary is clear and easy to follow.	Summary does not flow easily.	Summary is hard to understand in parts.

"What topic did we discuss today? What did we learn? What were the most important ideas that we learned? What else did we learn?" After the summary has been written, you might ask: "Did we include all the important information? Are there any ideas up there that we could leave out because they are aren't very important? Have we expressed our ideas clearly? Can we shorten our summary? Are there any unnecessary words that we might take out?" The summary need not be a formal paragraph; it might just be a title and a list of important facts.

Study Group Questions

- What are the key strategies in Locating and Recalling?
- What are my students' proficiencies in this area?
- What instruction do they need in this area? What is my plan for teaching strategies in this area?
- Which of the suggested approaches or techniques seem most promising? How will I use the techniques?
- How will I help students apply the skills? In what subject areas will they apply the skills?
- What materials will I use?
- How will I help students who are having a difficult time learning the skills?

Integrate and Interpret (Developing Interpretation)

Interpreting means that we must bring out own knowledge and experience to bear. It also involves a higher level of reasoning. Not only must we understand what we have read, we must integrate by making inferences, drawing conclusions, and making connections based on what we have read. Integrate and Interpret also includes comparing and contrasting, asking questions, and creating images. A key element in integrating and interpreting is the ability to support inferences, conclusions, and connections.

Inferences

Drawing inferences requires combining background knowledge and information from text. There are two kinds of inferences: schema-based and text-based. In a schema-based inference the reader uses prior knowledge plus information from the text to make an inference. For instance, if the students read that the man's hat blew off but a passenger sitting several rows behind him caught it before it fell into the lake, they can infer that it was a windy day and that the man was probably on a boat and that the boat was large enough to carry a number of people. In a text-based inference, the reader puts two or more pieces of information together to make an inference. To assess students' ability to make inferences, have them read the following or a similar selection. Tell them that you want them to make as many inferences as they can. In other words, based on the information in the passage, what can they infer or conclude?

The Life-Saving Elephants

The elephants were acting strangely. They seemed frightened. But of what? Their mahout couldn't tell. Speaking softly to the elephants, the mahout calmed them down. Now it was time for them to go to work. Their job was to take tourists for a ride. Now that they were calm, the elephants began carrying the tourists. But then they began trumpeting again, and then, with the frightened tourists hanging on tightly, the elephants began running up a nearby hill. Looking down to the beach, the mahout spotted a giant wave rushing for shore. Now everyone began running for the hill. Minutes later a giant wave known as a tsunami swept over the beach. But the wave did not reach the top of the hill. The elephants had saved hundred of lives (Gunning, 2006d).

Putting together pieces of information from the story, the reader can infer that the elephants sense the coming of the tsunami. Also using clues from the story, the readers can tell that the mahout is someone who takes care of elephants. Other possible inferences include concluding that the place is a vacation area, that it is probably in Africa or Asia because that is where elephants live, and the place is located near the ocean. At first, have students make inferences without any prompting on your part. If there are still inferences to be made, provide prompts. Start off with general prompts and move to more specific ones if necessary. Note the degree and nature of prompting required. This provides some insight into the kinds of instruction that students might benefit from. Discuss with students the inferences they made. Also ask them to support their responses. If need be, you might use prompts, such as the following, to draw out inferences:

> What ability did the elephants have? What could they sense?
> Where were the elephants? In what part of the world?
> What kind of an area was this?
> What makes you think that it is a place where people go on vacation?
> What is a mahout?

Chances are, students will surprise you and themselves with the number of inferences that they make. Students have been making inferences since they were small children. They were able to infer from tone of voice, facial expression, or actions how a person might be feeling. In their everyday experiences, students are continuously making inferences based on what they see and hear. However, they don't always transfer the ability to infer and conclude to the written word. Students might not realize that inferences are called for. They might be fixated on a literal level of understanding (Westby, 1999). They respond to inferential questions by complaining that they can't find the answer in the selection. For these students QAR (Question-Answer Relationship) might be a useful technique.

Using QAR

QAR was created to help students locate the sources of inferential as well as literal questions (Raphael, 1984, 1986). Through QAR, students identify the source of answers as being:

1. *Right there:* Answer is contained within a single sentence in the text.
2. *Putting it together:* It is necessary to put together information from several sentences to obtain an answer.
3. *On my own:* The answer is part of the student's prior knowledge.
4. *Writer and me:* The reader must combine personal knowledge with information from the text to construct an inference.

To introduce QAR, use the following or a similar exercise to show where the source of answers can be found.

> Jason jumped up. A wave had just washed over his feet. When he had fallen asleep, the waves were at least 30 feet away. Now they were lapping at his bare feet. How long had he slept? The sun was high in the sky when he had dropped

off. It must have been about noon. Now it was a red ball of fire slipping beneath the waves far out at sea. It must be after eight o'clock. Jason scanned the horizon. He hoped to see a rescue boat, but the horizon was empty. He figured he'd better build a shelter. Tomorrow he would work on his sailboat.

To show students where answers to questions can be found, ask questions of the following type:

- What had awakened Jason? (right there)
- How long had he been asleep? (putting it together)
- Why had the water gotten closer to Jason? (writer and me)
- Where was Jason? (writer and me)
- How do you think he got there? (writer and me)
- What time of the year was it? (writer and me)
- How would you feel if you were Jason? (on my own)

Discuss answers to the questions and the sources of the answers. Ask students to explain how they determined the answers to the questions. Emphasize the fact that answers are not always stated directly. Also stress reasoning processes. If students have difficulty with a question, use prompts to guide them. If students have difficulty answering the question, What time of year was it?, ask: "What time of year is it when the sun is still shining at eight o'clock at night?" Text-bound students need to see that they are expected to use their backgrounds and reasoning processes to answer open-ended questions. They need to see that what they have to say counts.

Just as some students are text-bound, others are bound by background knowledge. They overuse background and fail to use information from the text to answer questions. QAR also helps these students because it emphasizes the need to use the text to construct meaning.

Inferences vary in type and difficulty. Making predictions, which is inferring what will happen in the future, is more difficult than making inferences based on completed actions. Inferring character traits is one of the easiest to draw. Even young students have extensive experience from real-life experiences using inferring skills to make judgments about acts of kindness, friendliness, bullying, and selfishness. A good place to initiate instruction would be with inferring character traits and feelings. Drawing conclusions is a kind of an inference. However, a conclusion is generally based on a series of facts.

Making an inference is a two-part skill. Readers consider the details and/or background to make an inference, and they then provide support for the inference. In a highly successful series of lessons, students were taught how to use details to make inferences, how to support inferences, and then how to put both skills together (Hansen & Pearson, 1982). Initially, the teacher provided the details and showed students how to make an inference based on those details. The teacher then provided an inference and asked students to find support for the inference, and, lastly, the teacher asked students to make inferences and provide support for the inferences. Since making an inference is more difficult than supporting an inference, begin by providing inferences and requesting that students support them. Ask: "How-do-you-know?" questions. How do you know that Richard was taller than Tyrique? How do you know that Alyssa was traveling by plane? Students then find support for the inference. In so doing they learn how to use textual and experience clues. *Why* questions can also be used to draw out inferences. Why did William say, "Oh no!" when he saw his older brother?

Ultimately, students have to make their own inferences. They need to use information in a selection as a basis for inferring what kind of a person the characters in a story are. One helpful device is a graphic organizer known as "Getting to Know My Character" (Richards & Gipe, 1993). Using this device, the teacher places an excerpt that does a particularly good job revealing a character's traits. The excerpt is placed on an overhead or the chalkboard. In think-aloud style, the teacher explains that when reading a story, it is important to get to know the characters. The teacher tells students that authors sometimes directly tell what a character is like, or they might let us judge what kind of a person the character is by looking at the character's actions or what the character says about himself or herself or what others say. Or sometimes the author takes us into the character's mind so that we can see what the character is thinking.

After displaying a passage similar to the following one, note the facts that the author reveals about the main character, and place the facts in the Character Chart (Table 6.1). The facts are simply listed under "What the story says." In the next column, "What the reader can infer," the facts are interpreted. The teacher thinks aloud as she demonstrates how she makes inferences based on the facts. The teacher goes through the same process with actions, thoughts, conversations, and what others say.

Timothy

Instead as she [Mrs. Frisby] came out of the woods from Mr. Ages' house and reached the farmyard fence, she thought about Timothy. She thought of how his eyes shone with merriment when he made up small jokes, which he did frequently, and how invariably kind he was to his small scatterbrain sister Cynthia. The other children sometimes laughed at her when she made mistakes, or grew impatient with her because she was forever losing things; but Timothy never did. Instead he would help her

Table 6.1 ● Character Chart

Name of character _____

	What the Story Says	What the Reader Can Infer
Character's actions		
Character's thoughts		
Character's conversations		
What others say about the character		
What the author says about the character		

find them. And when Cynthia herself had been sick in bed, he had sat by her side for hours and entertained her with stories. He made these up out of his head, and he seemed to have a bottomless supply of them (From *Mrs. Frisby and the Rats of NIMH* by Robert C. O'Brien, 1971, p. 20).

For practice, have students read the following or similar paragraphs and complete a character chart for each person.

Chester Greenwood

One of six children in a farm family that didn't have much money to spare, Chester Greenwood began helping out at an early age. He went from door to door selling eggs laid by the family's hens. His egg route was eight miles long. To make extra money, Chester made candy at home and sold that along with the eggs. When he was just 15, Chester began making and selling earmuffs (Gunning, 2006d).

Sibyl Ludington

It was nine o'clock on a Saturday night in April of 1777. A messenger had just warned the Ludingtons that the British were near. At that time the British ruled America. But the people of America were fighting for their freedom. More than 2,000 British soldiers were marching toward the town of Danbury, Connecticut. They were planning to burn it down. Mr. Ludington wanted to stop the British. He was in charge of a group of soldiers, but his men were back in their homes. So he sent his daughter to call the soldiers together. Sibyl, who was only 16, rushed around the countryside on her horse, Star. "Meet at Ludington's!" she shouted to all the fighting men she could find. Sibyl rode all night. For ten hours she rode through farmland and forests. She had to be careful that the British didn't catch her. There were also lots of robbers around. She had to make sure they didn't catch her either. And she had to be careful that she didn't get lost or fall off her horse. The trail was muddy and slippery. During that long night, Sibyl rode for 40 miles. She made it home just in time to see her father and his men march against the British (Gunning, 2006d).

Using Writing to Develop Character Traits

Have students apply their knowledge of how authors reveal character traits by using actions, thoughts, and conversations to develop characters. Explain how it's often better to show rather than tell what a character is like. Have students collect examples of authors using actions, thoughts, and conversations to reveal character traits. To assist students in inferring character traits, discuss the main traits that characters might display and the kinds of actions that would suggest possession of those traits. Discuss how a kind or caring character might display kindness; a nervous character, nervousness; a courageous character, bravery. Compile and post a list of possible character traits. To extend students' learning, have them write about the positive traits of real-life people. They might write about a kindly uncle or a vivacious aunt or a determined cousin or a sensitive brother. As always, they should provide support in the form of examples and details.

If students are intimidated by words, have them make inferences from pictures. The pictures might be from a text they are about to read. From a picture of a person, they might infer the person's age, where the person is, what the person might be doing, what the person is thinking, whether the person is rich or poor, etc. You might also use wordless books and have students infer a whole story.

Once students feel comfortable with making inferences from pictures, have them move up to sentences (Yuill & Oakhill, 1991). Have them read the following sentences and ask: What might you infer from the following? What leads you to make that inference?

Alfred is still absent.

Students might infer that Alfred is a boy because Alfred is a boy's name. They might also infer that Alfred has been absent for a while because the word *still* implies that. They might infer that perhaps Alfred has a serious illness and that is why he is still absent. Use the following or similar sentences as prompts for inferring.

Juan ran for the school bus.
Jamie put on a hat with flaps that pulled down over his ears,
Alexia ran into her home when she saw the neighbor's dog.

Cloze

We don't like unanswered questions or unexplained phenomena. Seeing an unfinished jigsaw puzzle, we can hardly resist finishing it. In conversations, we supply words when the speaker hesitates and can't seem to think of the next word. Humans have a built-in need for completeness, for closure. Taking advantage of that penchant for completeness is a technique known as cloze. Originally used as a technique for assessing the difficulty level of texts, cloze is also a highly effective method for fostering inferential thinking (Dewitz, Carr & Patberg, 1987).

Traditional Cloze   In traditional cloze, words are deleted at random from a narrative or expository passage. The first and last sentences are left intact, and no proper nouns are removed; otherwise, every fifth, sixth, seventh, eighth, ninth, or tenth word is deleted. (Generally, the interval for word deletion should be no more than every fifth and no less than every tenth word.) Before attempting cloze passages, students need some orientation and practice. Filling in missing words is more difficult than reading intact passages. (Unless modified, cloze should only be used by students reading on a third-grade level or above.) Students should be informed, too, that the standard for excellence is much lower for cloze passages than it is for regular passages. When introducing cloze, explain the purpose of cloze and provide suggestions for completing cloze exercises:

- Read the entire passage first.
- Use all the clues given in a passage.
- Read beyond the blank to the end of the sentence. Often it is necessary to read the whole sentence to get the full benefit of the clue, or the clue might not occur until after the blank.
- If necessary, read a sentence or two ahead to get additional clues.
- Spell as best you can. You lose no points for misspelled words.
- Do your best, but do not worry if you cannot correctly complete each blank. Most readers will be able to fill in fewer than half the blanks correctly.
- After you have filled in as many blanks as you can, reread the passage. Make any changes that you think are necessary (Gunning, 2005a).

Scoring Cloze   **Exact Replacement**   There are two ways of scoring a cloze activity. When used as a test, only exact replacements are counted as correct. Otherwise, scoring is too time consuming and too subjective. Scores are lower on cloze exercises than they are on multiple-choice exercises; on cloze a score of 50 percent is adequate. Criteria for scoring cloze procedure are as follows:

Level	Percentage
Independent	> 57
Instructional	44–57
Frustration	< 44

Substitution Scoring   When cloze is used instructionally, substitution scoring is recommended. A response is considered correct if it fits both semantically and syntactically.

Modified Cloze   Modified cloze, which is also known as mazes, has a multiple-choice format. Instead of supplying the missing word, students pick from three or four options. This format is used by a number of commercial workbooks and some tests. Although providing valuable practice, multiple-choice cloze shifts the focus from predicting a word to considering which alternative is best. The task is changed from being one of constructing meaning to recognizing meaning, a subtle but significant alteration. However, modified cloze can be good preparation for completing traditional cloze exercises and provides excellent practice for students who are so focused on getting the words right that they fail to read for meaning.

Macro-Cloze   After students have grown accustomed to drawing inferences based on single sentences, have them try macro-cloze. In macro-cloze, students use background of experience and inferential reasoning to supply a missing sentence (Yuill & Oakhill (1991).

The team had hoped to play a game of baseball.

_____

_____

They played basketball instead.

Jeff thought he would finish his chores in less than an hour.

_____

_____

He didn't finish until three hours later.

Tanya thought she had gotten a hundred on the spelling test.

_____

_____

She made up her mind to study harder for the next spelling test.

Help students to see that the inferences that we make and conclusions that we draw are based on our background of experiences, the assumptions that we make, and our perspectives (Paul & Elder, 2001). Students might enjoy making up their own macro-cloze activities and sharing them with their classmates.

Making Inferences with It Says-I Say-And So

It Says-I Say-And So is a series of prompts placed in a chart that help students make inferences by taking them through the process step by step (Beers, 2003). Students complete four columns as in Table 6.2. Under the Question column, students write the question they are answering. Under "It Says," they respond to the question by writing information from the text. Under "I Say" students draw on their background of experience to write what they know about the text information recorded in "It Says." Under the "And So" column, they use both text and personal information to make an inference.

As with other approaches, model how you might use it and provide opportunities for guided and independent practice. Start with questions that are supported by just one piece of information and which would appear under "It Says." Start with brief selections. As students gain in proficiency, advance to questions that are supported by several pieces of information under "It Says" so that students make note of and analyze a number of details. Under your guidance, have students try out the technique with the following or similar paragraphs.

Table 6.2 ● It Says-I Say-And So Chart

Question	It Says	I Say	And So
Read the question.	Find information from the text that will help you answer the question.	Think about what you know about the information from the text.	Put together what the text says with what you know.
How did Monique feel at the end of the story?	Monique wiped away a tear as the bus pulled away. She would miss her big sister. But then she thought of having the room she had shared with her sister all to herself at least until Christmas vacation, and a smile broke across her face.	You cry when you are sad. And you get sad when your sister goes away. But getting your own room can make you happy. I remember how I felt when my brother went off to college and I had the room to myself.	And so that's why I think Monique had mixed feelings. She was sad and glad at the same time.

Brian Anderson

Watching a TV show saved Brian Anderson's life. While surfing near his home in Seaside, Oregon, Anderson felt something grab his leg. Pain shot through his body. Turning his head to see what it was, Anderson found himself looking into the killer eyes of a ten-foot-long great white shark. Then Brian remembered from a TV program that a shark's nose is very sensitive. Anderson wound up and belted the great white right smack in the nose. Nothing happened. He punched the shark again and again. Finally, the shark let him go. Bleeding and in pain, Anderson swam to shore. People on the beach called 911. Anderson was rushed to the hospital. He had deep teeth marks in his leg, but he was going to be OK (Gunning, 2006d).

Question	It Says	I Say	And So
Read the question.	Find information from the text that will help you answer the question.	Think about what you know about the information from the text.	Put together what the text says with what you know.
What kind of a person is Brian Anderson?			

Inferring Word Meanings from Context

One of the most useful inferential skills is the ability to use context clues to derive the meaning of an unfamiliar word. Through using context, average readers acquire hundreds of new words in a year's time. Unfortunately, students are able to use context only about 15 percent of the time. However, with instruction the ability to use context improves. The ability to use context also improves as students move up through the grades. And students are better able to use context if they are reading materials that are on their instructional level. Deriving the meaning of an unfamiliar word generally involves the following (Gunning, 2006d):

- Recognizing that a word is unknown (Nation, 2001).
- Deciding to use context to derive the meaning of the unknown word. Many readers simply skip unknown words. Even when not skipped, most use of context is spontaneous and virtually automatic (Rapaport, 2004). The reader is hardly aware of using context. The reader doesn't make deliberate use of context until she notes a disruption in meaning and makes a conscious decision to use context (Kibby, 2004).

- Using past experience. The reader notes whether or not she has ever seen or heard this word before.
- Using morphemic cues. The readers looks for prefixes, suffixes, and roots that might provide helpful clues to the word's meaning.
- Selecting clues to the word's meaning. From the passage as a whole and the particular sentence in which the word appears, the reader seeks information that might help reveal the word's meaning.
- Creating a hypothesis as to the word's meaning. Combining clues from the text, background knowledge, and reasoning, the reader creates a hypothesis as to the word's meaning. Although the text is used to provide clues, reader's background knowledge is often more of a factor than context. Context leads the reader to use her background of experience to make inferences about the word's meaning. The reader revises his hypotheses based on subsequent encounters with the word (Rapaport, 2004). One way to improve students' ability to use context is to show them how to make inferences about a word's meaning based on background knowledge (Rapaport, 2004). Deriving the meanings of words from context is often incremental. Each exposure provides another clue to the word's meaning. It might take five or six exposures to a word before the reader is able to derive an adequate meaning for the word (Kibby, 2004).
- Testing the meaning of the word. The reader tries out the hypothesized meaning to see if it fits the context. If it doesn't fit, the reader repeats the process.

Steps for Using Context

Step 1: Reread and gather clues: Reread the sentence and see how the target word is used. Look for clues to the meaning of the word. If there are no clues or the clues don't help, read the sentences before and after the target sentence.

Step 2: Determine the word's part of speech.

Step 3: Summarize. In your mind summarize what the text has said so far. Combine that with all clues that the text offered.

Step 4: Use background knowledge. Use what you know, the sense of the passage, and the clues you have gathered. Make a careful guess (hypothesis) as to the word's meaning.

Step 5: Check the careful guess (hypothesis) to see if it fits the context.

Step 6: Revise. If your careful guess (hypothesis) doesn't fit, try again. If the word is used in other places in the selection, get clues from those uses.

Model the process of using context clues. For practice in using context clues, provide students with passages that have especially helpful context. Many content area and informational books provide definitions of words. Show students how to use morphological clues along with context clues. Students might use the following questions to help them use context:

- What information in the selection will help me figure out what the unknown word means?
- How is the target word being used? (What is its part of speech?)
- What do I know that will help me figure out the meaning of the word?
- When I think about what I know and all the information given about the unknown word, what does it seem to mean?
- Does the meaning I hypothesize (guess) fit the way the word is used in the passage?

As a practical matter, the ability to use context is assessed on most high-stakes tests. For some items, students are assessed on their ability to use context to derive the meaning of an unfamiliar word. Typically, this is a multiple-choice item so students are only required to select the correct meaning from four options. In other items, familiar words with multiple means are presented, and the task is to select the meaning that best fits the way the target word is used in context. Both kinds of items call for a close examination of the way the word is used in the selection. To provide practice in the ability to respond to this type of item, have students complete exercises similar to the following:

Learning New Words

One of the best ways to become a better reader is to learn new words. In this article three words have been underlined. As you read, try to figure out what these words mean. Then answer the questions about each word's meaning. Circle the letter of the correct answer. If you aren't sure which meaning is the correct one, go back over the article and see how each word is used.

Keeping Safe

1. If you see a meercat, chances are it is standing up on its hind legs and looking all around. Meercats have lots of enemies. When they are outside their homes, at least one meercat acts as a guard or <u>sentry</u>. If it sees an enemy, it calls out a warning.
2. Meercats let out a barking cry if they spot an eagle or other birds of <u>prey</u> flying overhead. Meercats give a hooting sound if they spot a fox or other animal that is attacking from the ground.

3. Meercats don't always run from their enemies. If they spot a hawk, snake, or small fox, or other <u>predator</u> on the ground, they march at it. They growl and bark at the predator as loud as they can. As they get closer, they jump up and down. Most predators take the hint and run, fly, or crawl away.

1. As used in paragraph 1, the word <u>sentry</u> means
   a. animal.
   b. guard.
   c. helper.
   d. worker.

2. As used in paragraph 2, the word <u>prey</u> means
   a. animal caught and eaten for food.
   b strong animal that likes to fight.
   c. mean or cruel animal.
   d. animal that can fly.

3. As used in paragraph 3, the word <u>predator</u> means
   a. an animal that comes out only at night.
   b. an animal that hunts other animals for food.
   c. an animal that eats whatever it can find.
   d. an animal that is stronger than most other animals. (Gunning, 2006d)

Discuss students' responses. Emphasize the importance of selecting a meaning that fits the context. Provide frequent practice. One advantage of this activity is that it builds vocabulary while it develops the ability to use context, so it has a double payoff.

Predicting

Predicting is a powerful strategy. Predictions require students to use the clues provided in titles, headings, illustrations and the text itself to activate prior knowledge and, based on prior knowledge, to make predictions about text to be read. Predictions are ongoing. Students make predictions before reading a selection, but should modify predictions as they read the selection and acquire additional information. Predicting fosters comprehension because it activates schema and helps establish a purpose for reading: to see how predictions play out.

Students get out of predicting what they put into it. Carefully thought-out predictions are more productive than those that are little more than a guess. To direct students to base their questions on experience and textual clues, ask two questions: one that asks what the prediction is (What do you think will happen in the story? How do you think the main character will resolve her problem?) and one that asks for support of the prediction (What makes you predict that? What have you experienced, and what clues from the story lead you to make that prediction?) (Nessel, 1987). For nonfiction, students predict what they might learn about the topic.

The foundation of making effective predictions is in using text clues to activate one's background knowledge to help judge what is likely to come next (Benson-Castagna, 2005). To help students make the best use of text clues, teach them how to preview. Model how you use the title, illustrations, headings, story introduction, and/or summary as a basis for making predictions. Note how the elements you preview activate your background knowledge and help you to make reasonable predictions. In fiction, the most frequently used text clues are the title and the illustrations. If students look at both the title and the illustrations at the same time, they will probably place emphasis on the illustration, and this might be misleading or narrow their predictions (Benson-Castagna, 2005). Instead of having them look at the cover or first page of a text they are about to read and so see the title and illustration, write the title of the selection on the chalkboard. Have them use just the title to make predictions. Using the title *A Bad, Bad Day* (Hall, 1995), students make a variety of predictions. The illustration shows the main character missing the school bus. If they had seen the illustration, they might have predicted that the story tells what happened when the boy missed the bus. But that was only a small part of the story. The title *Stealing Home* (Stolz, 1992) should lead to a lively discussion because the word *home* in the title has a double meaning. After discussing the title, students can then preview the cover illustration. Have students make predictions based on the title and the cover illustration. If students have difficulty making predictions, have them preview added illustrations, the story introduction, or the first paragraph or two of the story (Gunning, 2008).

Model the process of making predictions. For a story such as *A Bad, Bad Day*, you might explain what you think a bad day would be and explain how you use your background knowledge to predict what might happen in the story. After making a prediction based solely on the title, you might explain how the illustration helps you to change your prediction a bit. You might predict some of the things that might happen because the boy in the illustration missed the school bus. You might also discuss how the illustration relates to the title.

For nonfiction, students preview the title and cover illustration, but they also preview headings, additional illustrations, and the table of contents, if there is one. Students continue previewing until they are able to make reasoned predictions. When reading informational text, it is especially important to activate prior knowledge. Oczkus (2005) prompts students to activate prior knowledge by first discussing the title to note the topic of the text and having students tell what they already know about snakes, lasers, lacrosse, or whatever the topic happens to be. Once they have discussed what they know about the topic, students are then better able to make predictions and better prepared for reading the text. For informational text, instead of predicting what the text will be about, since this is usually obvious from the title and illustrations, students predict what the author will tell them about the topic or what they will learn about the topic.

Since making predictions about informational text is somewhat different from making predictions about fiction, show and discuss how you would go about making predictions when reading informational text. Previewing the title of a selection entitled "Robots at Work," you might start by saying what you know about robots. "I know that robots help put cars together, but I don't know how they do that. Maybe the article will explain how they assemble cars. A friend of mine has a robot that vacuums his home. I wonder if there are robots that scrub floors. I predict that the article will tell what kinds of jobs robot do beside putting cars together and vacuuming floors. I predict that the author will also explain how robots are able to do certain jobs."

Some students have difficulty making predictions or are reluctant to do so. Have students make predictions about everyday occurrences: "Who do you predict will win the big game? Who do you predict will be elected mayor?" Provide lots of modeling and coaching. For younger children lift-the-tab books such as *Where's Spot?* (Hill, 1980) are especially good for making predictions. Other books for young readers that lend themselves to making predictions are *Where's the Bear?* (Pomerantz, 1984). For older students, detective stories, such as the Sebastian Super Sleuth series lend themselves to making continuous predictions.

If students are having difficulty making predictions, you might provide practice with illustrations. Students might look at illustrations and predict what the caption will say about the illustrations. They then check their predictions by reading the caption. Oczkus (2005) arranges for students to examine illustrations and has students complete this sentence stem: "I wonder what is going on in this illustration."

Predicting doesn't work well when students have little background to bring to a selection. When background is limited, have students do more previewing. They might preview additional illustrations, read the captions, and read the summary and then make predictions based on these.

To encourage the use of predictions and also supporting and modifying predictions, have them fill out a Prediction Chart (Table 6.3). As students become proficient at predicting, phase out the use of the charts.

Working in pairs, students can practice making predictions. To remind students how to make predictions, you might post the following:

To make a prediction for fiction:

- Read the title, and think what this story is going to be about or what is going to happen.
- Look at the illustration. Think about both the title and the illustration and think what the story is going to be about or what is going to happen.

To make a prediction for nonfiction:

- Read the title and see what this selection is going to be about. Predict what the author is going to tell you.
- Look at the illustration and think about the title, and predict what the author is going to tell you.
- Use headings as clues to help you make predictions. Ask: "What is the author going to tell me in this part of the selection?" Turn the heading into a question and read to answer the question you have made.

To make predictions more interactive, create book boxes in which items that play an important role in a story or informational piece are placed. (Yopp & Yopp, 2000). Display and discuss the items, and have students predict based on the items displayed what they believe might happen in the story or what they might learn from the article. Because the technique can be used to build background and vocabulary, it is especially helpful to ELL.

To provide practice, have students complete exercises similar to the following. Have students read the title and predict what the selection might be about. Ask: What do you think the elephants' cell-phone might be? Assuming that students see cell-phone as an indication that the article will discuss elephants' communication, ask: What do you think the author is going to tell us about the elephants' communication? What does the illustration show? Thinking about both the title and the illustration, what do you think the author will tell us about elephant communication?

Table 6.3 ● Prediction Chart

Prediction	Clues	Changes in Predictions
	What led me to make this prediction?	As I read the text, what changes did I have to make in my predictions?

Read the title. Read the article. See how your prediction turns out. Be ready to change it if necessary.

The Elephants' Cell-Phone

While studying elephants in a wild animal park, Caitlin O'Connell-Rodwell noticed that the animals were acting rather strangely. "I noted that the elephants appeared to pay a lot of attention to the ground with their feet, shifting their weight and leaning forward, sometimes lifting a foot off the ground." Later, O'Connell-Rodwell learned that another herd of elephants was coming toward the park. Were the elephants in the park using their feet to pick up signals from the approaching herd? Had the approaching herd made known what they were doing by stomping on the ground? Were the elephants communicating by sending and receiving vibrations in the earth? It was a very interesting idea. O'Connell-Rodwell began looking for proof for her fascinating theory.

Caitlin O'Connell-Rodwell photo. Used with permission.

O'Connell-Rodwell got herself a set of geophones. Geophones are used to pick up vibrations from the earth. Scientists use geophones to listen for earthquakes. Using her geophone, one of the first things O'Connell-Rodwell observed was whether mock charges set off vibrations in the ground. When a mother elephant's babies are threatened by a lion or other predator, the mother raises a fuss. She flaps her ears, screams, makes low rumbling sounds, stomps on the ground, and pretends that she is going to charge the predators. O'Connell-Rodwell found that the mother elephant's mock charges and rumbling cause vibrations that are carried in the ground. The screaming could be heard for 6 miles. But the vibrations could be picked up 20 miles away. By sending out vibrations elephants could warn other elephants who were far away.

O'Connell-Rodwell found that elephants have three kinds of signals. One is a warning, another is a greeting, and the third means, "Let's go!" Elephants might also be able to hear the vibrations caused by thunderstorms. One herd of thirsty elephants started heading in the direction of a thunderstorm that was a hundred miles away. The vibrations may have been signaling that rain was falling there. This meant that there would be water for them. For elephants, using vibrations is like having a cell-phone (Gunning, 2006d).

Using the DR-TA

A technique that is tailor-made for making and supporting predictions is the Directed Reading-Thinking Activity (DR-TA). The direct reading-thinking activity is based on the premise that students have a natural inclination to predict and make decisions (Stauffer, 1970). In the directed reading-thinking activity, students survey a selection and, based on their survey, make predictions. They then read silently in order to evaluate their predictions. They read flexibly. If their prediction is not working out, then they modify it. Students continue to read until they have gathered enough information to justify or reject or modify their predictions. Selections are typically read in parts. As envisaged by Stauffer (1969), students stop reading when the purpose they have set has been satisfied, when they are able to respond to their predictions. However, you might want to set stopping points. After students have read enough to evaluate their predictions, discuss with them how their predictions played out. Have them tell how they might have had to modify their predictions. Also have them support the accuracy of their predictions by citing support from the selection. As students discuss a section of the text, provide assistance as they justify their predictions or explain modifications. Also provide any other assistance as needed. Clarify confusing points and misunderstood passages. During the discussion, lead students to make predictions about the next section. Here is how a DR-TA is conducted:

Step 1   Through surveying and discussions students are led to make predictions. The teacher writes the title of the selection on the board: *Brave Irene* (Steig, 1988). Based on the title, students predict what the selection might be about. They discuss why Irene is called brave or what brave things she might do. Students' predictions are written down. Students are then shown the cover illustration, which shows Irene carrying a box in a snowstorm. Students then use the title and illustration to predict what will happen in the story. Students' revised predictions are written on the chalkboard. Students need not come to a consensus. Students can make up their own predictions or say which of the predictions written on the board they agree with.

Step 2   Once predictions have been made, students then read silently to assess their predictions. Students might have a set stopping point or they might continue to read until they are able to evaluate their predictions. This could be single page or a number of pages. Students read flexibly. They alter their predictions as they encounter information that suggests that they do so.

Step 3   Students' predictions are discussed. Students assess which predictions were on the mark or close to it and which needed to be modified. In one class most students predicted that Irene had an important package to deliver, but no one predicted that it was a gown. Most thought it was food or medicine. Students discussed how they modified their predictions and orally read to the group passages that support their modifications. During the discussion, the teacher clarified the specialized meaning of the word *ball* and took the opportunity to lead students to see what kind of a person Irene is. After discussing the section, students predicted what would happen next. They based their predictions on what they had read so far and also on their discussion of what kind of person Irene is. They then read the next section. *Brave Irene* was read in this way until students had read the entire book. If students have difficulty responding to the generic prediction question—What do you think will happen next?—rephrase the question. You might ask: "What danger or difficulties do you think Irene might face?" or "What do you think Irene's trip to the palace will be like?"

Steps 4 & 5   After the discussion, students might reread the text to dramatize it or put it in a readers' theater format or for another purpose. Students might also complete a follow-up activity.

To develop vocabulary and background while using the DR-TA, have students predict what words they might see in the selection. If students don't suggest words that you judge should be included, add them. If you have guided reading groups, you might use the DR-TA format from time to time. The DR-TA works best when students have enough background so that they can make predictions and also when they have established some independent work habits.

Predict-O-Gram and Possible Sentences

Still another way to foster predictions—and also to build vocabulary—is to use the predict-o-gram or possible sentences. In a predict-o-gram (see Table 6.4), you present and discuss key words from an upcoming short story such as "A Day's Wait" by Hemingway (Blachowicz, 1986). List the words on the chalkboard. Include familiar vocabulary along with unfamiliar words. After discussing the meanings of any unfa-

Table 6.4 ● Predict-O-Gram

Setting	Characters	Story Problem	Plot	Resolution
	Schatz	Fever	Thermometer	Miles
	Doctor	Germs	Die	Kilometers
	Narrator	Influenza	Capsule	98 degrees
		Temperature	44 degrees	37 degrees
			102 degrees	

miliar words, have students predict into which story grammar category the words should be placed: setting, characters, story problem, plot, or resolution. After all the words have been categorized, have students predict what the story might be about. After reading, students assess their predictions.

Possible sentences work well with nonfiction. Just as in the predict-o-gram, list 12 to 16 key words. The words should be ones that are used to convey the main concepts in the text. Include both new words and familiar words (Stahl & Kapinus, 1991). List the words on the board. Invite students to read them and tell what the difficult ones mean, but supply pronunciations and definitions if no one else can. Explain that the words have been drawn from a selection that students are about to read. Give the title of the selection. Ask students to predict what information the selection will present. Then invite students to compose sentences in which at least two of the words from the list will be used. The sentences should be ones that might appear in the text students are about to read. Model the creation of one sentence, explaining as you compose the statement why you think it might appear in the passage. Then have students create sentences. Explain that words may be used in more than one sentence. Write students' sentences, including those that are not accurate, on the board. Stop after all the words have been used. Students then read the selection to see how accurate their sentences are. After students have completed their reading, discuss the accuracy of their sentences. Edit or delete sentences that are inaccurate. Students may also expand sentences to include new information gathered from the selection.

Conclusions

Conclusions are a form of inferring. They usually involve considering several details and drawing a conclusion based on all the information. Conclusions should flow from the evidence. They should be logical, should have sufficient support, and should be based on all the available evidence. Conclusions should also be unbiased. Often, the same set of details can yield different conclusions. However, all the conclusions may not have equal support.

To introduce conclusions, role play a situation, and have students draw a conclusion about it. Say to the class: "Does anyone know what is on the lunch menu today? I should haven't skipped breakfast. I should have stopped and picked up something to eat on the way to school. I wish I had an apple or a sandwich. Even a cracker would help." Ask students to draw a conclusion about how you seem to be feeling. Ask them to support their conclusions. Lead them to see that all your statements support the conclusion that you are hungry. Explain to students that they will be studying conclusions. Explain that drawing a conclusion means that we look at or think about details and see what all those details add up to. What do those details suggest? Explain that asking about lunch; saying you skipped breakfast and should have stopped for something to eat; and wishing that you had a sandwich, an apple, or even a cracker lead to the conclusion that you are hungry.

Drawing Conclusions

Model the process of drawing a conclusion. You might read the following paragraph or an excerpt from one of the students' texts and do a think-aloud as you draw a conclusion. As you read the paragraph, think out loud about Matt's actions and what they say about the kind of person Matt is. Demonstrate to students that you use details from the paragraph to draw a conclusion about Matt.

> Before heading off to school, Matt shoveled the snow from the sidewalk of his next-door neighbor. He knew that Mr. Grisom had been sick and was unable to shovel snow. At school, Matt made it a point to talk to the new boy. He remembered how lonely he had felt when he was the new kid in the class. At lunchtime, Matt gave his piece of cake to Sandra, who had forgotten her lunch. After school, Matt and his friends planned ways to raise money for the victims of a flood.

To further develop the concept of drawing conclusions, write sets of sentences, such as the following, on the board and invite students to draw a conclusion based on them:

Teenagers work as clowns.
Young men and women have become clowns.

People in their 40s have become clowns.
Grandfathers and grandmothers work as clowns.

Two-thirds of a shark's brain controls its sense of smell.
A shark can smell a single drop of blood in the water from half a mile away.

By moving its head from side to side, the shark can quickly follow and locate the source of a smell.

Supporting Conclusions

An essential element in drawing conclusions is making sure there is adequate support for the conclusion. To get across the idea of adequately supporting conclusions, have students consider the following conclusion, which is supported by just one detail. Discuss with students the lack of adequate support for the conclusion. Have them suggest added support.

Computers have changed the way we live. Many people now shop online instead of going to stores.

Provide conclusions such as the following and have students supply support.

Football is the most exciting sport.
Baseball is becoming less popular.
Cats make better pets than dogs.

To provide added practice, have students read the following or similar passages and answer the questions, which ask students to select conclusions and provide support for the conclusion.

> Chester Greenwood was just 15 when he invented earmuffs. Over the years thousands of earmuffs made in his factory were sold. Louis Braille was the same age as Chester Greenwood when he devised Braille. Braille is a way of writing that uses raised marks so that the blind can read with their fingers. Philo Farnsworth was just 14 when he got an idea for sending and receiving moving pictures. His ideas were used in the invention of television. Frank Epperson was just 11 when he created a frozen fruit juice treat. He developed the frozen fruit juice treat into the Popsicle.

The information in the article best supports the idea that

a. young people can be inventors.
b. it takes many years to develop an invention.
c. inventions change the way we live.
d. inventions help solve problems.

List at least three details to support the conclusion you have chosen.

_____

_____

_____

(Gunning, 2006d).

There's a rule that says players can't be elected to the Baseball Hall of Fame unless they have been retired for five years. But the rule was broken for Roberto Clemente. Clemente was an outstanding fielder for the Pittsburgh Pirates. Fast on his feet, he caught just about everything that came his way. He also had a mighty throwing arm. With his rocket arm, he threw out dozens of runners. In his last season of play, Clemente became the eleventh player in major league baseball to get 3,000 hits. Clemente was at his best when the pressure was on. He got a hit in every World Series game in which he played. In 1972, only a few months after helping the Pirates win the 1971 World Series, Clemente lost his life in an airplane crash. The plane had been carrying food and other supplies to earthquake victims in Nicaragua. The following year Clemente was elected to the Baseball Hall of Fame.

The information in the article best supports the idea that

a. The Pirates were one of the best teams of all time.
b. Roberto Clemente was well liked by people.
c. Roberto Clemente was an outstanding baseball player.
d. Years ago, flying was more dangerous.

List at least three details to support the conclusion you have chosen.

_____

_____

_____

_____

More than ever before, students need to be able to draw logical conclusions. With so much data available, it is essential that they be able to put the data together and draw suitable conclusions. The added mental effort of drawing conclusions requires that they consider the information upon which their conclusion is based. This fosters understanding and retention. However, students must also see the need to be flexible so that they can revise conclusions in the light of new data that contradicts old data. They also need to know when they don't have enough data for a valid conclusion or the data is not reliable.

Imaging

Although not directly assessed on higher-level tests, imaging does play an important role in reading and responding. Imaging helps readers to picture characters, scenes, and actions in fiction and processes, places, and things in informational text.

Imaging also adds a little variety to instruction. Imaging can be especially helpful to students who are better with pictures than they are with words. Students who have been taught to use imaging have better comprehension. If they draw a person that they are going to write about, they produce a more elaborated piece (Olson, 1987). The drawing becomes a kind of a visual prompt for their writing. Students see and record details that might otherwise have been overlooked.

Imaging should be taught in the same way that other strategies are taught. Explain and model the strategy; discuss when, where, and under what conditions it might be used; and provide guided and independent practice and application. As a part of your guided practice, you might read aloud high imagery passages and have students close their eyes and try to picture the person or scene being depicted. They might also image associated sounds, smells, and touches. Students can describe and/or draw their images. As part of postreading discussions, include questions that ask students to tell how they pictured the main character or what the setting was like. Explain to students that each of us creates our own individual images. Imaging should follow these guidelines (Fredericks, 1986):

- Students create images based on their backgrounds. Images will differ.
- Teachers should not change students' images but might suggest that students reread a selection and then decide whether they want to revise their images.
- Students should be given enough time to form images.
- Through your questioning, encourage students to elaborate their images: What was the main character wearing? How big was he? What did he sound like?

Comparing and Contrasting

Making comparisons is a deceptively complex skill. On the NAEP, a national reading test, it is an area where students experience serious difficulty. Marzano and associates (2000) found that teaching comparing and classifying boosted students' performance on achievement tests by 45 percentile points. This represents a gain of about 1½ years. However, although making comparisons is an essential skill, it is sorely neglected.

Introducing Comparing

Root instruction in comparing in the real world. Even the youngest of students have extensive experience making comparisons. They compare pieces of cake to see which one is bigger; they compare classmates to see who is taller, faster, funnier;

they compare themselves with others; they compare books and authors and games and friends. Given a choice of two books, two games, or two TV shows, they usually have no difficulty telling which they prefer. However, they may experience more difficulty telling you why they prefer one to the other. To transfer the skill (which they obviously have when dealing with the outside world) to the academic world, make comparison questions a part of your discussions. Compare authors, books read, activities engaged in, lessons learned, performances watched, experiments demonstrated. Most important of all, discuss how items differ and/or are similar. Differences are easier to distinguish. It is easy to see how a dog is different from a cat. It's not quite so obvious how they are the same.

To teach comparing, have students compare items in which the differences or similarities are fairly obvious and concrete. Begin instruction by having students making comparisons on the basis of physical differences. Students might compare alligators and crocodiles, African and Asian elephants, moths and butterflies, or toads and frogs. To make the task easier, give them the dimensions for making the comparison: the experiences and the challenges faced by Sam from *My Side of the Mountain* (George, 1959) and Brian from *Hatchet* (Paulsen, 1987). As students become more adept at making comparisons, have them choose the areas for comparison (Marzano et al., 2000). When discussing students' comparisons, be sure to have them explain their responses and back up choices by citing supporting text or explaining their reasoning.

Make comparing and contrasting a part of your questioning. Some possible comparisons include:

- characters in the same story, characters from different stories, characters with real people
- settings from different selections and with real places
- events, themes, and plots from similar stories

In social studies, compare historical figures, events, eras, political parties, presidents, explorers, inventors, world leaders, ideas, war, and inventions. Also compare cities, states, countries, continents. In science, compare animals, insects, habitats, clouds, storms, discoveries, processes.

As part of your instruction, include the words of comparison: *compare, contrast, same, different, differences, similar*, and *similarities*. In quizzes and tests, ask students to compare and contrast: What are the major differences between the Republican and Democratic parties? Compare and contrast the Senate and House of Representatives. Also arrange for students to compose comparison/contrast pieces in their writing program.

To foster making comparisons, review the use of graphic organizers. As noted in Chapter 3, frame matrices (see Table 3.2) are especially effective for making comparisons. Frame matrices make it possible to compare several items among a number of features. Using the following or a similar exercise, guide students as they complete the following frame matrix (Table 6.5). Have students read additional selections in which there are comparisons and contrasts, and fill in frame matrices. Eventually, have students set up their own frame matrices. This would make a good activity for pairs of students or small groups. Before students set up a frame matrix, discuss the procedure for creating them. They must decide who or what is being compared. They must also decide the basis for the comparison: what the main characteristics are.

Larks and Owls

If you had your choice, when would you get up? When would be the best time of day for you to tackle a difficult task? If you prefer sleeping late and working late, you are an owl. If you like to get up early in the morning and you seem to have the most energy early in the day, you are a lark. Larks have a higher body temperature when they awaken than owls do. Their body temperature is highest at about 3:30 in the afternoon. Owls have their highest body temperature at about 8:30 in the evening. About 10 people out of 100 are larks. Their body clocks are set early. They get out of bed early in the morning. They think better and work better early in the day. Morning is the best time to get work done. By late afternoon, larks tire out, and they like to go to bed early. Owls, on the other hand, prefer sleeping late. About 20 people out of 100 are owls. Their energy peaks come in the afternoon or at night. The later it gets, the better they seem to feel. Owls get higher grades

Table 6.5 ● Frame Matrix: Larks and Owls

Characteristics	Larks	Owls
Waking up		
Going to bed		
Highest body temperature		
Best time to work		
Best time for taking a test		
Number of out of 100		

Comparing and Contrasting

on tests taken in the afternoon than they do on tests taken in the morning. The opposite is true for larks. Most people are neither extreme larks nor extreme owls. They are somewhere in between. They don't have much trouble getting up a little earlier or staying up a little later if they have to.

A key element in comparison/contrast questions is providing examples of differences or similarities. In addition to noting similarities and differences, students must be able to cite specific ways in which the persons or things being compared differ or are similar.

Making Connections

Readers can make three kinds of connections. They can connect the text they are reading with a text they have read. That connection can be internal. (This reminds me of an incident in the beginning of the story.) Or it could be external to the selection now being read. (This reminds me of the story that we read last week.) Students can make personal connections: This reminds me of the time my family was caught in a snowstorm. Or they can make connections with the outside world: This is like what is happening to the farmers because of the drought (Keene & Zimmermann, 1997). Connections should be text based and should go beyond mere opinion. They should also be significant. Students' connections might be ephemeral. The only connection might be that the main characters in both stories were the same age. Making a connection of this type is a start, but higher-level skills are built when the teacher models how to make more substantial connections and/or prompts the students to do so. One way to foster significant connections is to have students make connections that enable them to better understand the selection they are reading. As Collins (2004) explains,

> Besides teaching children about different ways that readers can connect to their texts I also want to extend or deepen their connections in a way that helps them to better understand the text. Instead of simply saying, "This reminds me of. . . ," my students can go further by adding "and this connection helps me to understand [the story, character, part, page] because . . ." (p. 176)

Another way of eliciting substantial connections is to prompt the student to say what the element in the book shares with the element to which the student is connecting. If a student says that the story reminds him of his dog, prompt him to tell what it is about the dog in the story that reminds him of his dog. Connections, especially ones that are substantial, are essential to comprehension because they are the basis of understanding. We understand what we read in terms of our past experiences and background knowledge. Connections activate knowledge and experience, and so enable comprehension.

Text-to-Self Connections

Usually, the easiest connections to make are text to self. When reading a story, students discover a main character who has problems or is facing difficulties that are similar to ones they are facing. Or one of the characters reminds them of a grandfather or uncle. Undoubtedly, students make many personal connections as they read, but these connections can be strengthened through modeling, prompting, and discussion. After reading aloud a story that has a special significance for you, discuss the connections that you might make. The grandfather in the story might remind you of your grandfather. The main character's fear of high places might remind you of your fear of high places. You might ask reader response questions such as:

- Does this story remind you of anything that has happened in your life?
- Are any of the characters like anyone you know?
- What feelings did the story stir up?

During discussions, as students talk over personal connections, they will help others make added connections or extend their connections. Students will hear connections that they hadn't thought of and so their understanding of and connection to the selection will be enriched. During discussions of personal connections be aware of students' right to privacy and be sensitive to delicate issues.

For nonfiction, personal connections might come in the form of using the information. Reading a selection on nutrition, students might examine their diets and perhaps decide to make healthier choices.

Text-to-Text Connections

When students make connections between texts, their understanding is taken to a higher level as they note similarities and differences, and make generalizations that encompass both texts. Making a connection between the resourcefulness shown by Karana in the *Island of the Blue Dolphins* (Odell, 1960) and the resourcefulness demonstrated by *Robinson Crusoe* (Defoe, 1706), they come to a deeper understanding of the concept of courage. Making connections between informational texts depends upon and extends students' knowledge and understanding of a topic. Making connections between a history text and a historical novel can put a human face on historical events. To foster text-to-text connections, you might ask the following or similar questions:

- Does this story remind you of any other stories that we have read?
- Does this story remind you of anything else that you have read or of any movies or TV shows that you have seen?
- Does the main character remind you of any other characters that we have read about or that you have seen in the movies or on TV?
- How is _____ (character in story a) similar to _____ (character in story b)?
- How does the information in this article compare with the information in your textbook?
- How would you compare the information provided by the two sources?

Text-to-World Connections

Students make text-to-world connections when they can make connections between their reading and what is happening in the world. Students make text-to-world connections when they read a book such as *December* (Bunting, 1997) and this helps them to better understand the problem of homelessness. To foster text-to-world connections, you might ask the following or similar questions:

- In what way is what happened in the story similar to what is going on in the world?
- How did this story help you to understand (note problem or issue)?
- What real-life problem did this story deal with?
- What real-life problem did this article explore?

Making Varied Connections

Students might also complete a Connection Chart as in Table 6.6 in which they note connections. In the first column, students identify the text that elicited the connection. They then choose whether their connection is text-to-self, text-to-text, or text-to-world and write their response in the appropriate column. Of course, they might make several connections for the same passage.

Students might use a stick-on note to indicate connections they have made. The connections might be marked as being t-s: text-to-self, t-t: text-to-text, t-w: text-to-world. If students are reading stories on the same themes, this helps them to make text-to-text connections. Also if they are doing a lot of reading, this helps them to make varied connections.

In their work helping students make connections, a group of middle school teachers discovered that the more connections students made, the more interested they became in their reading (Kendall & Khuon, 2006). Building on this observa-

Table 6.6 ● Connection Chart

What the Text Said	Text-to-Self Connection	Text-to-Text Connection	Text-to-World Connection

tion, they began focusing on materials that lend themselves to making connections. A good choice was the short story "Eleven" by Sandra Cisneros (1991). Since the story revolves around an embarrassing moment, it was easy for middle school students to make connections to it.

As noted earlier, not all connections are equal. Some get at the heart of the piece. Others are ephemeral and might actually be a distraction. Through prompting and discussion, help students to select connections that deepen their understanding of a selection. For a selection such as "Larks and Owls," have students make personal connections by discussing whether they are larks or owls or in-between. Lead them into a deeper understanding by having them explain how being a lark, an owl, or in-between affects their lives: the time they get up, the time they go to bed, the time they like best for doing work or playing. Also have students make text-to-world connections by identifying people they know who are larks or owls. They might come to some conclusions: young children tend to be larks, teenagers tend to be owls, and older people tend to be larks.

Study Group Questions

- What are the key strategies in Interpreting and Integrating?
- What are my students' proficiencies in this area?
- What instruction do they need in this area? What is my plan for teaching strategies in this area?
- Which of the suggested approaches or techniques seem most promising? How will I use the techniques?
- How will I help students apply the skills?
- In what subject areas will they apply the skills?
- What materials will I use?
- How will I help students who are having a difficult time learning the skills?

Making Judgments about Text

Making Judgments about text requires the reader to stand back and take a critical look. The reader uses standards and knowledge of literary techniques to analyze and judge literary works. The reader uses knowledge of text structure to analyze informational text. The reader looks at the author's purpose for writing and also the author's style, critically evaluating, comparing and contrasting, and understanding the effect of such features as irony, humor, and organization. There is some overlap with the Interpret category. The reader may, for instance, be called upon to compare two pieces of writing.

Critique and Evaluate

Critique and Evaluate requires teaching standards for literary pieces and also developing knowledge of the literary devices, such as figurative language, symbols, irony, and personification. For informational text, instruction should include instruction in the elements of effective writing of expository text and the concepts of fairness and credibility. Reading and writing instruction should be integrated. Just as students use knowledge of stylistic devices to understand text, they can also use stylistic devices to improve their writing.

Questions used to assess this aspect of reading require readers to stand apart from the text, consider it objectively, and evaluate its quality, appropriateness, fairness, and credibility. Questions ask readers to determine the usefulness of a text for a specific purpose, evaluate the language and textual elements, and think about the author's purpose and style. Some questions also require readers to make connections across parts of a text or between texts. For example, students might be asked to compare a poem and a story with the same theme or relate information from a first-person account to a textbook description of an event. Questions that assess this aspect of reading include the following:

- Compare the structure of this magazine article to that one.
- How useful would this be for _____? Why?
- Does the author use (irony, personification, humor) effectively? Explain.
- What is the author's point of view? Using the text, provide a sentence or two to support your response.
- Is this information needed for _____? Explain your reasoning.
- What other information would you need to find out about _____? Support your answer with information from the text.

Critical/Evaluative Reading

Never before have we had access to so much information. However, along with increased access to information, there is an increased need to be able to judge the usefulness and trustworthiness of that information. Information that appears in traditionally published books and periodicals is screened by editors and reviewers. However, much of the information on the Internet does not go through an editing or review process and is sometimes created by sources who are biased or who lack the necessary knowledge base to make authoritative statements.

To encourage critical reading, the teacher must create a spirit of inquiry. Students must feel free to challenge statements, support controversial ideas, offer divergent viewpoints, and venture statements that conflict with the majority view. When they see that their own ideas are accepted, they are better able to accept the ideas of others. The program, of course, must be balanced. The idea is not to turn students into mistrustful young cynics but to create judicious thinkers (Gunning, 2005a).

Uses of Language

The most basic critical thinking skill is to determine how words are used, Words are used in four main ways: to describe, to evaluate or judge, to point out, and to interject (Wilson, 1960). The words *house, see*, and *elephant* describe objects or actions. The words *evil* and *lie* evaluate. They express a judgment. Some words both describe and evaluate: *rude, rob*, and *pest* describe objects and actions, but they also incorporate unfavorable evaluations. Words such as *and, in, for, to* are words that show relationships. They have very little meaning. Words such as *hurrah* and *gosh* are interjections and are simply used to express emotions. In this selection only words that describe or evaluate or do both will be considered. A key strategy in critical reading is to note whether words offer neutral descriptions, evaluations, or both. To introduce the concept of the uses of words, write a series of sentences similar to thefollowing on the board:

The male lion <u>weighs</u> 500 pounds.
The male lion <u>guards</u> the pride.
The <u>lazy</u> male lion lets the female lions do the hunting.
The <u>selfish</u> male lion eats first.

Discuss which words just tell about the lion and which judge it. Guide students as they locate words in their texts that describe, judge, or do both. While discussing selections that students have read, call attention to words that are used to judge. Once students have grasped the concept of uses of words, introduce the concept of connotations. Discuss words that have favorable connotations (*thrifty, slim*) and those that have unfavorable ones (*selfish, skinny*). For younger students, use phrases like "sounds better" and "sounds worse," instead of "favorable connotations" and "unfavorable connotations."

Have students note which of the following words in each pair sound better.

1. Who owns that (beast, dog)?
2. That dog is (greedy, hungry).
3. That dog is (bony, thin).
4. That dog is (curious, nosy).
5. That dog is (clever, sneaky).
6. His dog is (frisky, wild).
7. The new student is (enthusiastic, noisy).
8. Maria (scrawled, wrote) a few sentences on a piece of paper.
9. Luis was (sipping, slurping) his soda.
10. We (chatted, quarreled) for more than an hour.

Using students' growing knowledge of the power of words, discuss persuasive language. Write the words *new* and *improved* on the board. Ask students where they have seen these words. Lead them to see that these words often appear in ads on TV and in newspapers. Bring in print ads or clips of TV ads. Have students locate words that sell or persuade—*fresh, delicious, better, exciting*, and *adventure*. They might try their hands at composing persuasive ads.

Understanding Facts and Opinions   The ability to identify statements as facts or opinions is a simplification of the sophisticated skill of classifying statements as empirical, analytical, attitudinal, or value-laden. Facts can be verified by empirical or analytical means. Facts can be verified as accurate or inaccurate by counting, measuring, weighing, touching, hearing, observing, or analyzing. Opinions are statements that express an attitude or a value and cannot be proved. The terms *fact/opinion* are imperfect descriptions. The word *fact* suggests something that can be proved with objective evidence and suggests something that is true. For example, a new way was recently found to measure Mt. Everest. In the past it was stated that Mt. Everest was 29,141 feet high. That is an empirical, or factual, statement. It can be proved by measuring Mt. Everest. Using an improved measuring technique, scientists found Mt. Everest to be higher. The first statement does not become an opinion because it was proved to be inaccurate. It does not become an attitude or a statement of feeling; the statement is still empirical. An empirical statement is simply one that can be proved to be accurate or inaccurate. An attitude or value (opinion) statement cannot be proved. It can be strongly held, defended, explained, and rationalized, but there is no objective way that the statement can be proved right or wrong.

Write factual statements on the board similar to the following:

1. There are more than 500 students in our school.
2. Our school has 20 classrooms.
3. Our school's outside walls are made of red brick.
4. Our school is outstanding.

Ask students to tell which of the sentences can be proved either right or wrong. The first two can be proved or disproved by counting and the third by looking at the outside wall. However, the fourth sentence cannot be proved. It simply tells how someone feels about the school. Model the process of distinguishing between facts and opinions by showing the thought processes you go through. Tell students that sentences that can be proved or disproved are known as factual sentences. Sentences that cannot be proved or disproved are opinion sentences. Show students that the first three sentences can be proved in some way, but the last one cannot. It is simply an opinion, a statement that tells how someone feels. Help students locate statements of fact and opinion in their texts.

Present words that signal opinions, such as *good, better, best, wonderful marvelous, spectacular, bad, worse, worst, awful, terrible, like (verb), believe, enjoy, should*, and *ought*. Ask students to use these and other signal words in differentiating between facts and opinions. Also introduce the concept of verifying factual statements. Explain to students that factual statements can be proved in some way—by measuring, weighing, observing, touching, hearing, counting, and so on. Bring in a lacrosse ball or other object and make statements about it. The ball is heavier than a tennis ball. The ball bounces higher than a tennis ball. The ball is white. The ball is _____ inches around. The ball weighs _____ ounces. Discuss how each statement might be proved. Bring in a scale and a measuring tape so that the ball can be weighed and measured. Have students make other factual statements and tell how they might prove them; that is, whether they would mainly count, measure, weigh, touch, listen, or observe to prove the statements. For some statements it would be necessary to consult an encyclopedia or other reference.

Have students identify whether the following are factual or opinion statements. For those that are labeled as being *factual*, have students tell how the statements might be proved. For those that are opinion statements, have students see if the statement contains words that signal a judgment or opinion.

1. One of the best birds is the whooping crane.
2. The call of the whooping crane travels a long distance.
3. The bird's loud whoop is one of the worst noises you will ever hear.
4. The whooping crane's windpipe is nearly five feet long.
5. With its long neck and thin legs, the whooping crane is a silly-looking bird.
6. Whooping cranes are five feet tall.
7. Their wingspan is about seven feet.
8. A whooping crane in flight is a wonderous sight.

On an ongoing basis, have students identify key statements as being factual or expressions of opinion. Lead students to see that although opinions can't be proved, some opinions can be supported with facts. The statement that "William Shakespeare was the greatest writer in the world" can be supported with facts: he wrote a large number of plays and sonnets. His plays are still being read and performed, he is rated as number one by a survey of educated people, etc. In writing and discussions, encourage students to support opinions and judgments with facts whenever possible.

Not all factual statements can be verified by counting, measuring, or observing. Some statements are analytical. The statement is proved by analyzing it. Statements such as "There are twelve in a dozen" or "A flock of geese is known as a gaggle" are verified by examining the context in which they are used.

To reinforce the concept of factual information, obtain and discuss references such as almanacs, encyclopedias, *Guinness Book of World Records*, and some of the many informational books that present "amazing" facts. Students might begin composing a book that contains facts about an area of interest.

Biased Communication

Much of the text, oral and written, that students encounter will be biased in some way, or at least, will have a particular point of view. This is especially true of talk shows on radio and TV, commentaries, and press releases. Those in favor of an idea or program put a positive spin on an event; those opposed put a negative spin on the same event. Slanted or biased writing uses emotionally loaded words and carefully chosen words to cast a subject in a favorable or unfavorable light. Slanted text might contain facts, but the facts might be distorted or it might just present the facts favorable to its position. Slanted writing is frequently found in sports writing, in biographies, and in autobiographies. To convey the concept of emotionally loaded words, you might have students consider pairs of animal names and tell which ones elicit a favorable response and which an unfavorable one.

killer whale—orca
groundhog—woodchuck
dog—mutt
snake—viper
chickenhawk—red-tailed hawk
mouse—rodent
skunk—polecat
hagfish—slime eel

To provide practice analyzing slanted text, have students compare the following two selections and respond to the questions that follow. Discuss the details and words used to make the trip sound favorable and those used to make the trip sound unfavorable. Discuss, too, what a balanced, unbiased article would include. As a cooperative project with you providing guidance, have students combine information from both paragraphs to present a balanced description.

Selection 1

In the mid-1800s thousands of families headed west. For many young people, the trip west was a wonderful adventure. They climbed steep mountains, forded deep rivers, and crossed wide deserts. During these exciting journeys, the children saw huge herds of thundering buffalo. The families saw antelope, bobcats, prairie dogs, and other wild animals. The pioneers met and traded with Native Americans. Pocketknives, mirrors, and other treasured goods were traded for baskets or deer-skin moccasins. Even chores were fun. Gathering firewood became a game. The children would choose sides to see which team could collect the most firewood.

Selection 2

In the mid-1800s thousands of families headed west. For many of the children in the families, it was a trip they would never forget. At first the journey seemed to be an adventure, but it soon grew boring and difficult. Families lived in crowded covered wagons. There was a sameness about the land. Often there was nothing to see for mile after tiresome mile but dying trees and scorched grass. Children as young as 10 years old had to do the work of an adult. They had to carry heavy loads of firewood, search the hot desert for water, and care for stubborn cattle. During the day the blazing sun burned the children. At night clouds of insects swarmed over the campsite. The children's young bones ached from the day's work, but often the children had trouble falling asleep because of the bothersome insects.

1. Which selection, 1 or 2, is slanted in favor of the trip west?
2. From the selection slanted in favor of the trip, what are some words that make the trip sound good?
3. From the selection slanted against the trip, what are some words that make the trip sound bad? (Gunning, 2006d)

Encourage students to bring in examples of slanted text and also text that they feel is balanced. Discuss the techniques used by these examples to slant the text. From time to time, bring in examples of slanted writing that you notice in children's books, periodicals, or other sources. Also bring in examples of balanced writing. In their writing and discussions, encourage students to make balanced presentations.

Author's Purpose The three main purposes for writing are to inform, to entertain, and to persuade. News stories, encyclopedia articles, almanacs, and most nonfiction books inform. Novels, plays, poems, short stories, and humorous essays entertain. Advertisements, editorials, letters to the editor, and serious essays persuade. Writing can have more than one purpose. Nonfiction books can be entertaining. Nonfiction books can also be designed to persuade. In addition to conveying information, a book about global warming, conservation, or energy may attempt to persuade the reader to sympathize with a certain cause. Even fiction sometimes attempts to persuade. A novel, in addition to presenting an interesting story, may try to convince the reader to adopt a certain viewpoint or take a certain course of action. Upton Sinclair's (1906) novel *The Jungle*, for example, led to reform in the meat-packing industry.

To introduce the concept of author's purpose, bring in an informational book about bicycles, a fiction book that involves bicycles, and an ad for bicycles. Tell students that you are going to read three selections that have to do with bikes. Have students see if they can tell why each selection was written. Read excerpts from the informational book and the fiction book. Read the whole ad. Discuss with students why each selection was written. Lead students to understand that the nonfiction book was written to inform, the fiction book was written to entertain, and the ad was written to persuade. Have students read the following three paragraphs and decide the author's main purpose for each.

Selection 1

Tiger sharks are sometimes known as the ocean's garbage cans. They will eat anything. Tiger sharks will eat any object that they can bite. Trash, bottles, potatoes, rocks, dogs, birds, and even parts of old tires have been found in the stomachs of tiger sharks.

Selection 2

The book *Great White* describes in words and pictures the great white shark, the most feared creature in the world. Read about this amazing animal's keen sense of smell, its speed, and its huge size. Find out about people who have been attacked by this shark and who have lived to tell their tales. Once you pick up *Great White*, you won't be able to put it down. Just $9.95 at bookstores everywhere.

Selection 3

"Shark!" I screamed. I had spotted a fin slicing through the water. I screamed once more, but no one on shore heard me. With my heart pounding, I raced for shore. The fin was getting closer now. I swam harder. The creature was too fast for me. "This is it!" I thought. Suddenly, the beast leapt out of the water. "That's a dolphin," I thought to myself. I didn't know whether to laugh or cry, so I did both (Gunning, 2006d).

During discussions of texts that students read, have them identify the author's purpose. Go beyond identifying categories and invite students to tell more specifically what the author is trying to persuade the reader to do or believe, or how the author is entertaining the reader, or what main information the author is trying to give to the reader. As part of their writing have students compose a piece that informs. This could be a report or an article. Also have them write a letter to the editor, an advertisement, an essay, or another piece that persuades.

Judging Sources

The competence of a source of information is dependent on a number of factors. First, the expert or source should have a depth of knowledge about the particular subject in question. Second, the information should be current. Third, the source must be completely unbiased. An expert who has something to gain by making a certain recommendation cannot be completely objective.

To introduce the concept of judging sources of information, discuss with students where they might go if they have questions about the following:

What kind of digital camera is best?
Do I need glasses?
What is the best bicycle?
How can I become a better basketball player?
How can I improve my writing?

Discuss your experience seeking expert advice and how you select expert sources. Talk over why you would go to certain sources. Lead students to see that when you go to get information, whether it is from a person, a book, or a website, you want the information to be accurate, fair, and up to date. Discuss how you might judge the qualifications of a source. Show students books that have been written by obvious experts and whose qualifications are described somewhere in the book (a book by Eugenia Clark on sharks or Jane Goodall on chimps would be a good choice). Read the author's qualifications to students. Discuss what the author's qualifications are and whether the person is an expert. Have students examine informational books in the class or school library and determine whether the authors are experts or have access to expert information. Discuss the other criteria for judging a source: whether the source is unbiased and whether the information is up to date.

Encourage students to examine their textbooks to see if they are written by experts and are up to date. When students read informational books, have them note who wrote the information and then examine the book jacket or another source of information to see if the author seems to be an expert. Since websites might not be checked the way print material is, students should be especially critical when consulting Internet sources. For a website, students should see if the author's name or sponsor is given and whether the author's credentials are provided. Students should also check the date of creation and any updates. Also, discuss the issue of author or sponsor bias. Discuss why an oil company or a conservation group would most likely provide information on fuel sources from their point of view. When using the Internet, students might also determine what the URL tells them about a site. Students can tell if the site is educational (edu), governmental (gov), an organization (org), or commercial (com) (Caruso, 1997). A tilde (~) generally indicates a site operated by an individual. One might have more trust in a site sponsored by a library, university, or government agency than in one sponsored by a commercial entity or individual. Discuss why government and library sites might be especially trustworthy.

Websites should fulfill the students' purpose. They should help the student answer the question he is asking. Websites should also be well designed and easy to use. The American Library Association (www.ala.org) has an excellent set of criteria for choosing websites. It also has a list of recommended websites for students up to 14 years of age. Recommendations are made depending on age level. Approximately 500 sites are recommended.

Detecting Assumptions

Assumptions are ideas or beliefs that are accepted as being true. We make many assumptions, some of which turn out to be true, and some of which don't. If we ask a person for directions and the person gives them to us, we assume that the person knows how to get to our destination and the person has given us the best route. If we are invited to someone's home at dinnertime, we might assume that we will be fed. To see how assumptions sometimes work, try this riddle: A father and his son are in a serious accident. The father is killed and the son is rushed into emergency surgery. The surgeon looks at the boy's face and says, "I can't operate on this boy; he's my son." Explain the riddle (Kies, 2005).

The surgeon couldn't operate because she was his mother. Many people make the assumption that surgeons are males and so have difficulty with the riddle or offer other solutions. Assumptions may be directly stated or implied. They might be supported or not supported. Reasonable assumptions are said to be warranted. Those that are not are unwarranted. The problem with assumptions is that young readers often accept them as facts. Assumptions need to be examined and evaluated. To introduce the concept, present paragraphs similar to the following to students:

> No wonder today's students can't read as well as we did when we were in school. They don't spend as much time reading books as we did. They spend too much time watching TV, playing computer games, surfing the net, or talking to their friends on cell phones.

Discuss the paragraph and lead students to see that it makes statements for which the author offers no proof: "Today's students can't read as well as we did"; and "They don't spend as much time reading books as we did." Also discuss the implied assumption: Reading books is better than reading items from the Internet.

Model the process of identifying assumptions, and discuss why it is important to question them. The reader must decide whether assumptions are warranted and whether to accept them or to withhold judgment. Students should examine and discuss additional examples of assumptions. Once they have grasped the concept, have them note assumptions in periodicals and expository books and in their textbooks.

Using Evaluative Criteria

Once students seem to grasp the concept of judging sources for fairness, help them develop a set of questions that they might use to assess printed sources and websites they consult:

- Is the source up to date?
- Who is the author?
- Is the author an expert?
- Is the author unbiased? Is there any reason that the author would be in favor of one side or one position?
- Is the writing fair, or does it seem to be slanted?
- Does the author make assumptions?
- Does the author give enough proof for all conclusions?

You might post these questions as a reminder for students to use them when they are reading. In adapted form, the questions might also be used for evaluating speeches and informational TV programs.

Teaching Students to Use Language with Care

As part of developing higher-level literacy, teach students to use language with care and to analyze language. A universal example of erroneous use of language is the careless use of absolutes, such as *always, never*, and *all*. "*Everybody* had trouble with the homework you gave us. You are *always* punishing the boys. You *never* give us any free time." This careless but ubiquitous use of absolutes ties in with the concept of verifiable statements. One of the most basic thinking skills is to teach students the difference between statements that are verifiable and those that are opinions or judgments. The statement "Everybody had trouble with the homework" can be checked by asking how many had trouble with the homework and counting to see if indeed it was everyone. Of course, defining what is meant by "trouble with" introduces another thinking issue. Clarifying statements is a related thinking skill.

Developing Aesthetic Judgment

As children gain depth in their response to literature, they should also develop standards by which to judge what they read. For a piece of fiction, they should judge the quality of the character development, plot, theme, author's style, and setting.

- *Character development.* In most pieces of fiction, character development is key. As Lukens explains, well-developed characters are rounded; they are not flat or one-dimensional, nor are they all good or all bad. They seem real enough to us so that we can identify with their struggles, bemoan their defeats, and glory in their victories. Most of all, they are memorable—they stay with us long after the final page has been read.

- *Plot.* Students thrive on action and adventure, so well-plotted stories will gain and maintain their interest. Twists and turns in a story grab students' attention, and plot developments must be plausible and have a measure of originality. Predictable plots are boring, but contrived plots leave readers feeling tricked or cheated.

- *Theme.* The theme may be implicit or directly stated, but as the main idea or central meaning of a work, it provides coherence to a story that otherwise would simply be a collection of episodes. Themes are most evident in traditional tales in which love conquers all, virtue is rewarded, and evil is punished. However, a theme should not be preachy. A tale written to demonstrate the evils of drugs or selfishness falls flat. Genuine themes arise out of the credible actions of believable characters (Lukens, 1995).

- *Author's style.* Style is simply the way an author writes. Authors may have a simple style, an ornate or flowing style, a plodding style, or a brisk style. Good writing is distinguished from poor writing by its forcefulness and originality of style, including choice of words, aptness of description, presence of original figures of speech, and imagery used to create pictures in our minds.

- *Setting.* Setting includes the time and place of a story and the mood that the author creates. For example, in a horror story, the author must create a sense of impending supernatural occurrence as well as depict a deserted castle in a far-off place. When the setting is an integral part of a story, as it would be in a survival tale set in the Arctic, the author must make the setting come alive.

Questions and Activities That Elicit Aesthetic Judgment   First and foremost, readers must learn to respond personally and emotionally to a piece of writing. Aesthetic judgment should build on that base. Because these responses and the reader's construction of meaning are part of a continuous process, Langer (1990) refers to them as envisionments. An envisonment is "the understanding a reader has about a text—what the reader understands at a particular point in time, the questions she has, as well as her hunches about how the piece will unfold" (p. 812). As readers build an envisonment, they go through a series of stances, or changing relationships with the text.

1. Being Out and Stepping In
2. Being In and Moving Through
3. Being In and Stepping Out
4. Stepping Out and Objectifying the Experience

Phase 1: Being Out and Stepping In   In addition to their background knowledge and knowledge of the unfolding story, students use their knowledge of the genre (they have different expectations for a mystery than they would for a science fiction piece) to make "initial acquaintance with the characters, plot, setting—and how they interrelate" (p. 813). They are trying to "step into" the world of the story.

Phase 2: Being In and Moving Through   Having gotten a foot in the door, students are building meaning and trying "to go beyond what they already understand" as they make inferences about "motivation, causality, and the implications of events" (p. 813). They "try to understand why characters behave as they do, why events are unfolding as they are, and what is likely to happen" (Temple et al., 1998, p. 63).

Phase 3: Being In and Stepping Out   Readers step away from the story, stand back, and think about their own lives in terms of the story. "They use what they read in the text to reflect on their own lives, on the lives of others, or on the human condition in general" (Langer, 1990, p. 813).

Phase 4: Stepping Out and Objectifying the Experience   Students compare the text to other texts they have read and evaluate it in terms of their experiences and their expectations and literary standards. They "distance themselves from the text world and talk about the work as a crafted object, and about other texts the story reminds them of. . . ." (Temple, et al., 1998, p. 64). Careful questioning can help students develop their envisonments. Langer suggests that teachers engage in four types of questions.

1. *Initial understandings.* Ask typical reader response questions, which enable students to share their reactions to the piece. Which part of the work stands out in your mind? Was there anything in the work that bothered you? Was there anything in it that surprised you? Do you have any questions about the work?

2. *Developing interpretations.* Ask questions that encourage students to think more deeply about the story. These questions can help students think about motivations, character development, theme, or setting: Do you think the main character acted responsibly? What do you think made the main character confess, even though he was innocent? What is the author trying to say here? Helping students develop interpretations of character is especially important. As Westby (1999) notes, "Understanding of characters' emotions, thoughts, and beliefs are the glue that ties the action of stories together" (p. 172). Students may experience difficulty drawing inferences about characters because they focus on action rather than inner states, they misinterpret the character's emotions and motivations because they mistakenly believe the character is just like them, they fail to consider the whole story, or they focus on the perspective of just one of the characters (Westby, 1999).

3. *Reflecting on personal experience.* Ask questions that help students relate what they have read to personal knowledge or experience. These questions can help them reconsider current or previous understandings or feelings. Some of the reader response questions will work well here. Does the main character remind you of anyone you know? Have you ever been in a situation similar to the one he was in? How would you have handled it? Does this story make you think of anything that has happened in your life?

4. *Evaluating.* Once students have responded to the work and refined their interpretations and looked at the work in terms of their own background knowledge and experiences, help them step back and take a critical look at the piece as a work of art. They might compare it with other pieces they have read and evaluate it in terms of character development, originality, and plausibility of the plot, development of the theme, suitability of setting, style, and overall impact. Students should consider the author's craft so they might come to a better understanding of the creative process and perhaps apply some of the techniques they experienced to their own writing. Some questions that might be asked include: Does this piece remind you of anything else that you read? What was the best line or paragraph in the piece? Did the characters seem real? What made them seem real? Was the plot believable? What special words, expressions, or writing devices did the author use? Which of these did you like best? Least? If you were the author's editor, what would you say to the author? What changes might you ask the author to make?

Over time, students should be able to recognize a well-plotted book, original style, universality of theme, well-developed characters, and—above all—how all the elements work together to produce a superior work. However, response and enjoyment should be at the heart of instruction. Analysis and critical evaluation should only come after students have personally interpreted and responded to the text (Gunning, 2005a).

Study Group Questions

- What are the key evaluative/critical thinking skills?
- Which of these skills do I teach?
- Which of the evaluative/critical thinking skills have my students mastered? What are my students' needs in this area?
- Which skills will I present? How will I present them?

Integrating Higher-Level Literacy Strategies

Although previous chapters presented techniques and activities for introducing single strategies, strategies are applied in integrated fashion. There are a number of techniques designed to show students how to integrate strategies.

Approaches That Integrate Multiple Strategies and Discussions

A number of approaches combine integrated use of multiple strategies with some form of cooperative learning. Cooperative learning can intensify the development of higher-level strategies and skills.

The Role of Questioning in Cooperative Learning

"Generating questions is a guide that supports learners as they develop internal cognitive process" (Ciardiello, 1998, p. 212). Asking questions requires that students comprehend what they read and also that they determine what are the key ideas so that they can ask questions about them. As Ciardiello explains, Question generation, "requires students to search or inspect the text, identify main ideas, and make connections among ideas as a basis for raising questions" (p. 212). Self-questioning is also the most effective monitoring strategy. It is more effective than clarifying or summarizing (Rosenshine, Meister & Chapman, 1996). Questioning plays a key role in cooperative learning and the fostering of thinking skills. To a large extent the quality of the questions posed in discussion groups determines the quality of the learning. Because of the importance of questions, students should be taught how to construct them, especially higher-level questions. Listed below are examples of questions at varying levels.

Locate and Recall   Locate and Recall consists of comprehending main ideas and details, and basic story elements such as setting, characters, and plot. Except for deriving main ideas, questions at this level are literal and text explicit. Question words include *who, what, where, when*, and *how*.

> Explicit detail: Who was Philo Farnsworth?
> Explicit detail: What did Philo Farnsworth invent?
> Explicit detail: Where was Philo Farnsworth born?
> Explicit detail: When did Philo Farnsworth begin working on his invention?
> Explicit detail: How did Philo Farnsworth's invention work?
> Main idea/details: What is the main idea of that section? What was the author telling us in that passage?
> What could be another title for that article?
> Summarizing: What did you learn about Farnsworth's role in inventing TV?

Integrate and Interpret   Integrate and Interpret consists of establishing relationships among ideas. This includes why questions as well as questions that ask for inferences, comparisons, contrasts, conclusions, and connections.

> Conclusion/Support: Based on what you have read, who should get credit for inventing TV? Be able to defend your choice with facts.
> Comparison/Contrast: Compare Philo Farnsworth's TV with Baird's TV. How were they similar? How were they different?
> Inference: Why do you think that very few people have heard of Philo Farnsworth?
> Inference/Support: What kind of a person was Philo Farnsworth? What proof or examples can you give to support your judgment?
> Inference: What do you think Farnsworth would say about television if he were alive today?
> Predict: What do you think television will be like ten years from now?

Connections   Connections require seeing similarities between something the student has read and personal experiences, other texts, or the world.

Text-to-Text: Connection (text-to-text): Which of the inventors that we read or talked about does Farnsworth remind you of?

Personal Connection: Has there ever been a time when you or someone you know didn't get full credit for something you or the person had accomplished?

Critique and Evaluate   Critique and Evaluate requires taking a critical look at the text and evaluating the fairness of the author's message or the literary quality of a selection.

Accuracy/Reliability: How would you judge the accuracy and reliability of the information in the article on Philo Farnsworth?

Author's Qualifications: What are the author's qualifications?

Author's Purpose: What seems to be the author's purpose in writing this article?

Fairness: Does the author seem to have any reason to be biased?

Fairness: Is the article balanced, or is it biased for or against its subject?

Assumptions: Are there any assumptions in the article?

Slanted language: Are there any examples of emotional use of language or slanted language?

Fairness: Are both positive and negative facts given?

Introducing Question Generation

To introduce question generation, discuss the value of questions. Model how you self-question as you read. Demonstrate how you sometimes mentally ask the author questions, including questions about the accuracy or judgment of the author. Discuss with students questions that they ask as they read. Discuss the value of self-questioning and also the value of questioning during discussions. Using a factual paragraph, such as the one that follows or a similar one, guide students as they construct a series of factual questions. Emphasize the desirability of asking questions about key information.

Cars That Drive Themselves

One day there will be cars that can drive themselves. The driver will just have to punch some buttons to tell the car where she is going. The car will do the rest.

One of the first cars to drive itself was Stanley. How did Stanley drive itself? Stanley had a device that kept track of where it was. Another device showed what the road looked like. A third device detected other cars, large rocks, or other things that might get in Stanley's way. Stanley also had six computers. The computers used the information from the devices to guide Stanley. The computers also had a map that showed the starting point, the route that Stanley was to take, and the finish line.

> Stanley didn't drive on a highway. That would have been too dangerous. Stanley drove across 130 miles (210 kilometers) of desert land. Stanley didn't drive fast. Stanley's speed was only about 19 miles (30 kilometers) an hour. But that's not bad for a car without a driver.
> Cars without drivers will be safer. They will have a device that slows them down if they are getting too close to another car. That device will stop them if they are in danger of crashing. Another device will keep them from getting in the wrong lane or going off the road (Gunning, 2006d).

Discuss the importance of asking questions that establish basic information about the topic because this provides the basis for higher-level questions. Basic questions include Who, what, where, and when? as in these questions:

- Who is Stanley?
- What is Stanley?
- What can Stanley do?
- When and where did Stanley drive itself?

As a next step, provide students with examples of why questions. Then encourage them to generate why questions. As a sample question, you might ask them: "Why did Stanley need so many computers?"

Other possible why questions include:

- Why did Stanley go so slowly?
- Why did Stanley ride in the desert instead of on a real road?
- Why might cars that drive themselves be safer?
- Why was the car called Stanley? (Students might consult a history of the car and find that one of the earliest cars was a Stanley Steamer.)

Students might also discuss whether or not they agree with the author's first statement: One day there will be cars that can drive themselves. Over time guide students in the generation and discussion of a variety of questions at all levels. One device that you might use to model and motivate the generation of questions is ReQuest.

ReQuest

ReQuest (reciprocal questioning) (Manzo, 1969; Manzo, Manzo & Albee, 2004) is an approach in which the teacher and students take turns asking questions. Although originally designed to be used one-on-one, ReQuest can be used with groups. Because it is as effective as it easy to use, ReQuest is an excellent technique for using discussion to improve thinking skills. ReQuest can be implemented by following these steps.

Step 1: Select a text that is on the students' level but is challenging enough so that it is possible to generate a number of questions about it.

Step 2: Explain the ReQuest procedure to students. Tell them that good readers ask questions as they read. Explain that in ReQuest, they will practice asking and answering questions. Tell them that they will get a chance to be the teacher because they and you take turns asking questions.

Step 3: Preview the text with the students and make predictions based on the preview.

Step 4: Direct students to read the first significant segment of text. As originally constructed, this was the first sentence, but it could be the first paragraph or section. Tell students that as they read, they are to make up questions to ask you. Explain that they can make up as many questions as they wish. Tell them to ask the kinds of questions that a teacher might ask (Manzo, Manzo, & Albee, 2004). If ReQuest is used with a group, students may write their questions, so that everyone participates. Both teacher and students read the segment.

Step 5: Students ask their questions. The teacher's book is placed face down. Students determine whether answers are accurate and satisfactory. However, students may refer to their texts. If necessary, questions are restated or clarified. Having students first ask questions on a section of the chapter offers an opportunity for the teacher to gauge the level of their thinking and then to model questions on the appropriate level (Bean, 2003).

Step 6: After responding to student questions, ask your questions. Pupil's books are face down. Model higher-level questioning by asking for responses that require integrating several details in the text or making an inference. After going through two or three sentences, you might ask questions that require students to integrate the information in these sentences: "Based on what the first three sentences have told us, why do you think the St. Bernard was a good choice for a rescue dog?" Your questions can be geared to the skill or strategy you wish to introduce. For instance, if you wish to reinforce the concept of main idea, as you are asking questions about the last sentence, you can ask students to tell what the main idea of the paragraph is. If you are reinforcing summarizing, you can ask them to summarize the paragraph. If students are unable to respond to one of your questions, encourage them to explain why they find the question difficult to answer (Manzo, 1998). If difficult concepts or vocabulary words are encountered, they should be discussed. Inform students that they can ask questions about the pronunciations and meanings of words: "How do you say the word that is spelled a-r-i-d? What does *arid* mean?" Throughout the interaction, students are reinforced for imitating the teacher's questioning behavior. Reinforcement can be direct or indirect. You might state, "That's a good question!" Or you might use the question as an example and ask, "Can anyone ask another question like that one?" (Manzo, 1998).

Step 7: Advance to the next segment. The questioning proceeds until enough information has been gathered to set a purpose for reading the remainder of the text. This could be in the form of a prediction: "What do you think the rest of the article will be about?" You can help set up a purpose question by prompting students to convert their "thoughts and speculations or hypotheses into questions" (Manzo, 1998). For example, before students read a selection on ancient structures, the teacher might ask, "What question do you suppose this article will answer regarding the relationship between arches and domes?" (Manzo, 1998).

Manzo, Manzo, and Albee (2004) recommend that the questioning be concluded as soon as a logical purpose can be set but no longer than ten minutes after beginning. However, Bean (2003) has adapted ReQuest so that it is used to introduce and discuss a portion of a novel segment by segment. In this adaptation of the procedure, students are guided to ask higher-level questions.

Step 8: After the rest of the selection has been read silently, the purpose question and any related questions are discussed. Here is an excerpt from a ReQuest lesson based on the following passage.

Acid Rain

Acid rain harms lakes, streams, trees, buildings and statues, and public health. Acid rain refers to acid that falls out of the atmosphere. Acid is formed in the atmosphere when pollutants from earth mix with water and chemicals in the atmosphere. Because it refers to more than just rain, acid rain should be called acid deposition. Acid deposition can be wet or dry. Acid deposition is wet when acid mixes with water and falls to earth as rain or snow, and it is dry when acid gases and particles fall to earth (Gunning, 2006d).

Teacher: Today we are going to try a new technique in which you get to ask questions, instead of just answering them. This technique is called ReQuest, and here's how it works. We look at the title and any illustrations and predict what the article will be about. Then we read the first part sentence by sentence. We read the first sentence, and then I turn my book over, and you can ask me any questions you want about that first sentence. You can even ask me what words mean if you want. You can ask as many questions as you want. After you have finished asking questions about the first sentence, then I ask questions. After I have finished asking questions, we go on to the next sentence. We do this until we have gone through the first paragraph. Then you read the article on your own. Let's read the title. What do you think this article might tell us about acid rain? Now let's read the first sentence.

Teacher: Now I will turn my book over and you ask me questions about the first sentence.

Student:	What does acid rain harm?
Teacher:	Lakes and streams and trees and buildings and statutes and health.
Teacher:	What is public health?
Student:	I think that means people in general.
Teacher:	Let's read sentence two now.
Student:	What is acid rain?
Teacher:	Acid rains is acid that falls out of the atmosphere.
Student:	What is the atmosphere?
Teacher:	I believe that is that air that surrounds the Earth.
Student:	How is acid rain formed?
Teacher:	Acid rain is formed when pollutants from earth are carried up into the atmosphere and mix with water and chemicals.
Teacher:	What would cause an increase in acid rain?
Student:	Having more cars and factories.
Student:	What should acid rain be called?
Teacher:	Acid deposition.
Teacher:	Why should acid rain be called acid deposition?
Student:	Because acid rain is more than just rain.
Teacher:	What familiar word do you see in the word *deposition*?
Student:	*Deposit.*
Teacher:	What do you think *deposition* means in this article.
Student:	To put or place something somewhere.
Student:	What are the two kinds of deposition?
Teacher:	Wet and dry.

The discussion is continued until key concepts and vocabulary have been developed. At that point, the students predict what the rest of the article might say about acid rain and read on their own.

Students enjoy playing the role of the teacher and asking questions. However, ReQuest can be made even more effective if students are taught to ask questions. Ciardiellio (1998) added a question training component to ReQuest. In his question-teaching procedure, which he termed TeachQuest, Ciardiellio (1998) explained the importance of questions and described four levels of questions. In his descriptions he included sample questions and signal words. Students then identified and classified questions. Through modeling and guided practice, students were taught how to compose higher-level questions. Once they were able to generate higher-level questions, students then applied this skill using ReQuest.

Highly motivational, ReQuest is virtually a sure-fire technique. Although valuable in and of itself, ReQuest provides preparation for a well-researched, highly effective procedure: reciprocal teaching.

Reciprocal Teaching

Reciprocal teaching is first and foremost a conversation between teachers and students, the purpose of which is to construct an understanding of the text they are reading (Palincsar & Brown, 1986). Reciprocal teaching incorporates four key strategies: predicting, questioning, summarizing, and clarifying. Known as the fab four (Oczcus, 2003), the strategies foster comprehension and structure the dialogue. In classical reciprocal teaching lesson, students take turns leading the discussion. The discussion leader makes predictions, asks questions, summarizes, and clarifies. However, other students can also clarify or request a clarification.

Each strategy was carefully chosen for the following reasons and to accomplish the following purposes:

Predicting: This activates prior knowledge and sets a purpose for reading. If the selection is being read in segments and a segment has already been read, the prediction is based on what has already happened or information already conveyed. The prediction functions as kind of summary and a check on understanding because the text serves as a basis for the prediction.

Questioning: Students compose questions about the selection. This leads students to consider the main points of the text. It also fosters enhanced comprehension. Asking good questions requires good comprehension. In order to ask effective questions, students must identify key information in the passage. Then they must formulate a question. When others respond to their questions, students must decide whether the answer is adequate. They must reflect on the information. They might also provide assistance to students as these students attempt to answer questions. When students pose questions, they have a greater involvement in the responses. Constructing and answering questions are also devices for monitoring meaning. Students will soon realize that they will have difficulty answering questions if they don't understand the selection.

Summarizing: Students give a brief summary after each segment read. This highlights main ideas and key details and serves as a check on comprehension. If you can't summarize, your comprehension is lacking.

Clarifying: Students monitor for meaning and become aware when meaning breaks down. They also use fix-up strategies to repair comprehension. Clarifying highlights the importance of being aware of one's understanding of text and the importance of using strategies to ensure comprehension. During the discussions students can report steps they took to repair comprehension and can also call for clarification of puzzling words or passages that they were unable to handle.

Introducing Reciprocal Teaching   Many of these strategies would most likely already have been taught. However, when introducing reciprocal teaching, you might want to review them. You also will want to show how they work together. Questioning is probably the most difficult strategy to use. In preparation, you might spend some time teaching students how to construct questions. Formulating questions poses a special difficulty for ELL. Asking questions, especially higher-levels ones, is a difficult linguistic task. ELL may need extra instruction on formulating questions. When introducing reciprocal teaching, explain to students that they will take turns acting as the teacher. In the beginning, provide students with needed guidance. As they become more proficient at making predictions, summarizing, and asking questions, and clarifying or asking for clarification, gradually give them more responsibility. Also have patience with the technique. Reciprocal teaching is fairly complex. You might not see much payoff until after several weeks. But it should be worth the wait. The payoff from reciprocal teaching can be quite substantial.

Developing Dialogue   Strategy use develops over time. It requires instruction, guided practice, and application. Students move from awareness of the strategy to initial acquisition to adept application and integration with other strategies (Benson-Castagna, 2005). However, strategy application is only part of reciprocal teaching. You also need to develop dialogue along with strategies. Although teacher-student dialogue might predominate at first, student-to-student dialogue should also increase. The ultimate objective is to develop students' self-awareness of their learning and to turn thinking into language, so that they can become more aware of their thinking and share their thinking with each other. To assist students with their dialogue, you might provide them with stem starters. Stem starters adapted from Beers (2003) are presented in Table 8.1.

Working with Pairs   One way of easing into reciprocal teaching is to have students work in pairs. Working with pairs, students can practice applying strategies. Working with pairs helps students develop their reflecting and discussion skills. As they explain their thinking, they become more aware of their thinking. As they construct oral responses, they are preparing themselves for taking part in discussions in larger groups. They are also preparing themselves to construct the

Table 8.1 ● Stem Starters

Stem Starters	
Predicting	I predict ____.
	I think_____.
	Based on what has happened so far, I think that ____ will happen.
	I predict that the author will explain _____ or tell _____.
Questioning	Who is _____?
	Who did _____?
	What happened _____?
	What are _____?
	When did _____?
	Where is _____?
	Where did _____?
	Why did _____?
	How did _____?
	What is the author trying to say here?
	What does this mean?
	What do you think about _____?
Summarizing	This section explained _____.
	This section told _____.
	In this section _____.
	The main ideas in this section were _____.
	This was about _____.
Clarifying	I am not sure what _____ means.
	I found _____ confusing.
	Can anyone tell me what _____ means?
	Can anyone explain how this process works?
	The author seems to be saying _____.
	I didn't understand the part where _____.

kinds of written responses demanded by high-stakes tests. As they listen to another person sharing thinking, they develop their ability to consider other viewpoints, thus broadening their thinking. After students have some experience working in pairs, you can ask two pairs to share so that now they are working in a small group of four (Benson-Castagna, 2005). Below is a practice reciprocal teaching lesson for you to try out with your students.

Teaching/Practice Reciprocal Teaching Lesson

Step 1. Introduction   Tell students that they will be using a technique in which they take over the role of the teacher. Explain the purpose of the technique: to increase comprehension by using four of the best comprehension strategies and discussing a selection. Inform students that they will be taking turns leading the discussions.

Step 2. Teaching Key Strategies   Introduce and explain each of the four strategies: predicting, questioning, summarizing, and clarifying. If students are already familiar with these strategies, review them.

- *Predicting.* Explain to students that predicting helps them to think about the key ideas in a selection, and that it gives them a purpose for reading. Modeling the process, show students how you would use the title or heading, illustrations, and introductory paragraph, if there is one, to make predictions about the upcoming content. If the prediction is about a segment in the middle of the selection, you would use your knowledge of what had happened or the information given so far and headings to make a prediction. Provide opportunities for guided practice.
- *Questioning.* Show students how you create questions as you read. Also explain that you ask questions about the most important ideas in a selection. Provide sample questions and guided practice.
- *Clarifying.* Explain the need for clarifying, and show what you do when you encounter a word, phrase, or passage that you find puzzling. Encourage students to locate words, expressions, or concepts in a sample selection that need clarifying. Discuss what might be done to provide clarification: rereading, using context or glossary to derive the meaning of a difficult word, using illustrations, etc.
- *Summarizing.* Explain to students that summarizing may be the most important reading strategy of all because it helps them concentrate on important points while reading. It also helps them review the main points and check on their understanding. Explain to students that if they can't summarize a passage, this is a sign that they may not have understood it and should go back and reread it. Provide guided practice.

Distribute the selection to be read (a student copy can be found in Appendix A). Tell students that they will be reading an article about Ireland. Tell them that Ireland is a small country in Europe. Ask students to find Ireland on the map. Ask: What country is it near? Read the title to students. Have the leader take over. Remind the leader to do the following for each section:

- Make a prediction.
- Make up questions about what you have read.

- Ask for clarification of anything that is not clear.
- Summarize what you have read.
- Predict what the rest of the selection might be about.

The following section is read silently after the leader has made a prediction.

Potatoes for Breakfast, Lunch, and Supper

Do you like potatoes? Would like to eat potatoes at every meal? Years ago, in Ireland, people ate potatoes for breakfast, lunch, and supper. Each person ate between seven and fifteen pounds of potatoes a day. The Irish ate baked potatoes, fried potatoes, mashed potatoes, boiled potatoes, and roasted potatoes. They ate potato soup, potato pancakes, and potato cakes. Why did they eat so many potatoes? They were very poor. Most families had tiny bits of land on which to grow their food. They grew potatoes because it was possible to grow a lot of potatoes on a small piece of land. Storing potatoes was easy. They were kept in pits in the ground and were dug up when needed.

(Leader asks questions, summarizes, and predicts what the next section will be about. Leader or anyone in the group can ask for clarification. Leader can do next section, or a new leader can take over.)

A Kindly People

Although the Irish were poor, they were a kindly people. Even though they barely had enough to eat, they would feed anyone who came to their door. If a stranger came to dinner unexpectedly, they figured they could put another potato in the pot or cut a potato in half to share with the stranger. They had a saying about feeding others: "We've an extra potato right hot on the fire, for one who travels through wet bog and mire."

(Leader asks questions, summarizes, and predicts what the next section will be about. Leader or anyone in the group can ask for clarification. Leader continues, or a new leader is chosen.)

The Great Famine

Disaster struck the Irish people in 1845. Their potato crop was hit by a plant disease known as a blight. Potatoes began rotting in the field. Not having enough to eat, more than a million men, women, and children died of starvation. To escape the famine, millions more sailed for the United States, Canada, or Australia. The blight wasn't over until 1854. Before the blight Ireland had 9 million people. After the blight, there were just 5 million left (Gunning, 2006d).

(Leader asks questions, summarizes, and predicts what the next section will be about. Leader or anyone in the group can ask for clarification.)

Other Forms of Reciprocal Teaching   Reciprocal teaching can be used in literature circles and other book discussion groups. Oczkus (2003) decided to use reciprocal teaching with literature circles because she found that many of the students she was working with were not fully comprehending what they read. "Reciprocal teaching adds a 'read and learn to comprehend' dimension to literature circles because it gives students the basics for comprehending well" (p. 134). Some teachers introduce reciprocal teaching in small groups or the whole class early in the year and by spring have students use reciprocal teaching in their literature discussion groups. If you do use reciprocal teaching in book discussion groups, you might also want to add other activities, such as making personal connections, making connections with other texts, inferring character traits, evaluating the credibility and fairness of the text, and appreciating the author's craft. You might want to use reciprocal teaching in book discussion groups with nonfiction and use the more typical book discussion format with fiction. If you use role or job sheets with your literature circles, you might incorporate the fabulous four so that you have a role sheet for a predictor, summarizer, clarifier, and questioner (see Figures 8.1 and 8.2, and Tables 8.2 and 8.3).

Previewing and Wondering   To provide students with practice activating background knowledge and setting up purposes for reading, have them preview an article and complete a What I Know strip. A strip is simply a slip of paper on which students write their responses. Based on their preview, have them complete a What I Wonder strip (Oczkus, 2003). A heading, a photo, or a chart might be the basis for their wondering statement. Strips might be posted and discussed. Talk over what things students already know. Also discuss what kinds of things

Figure 8.1 ● Summarizer Job Sheet

The summarizer's job is to tell what happened in the story so far. Don't try to tell every little detail. Tell only the most important things that have happened. Focus on what has happened to the main character. If you are summarizing nonfiction, summarize the most important information. Begin with the main idea of the nonfiction piece.

_____

_____

_____

_____

Figure 8.2 ● Questioner Job Sheet

The questioner's job is to ask questions about the part of the book or the article or story that your group will be discussing. Ask questions about the important parts of the story or the main information in the article. Ask questions that get the others to think carefully about what they read. Ask questions that help them make connections to the story or article. Here are some possible questions for fiction:

> After reading this part of the story, what stands out in your mind?
>
> Was there anything that bothered or surprised you?
>
> Do you agree with the main character's actions?
>
> What connections can you make with the characters or events in the story?
>
> If the author were here, what would you ask her or him?

Here are some possible questions for nonfiction:

> After reading this article, what stands out in your mind?
>
> What did you learn from the article?
>
> How might you use this information?
>
> What else would you like to know about this subject?

Write your questions on the lines.

_____

_____

_____

_____

they are wondering about. The discussion provides an excellent opportunity to build background, concepts, and vocabulary in preparation for reading the selection. Model the process. If students are familiar with KWL, they might use their knowledge of that technique to help them understand this activity. Students can work individually, in pairs, or in small groups. By examining the strips, you can assess students' background knowledge and their ability to make predictions based on their previews.

Reciprocal Teaching in the Early Grades Pamela N. Myers (2005–2006) tells the story of one of her students, a shy English-language learner who approached her the day after Myers read aloud *Miss Nelson Is Missing* (Allard, 1977). He said that he had a Clara Clarifier question. He didn't understand why Detective McSmogg was now looking for Viola Swamp at the end of the story. The student hadn't realized that Viola Swamp was Miss Nelson in disguise, which is the main point of the story.

Table 8.2 ● Predictor Job Sheet

If you are reading a story, your job is to read the title and look at the illustration, if there is one, and predict what might happen in the story. If your group has already read part of the story, then you make a prediction based on what has happened so far. If you are reading nonfiction, use the title, heading, and illustrations to predict. Predict what the author will tell you in the article or what you will learn from reading the article. Fill out the prediction chart. Write your prediction and the clues that helped you make the prediction.

Prediction	Clues: What led me to make this prediction?

The student's question helped Meyers realize that the student was experiencing some confusion that needed clarifying. Meyers had adapted reciprocal teaching for use with younger students. She read selections to the children and used puppets to personalize the reciprocal-teaching strategies. The Princess Storyteller summarized the story, Quincy Questioner asked questions. Clara Clarifier requested clarification, and the Wizard predicted what would happen next in the story. Each strategy was modeled during reading alouds for the first month of school.

Myers and her colleagues were concerned that comprehension was being short-changed in the primary grades. As she explained, "With so much emphasis on de-coding in the primary grades, comprehension issues have often been ignored; yet even with very young students, comprehension of text is critical. It is, therefore, es-sential that kindergarten teachers teach students the comprehension skills they need to succeed as future readers" (p. 314). Actually state standards required that kinder-garten students be able to make predictions, answer questions, and retell stories. All of these were encompassed by reciprocal teaching. Although reciprocal teaching is typically used with text that students are encountering for the first time, Myers used the technique with stories that had been read several times. She found that her ELL students were better able to comprehend selections after they had heard them several times. Strategies were introduced one at a time. However, strategies were reinforced on an ongoing basis. Since kindergarteners often don't distinguish between a state-ment and a question, there was much modeling of asking questions. Students were also encouraged to ask questions during pauses in read-alouds if there was anything they didn't understand. Because young children tend to ask clarifying questions only about words they don't understand, Myers modeled seeking clarification. Stopping at potentially confusing parts of a shared read-aloud story, she would think aloud

Approaches That Integrate Multiple Strategies and Discussions

Table 8.3 ● Clarifier Job Sheet

The clarifier's job is to make a note of any words that might be hard for readers or any parts of the story or article that might be confusing. Write each hard word, the sentence in which it appeared, and the meaning of the word. You can look these up in the glossary or in a dictionary. Make sure you consider how the word was used in the story or article when choosing a meaning. Many words have several meanings. If you can't decide on the meaning of a word, get help from the group.

Hard Word	Sentence in Which It Appeared	Meaning

For confusing parts, write down in the chart below any part that you found puzzling or that you think the other students will find confusing. If you can figure out confusing parts, write down in the chart below what you think they mean. If you can't figure out the confusing parts, get help from the group. If the group can't figure out the confusing part, get help from the teacher.

Confusing Passage	What It Means

about her confusion and ask students to help her. Students took turns assuming the roles. Instead of one student acting as leader, each of four students assumed one role. Students assumed a role at least once a week. Those who didn't have roles were able to respond to questions and ask for clarification.

Over the course of the three-month study, students' comprehension and ability to talk about stories increased. They also learned that stories should make sense and that they should seek clarification when something was confusing. Perhaps, most importantly, the study demonstrated that young students can learn to use key strategies and are capable of monitoring for meaning. The study demonstrated, too, the importance of teaching young children comprehension strategies. At the beginning of the study, students were often not aware when they weren't understanding. By the end of the study, they were able to identify confusing parts. Knowing that they didn't know, they were then in a position to take corrective steps.

Reading Seminar

Once students are doing well with reciprocal teaching, they might graduate to Reading Seminar. In Reading Seminar (described more fully in Chapter 9), using higher-level talk, they add information, ask for supporting or clarifying sentences, and add their own input. Interchanges are student to student as well as student to teacher. Students learn to express their points of view and to consider other points of a view in an accepting environment.

Study Group Questions

- To what extent do I integrate the teaching of higher-level thinking strategies?
- What are my students' major needs in this area?
- How might I use ReQuest and Reciprocal Teaching to integrate and foster higher-level literacy skills?

chapter 9

Using Talk to Build Higher-Level Literacy Skills

One of the best ways to develop higher-level thinking skills is through discussions. Discussions require us to think through and clarify our ideas. They also provide us with the perspectives and insights of others. Discussion programs designed to foster higher-level thinking are based on Vygotsky's (1981) theory that "the higher functions of child thought first appear in the form of argumentation and only then develop into reflection for the individual child" (p. 157). As Chinn, Anderson, and Waggoner (2001) explain, "We expect that when children express and hear arguments and counterarguments in groups, they will develop an internalized ability to formulate arguments and counterarguments on their own" (p. 385).

Accountable Talk

In order to be effective at building higher-level skills, discussions need to incorporate the kinds of elements that are fostered by accountable talk. Accountable talk is a program in which students are taught to think carefully about what they say and to provide support for their assertions. They also learn to listen attentively and to respond to others in conversations that build knowledge and understanding (Resnick & Hall, 2001). Accountable talk is an essential element in teacher-student conferences, in small-group and whole-class discussions, and in student presentations. Teachers foster accountable talk through direct instruction, modeling, and coaching. They make judicious use of questions and prompts designed to foster accountable talk (see pages 152–153 for a listing of prompts). Teachers

- seek clarification and explanation when called for.
- ask for proof or justification for positions or statements.
- help clarify erroneous concepts.
- interpret and summarize students' statements (Resnick & Hall, 2001).

Students are accountable to the learning community, to knowledge, and to rigorous thinking.

Accountability to the Learning Community

Students establish as a goal the development of a topic or idea. Students take deliberate actions to reach that goal. They listen attentively to each other, acknowledge and build on others' contributions, and they paraphrase or revoice the contributions of others. All students are encouraged to join in the discussions. If a student is not responding, others might invite him to make a comment or volunteer a response.

Accountability to Knowledge

Students support their assertions. They might cite a passage as support for their conclusion. When using information from outside sources, they take steps to verify its accuracy. As needed during discussions, students request clarification of unfamiliar words and ideas. They also request support for assertions. They might challenge statements but not persons. Students also request added information when necessary.

Accountability to Rigorous Thinking

Students engage in higher-level thinking and discussions. They attempt to draw logical conclusions and supply support for them. They assess what they read. They note evidence of author's bias and entertain other viewpoints. They seek multiple sources of information and compare and contrast the information they obtain from these sources. Most important of all, they boost each other's understanding and thinking.

Discussion Approaches

The discussion approaches explored here are based on the principles of accountable talk and also an analysis of more than a dozen discussion approaches. Most discussion approaches work best with fiction. However, Reading Seminar, which is explained below, has been designed for informational text. Discussion approaches can be categorized as being teacher-led or student-led, although there is some over-lapping. Within teacher-led approaches, the amount of freedom given to students to discuss can vary considerably. As students become more proficient, the teacher can gradually cede more responsibility to them.

Reading Seminar: Intensive Reading Instruction

Based on Accountable Talk and other collaborative discussion approaches, such as Questioning the Author (Beck & McKeown, 2002), Reading Seminar fosters higher-level reading, thinking, and discussion (Gunning, 2003). It also builds both back-ground and strategy use. It is collaborative because the teacher and students work closely together to construct meaning. At times the students are apprentice construc-tors as they imitate the strategies that the teacher models or suggests. At other times students take the lead. Student-to-student as well as teacher-to-student discussions are fostered. At all times the teacher builds on what the students know. The teacher finds out what knowledge students bring to the topic and builds on that knowledge. The teacher also finds out what strategies the students are using and builds on these. Reading Seminar is used primarily with informational text.

Reading Seminar uses the same levels of reading discussed throughout the text: preparing, locating and recalling, integrating and interpreting (including connecting), critiquing and evaluating, and monitoring. Preparing refers to processes that readers use before reading a text and include surveying, predicting, activating prior knowledge, and setting goals and purposes. Locating and recalling consist of comprehending main ideas and details, and basic story elements. Integrating and interpreting include why questions as well as questions that ask for inferences, comparisons, contrasts, conclusions, and connections. Critiquing and evaluating involve taking a critical look at the text and evaluating the fair-ness of the author's message or the literary quality of a selection. Monitoring in-volves checking comprehension and taking corrective steps when comprehension fails. All levels of comprehension include monitoring. Students should always be aware of whether what they reading is making sense, and they should be pre-pared to take corrective action if it isn't.

Not all levels are included in any one session. However, during the course of instruction all levels are presented and practiced. In any one lesson or series of les-sons, the teacher might guide instruction and discussion in such a way as to focus on a particular level or strategy. In a sense, reading seminar includes all the techniques and principles for building higher-level literacy that have been explored in the text.

Using Prompts   A key element in reading seminar is the use of prompts. Prompts guide the students' thinking and responding, provide structure and scaffolding, and also affirm and encourage. Suggested prompts are listed below. However, these should be adapted to fit your situation. Only use those prompts that are appropriate. Use a limited number of prompts so that your discussion has focus.

Preparational Prompts: Previewing, Predicting, Accessing Prior Knowledge, Setting Goals (before reading)

- Look at the title, illustrations, and subheads. Based on your survey, what do you think this selection might be about? What do you think this article will tell you?
- As you surveyed the text, did you come across any vocabulary words that were unknown?
- What do you know about this topic?
- What would you like to find out?
- What strategies might you use to help us understand this section? (optional)
- How might you go about reading this? (optional)

Locating/Recalling Prompts (during/after reading) (choose two or three prompts)

As they read, students should have a question in mind. Usually the question is based on the prereading survey. If headings are used, students can turn the heading into a question and read to answer the question.

- What is this part of the selection telling you?
- What seems to be the author's main point(s)?
- How does the author prove or explain his point(s)?
- What did you learn from this selection?
- How might you organize this information to help you understand it better?

Integrating/Interpreting Prompts (choose one or two prompts)

- What important information did the author imply but not state?
- What questions came to mind as you read this selection?
- Based on the information in the selection, what conclusion might you reach?
- How would you support that conclusion?
- How does this information fit in with what you already know?
- How might you use this information?
- How was the information organized?
- How did this organization help you to understand the information in the article?
- Which of the graphic organizers might we use to display this information?

Connecting Prompts

- What connections can you make between the information in this article and other texts that you have read?
- What connections can you make between the information in this article and your own experience?
- What connections can you make between the information in this article and what's happening in the world?

Critiquing/Evaluating Prompt

- Was the information presented fairly?
- Was there any evidence of bias? Has the author provided both sides of the question?

Monitoring Prompts (choose one or two prompts)

(Students might be encouraged to put a stick-on note on any passage that is not clear.)

- Was there anything in the article that was confusing?
- Were there any passages that weren't clear? What was it about the passage that puzzled you?
- Were there any words that weren't clear?
- Do you have any questions about anything that you read?

Strategy Prompts

- What helped you to understand this section?
- What strategies did you use to help you get the meaning of this section? (Students or teacher might explain and model helpful strategies.)
- How did you go about reading parts that weren't clear to you at first?
- How did you go about reading words that were difficult?

Text Connecting (Integrating) Prompts

These should be asked after reading more than one section. To connect information from a previous section, ask the following questions:

- How does this fit in with what was said in the section (or sections) that we have already read?
- Putting together the information from all the sections that we have read, what have you learned so far?

Discussion Prompts   During discussions, use prompts to scaffold instruction, discover and clarify confusions, encourage students, and keep the discussion moving forward. Listed below are some suggested prompts. They should be used as needed.

Focusing Prompt   In a focusing prompt, you direct the students' attention to a particular event or idea (Taba, 1965). You guide them so that they focus on specific information. These are who, what, where, when, and how questions.

Expanding Prompt   If a student does not provide sufficient information, ask: "Can you tell me more?" If that doesn't produce a response, follow up with prompts that are more specific. "What did he do next? What else happened? What are the other sources of alternative energy besides solar power?"

Clarifying Prompt   If a response is not clear, use a prompt in which you re-state what you believe the student said and then ask if your restatement is correct: "You seem to be saying that having a pet gave Tyrique a sense of responsibility which carried over to his school work." The purpose of a clarifying prompt is to help the speaker clarify her or his thoughts. It can also be used to keep the speaker on track if she or he has gotten off the subject (Hyman, 1978).

Rewording   Reword the prompt if you believe the student may not understand it. Use simpler terms or simplify the question.

Lifting   In a lifting prompt, you lift the discussion to a higher level (Taba, 1965). After students have responded with the basic facts, you might ask them to make an inference, come to a conclusion, make a comparison, or generalize. "When we see that sugar sweeteners are called by a number of names and are found in bread, cereal, applesauce, and even ketchup, what can we conclude about the amount of sugar we are eating?"

Substantiating   Substantiating questions ask students to provide evidence for their assertions: "What makes you say that many people are making unhealthy food choices?" Students might be asked to tell what led them to a conclusion, how they determined a character's major traits, or what standards they used to judge a piece of literature or the fairness of a piece of writing. Substantiating questions are at the heart of higher-level thinking.

Summarizing   A summarizing prompt provides a recap of the discussion. "Here is a summary of what the article said. What main points did the author make? What did you learn from the article? What were the highlights of the story?"

Affirming   An affirming prompt highlights effective use of a strategy or procedure. "I like the way you explained how Maria earned money to take her pet to the vet."

Scaffolding Prompts   Be aware of students' difficulties and pose questions that guide students' thinking. Use responsive elaboration (Duffy & Roehler, 1987). In responsive elaboration, you elaborate or build on the student's response. Instead of asking yourself, "Is this answer right or wrong?" ask: "What thought processes led the student to this response?" And, if the answer is wrong, "How can those thought processes be redirected?" Instead of calling on another student, telling where the answer might be found, or giving obvious hints, teachers ask questions or make statements that help put students' thinking back on the right track. The key is asking yourself two questions: "What has gone wrong with the student's thinking?" and "What can I ask or state that would guide the student's thinking to the right thought processes and correct answer?" (Gunning, 2005a).

The following is a scripted example of how a teacher might redirect a student who has inferred a main idea that is too narrow in scope:

Student (giving incorrect main idea): Getting new words from Indians.

Teacher: Well, let's test it. Is the first sentence talking about new words from the Indians?

Student: Yes.

Teacher: Is the next?

Student: Yes.

Teacher: How about the next?

Student: No.

Teacher: No. It says that Indians also learned new words from the settlers, right? Can you fit that into your main idea?

Student: The Indians taught the settlers words, and the settlers taught the Indians words.

Teacher: Good. You see, you have to think about all the ideas in the paragraph to decide on the main idea (Duffy & Roehler, 1987, p. 517).

Wait Time One of the most effective ways to improve students' responses is to do absolutely nothing—for about five seconds (Lake, 1973; Rowe, 1969). After posing a question, wait five seconds. Don't call on anyone. This gives the students time to gather their thoughts. Pausing in this way is known as wait time. Because it gives students time to think, wait time produces longer, more elaborate, higher-level responses. There are also fewer no-responses and I-don't-knows. Also use wait time with individual students. After calling on a particular student, give her five seconds to formulate a response. And provide wait time after a student has responded. After the student has apparently said all that she has to say, continue to focus on that student for three to five seconds. Maintain eye contact and ignore all those hands waving in the air, indicating that other students are waiting to jump in with their comments (Christenbury & Kelly, 1983). Maintaining contact for an added five seconds after the student has responded provides the opportunity for added elaboration or explanation. As a significant side benefit, using wait time enables teachers to develop their ability to help students clarify and expand their responses (Dillon, 1983; Gambrell, 1980).

Implementing Reading Seminar   In Reading Seminar, students meet to read and discuss a selection under the teacher's direction. Since this approach to instruction might be unfamiliar to students, it will need to be explained and modeled. Begin by explaining to students that they will be using a new way of reading. Explain that it is a way of reading in which people help each other understand a difficult story or article. It is called Reading Seminar. Explain that in Reading Seminar, a group reads and discusses short sections of a selection. (The seminar can include the whole class or, preferably, a small group.) Explain that the seminar group will be reading brief sections so that they can thoroughly discuss and understand a section they have read, before they move on to the next section.

- To prepare a selection for Reading Seminar, analyze the text and decide what you want students to learn as a result of reading the selection. What ideas or understandings do you want them to come away with? List two or three of these. Then gear all instruction and activities towards helping students achieve those understandings. Also note any key words that might pose problems for students and which you judge they will not be able to get from context. Note, too, difficult concepts or unfamiliar background that may need to be introduced.
- In light of these target understandings, the nature of the text, and the students' abilities, segment the text. Segment the text into sections that you think students can handle. Difficult text that contains many key concepts would be read in shorter segments.
- Once the text has been segmented, decide on the question or questions that you will use to introduce each segment and the questions you will use after each segment has been read.
- Before students begin reading the first section, introduce the entire selection or conduct a preparatory discussion. Then introduce difficult vocabulary and concepts, and provide needed background for the segment they are about to read. If you are working with older students, you might involve them in selecting difficult vocabulary. You might invite them to quickly survey the selection and note any words that might be difficult (Anderson & Roit, 1993). Discuss these words beforehand.

Introductory Lesson   Use a brief, but interesting article to demonstrate Reading Seminar. Use the preparatory prompts and selected prompts from locate/recall. In the next lesson add prompts for monitoring. Later add prompts from integrate/-

interpret and evaluate/critique. Also gradually add discussion prompts. Start using wait time and scaffolding responses. Adapt the prompts to fit your teaching style.

As with any new approach, it is best to start out gradually. Once you and your students feel comfortable with the basic elements, move on to more advanced ones. Also feel free to adapt the approach to fit your situation (Gunning, 2003).

Segment 1

Mill Child

After Lucy Larcom's father died, her mom sold their home and opened a boarding-house in Lowell, Massachusetts. The boardinghouse was a place where the girls and young women who worked at the cotton and wool mills lived and ate their meals. But with eight children to support, Mrs. Larcom needed more money than she made at the boardinghouse. To help out, Lucy Larcom went to work in one of the mills. It was 1837. Lucy was just eleven years old at the time.

Years later, Lucy Larcom told what it was like to go to work at such a young age. "I went to my first day's work in the mill with a light heart. The novelty of it made it seem easy, and it really was not hard, just to change the bobbins on the spinning-frames every three quarters of an hour or so, with half a dozen other little girls who were doing the same thing. When I came back at night, the family began to pity me for my long, tiresome day's work, but I laughed and said, 'Why, it is nothing but fun. It is just like play."

Segment 2

Lucy's Disappointment

Even though she was working, Lucy was given time off to finish her schooling. "When I took my next three months at the grammar school, everything there was changed, and I too was changed. The teachers were kind, and thorough in their instruction; and my mind seemed to have been ploughed up during that year of work, so that knowledge took root in it easily. It was a great delight to me to study, and at the end of the three months the master told me that I was prepared for the high school.

"But alas! I could not go. The little money I could earn—one dollar a week, besides the price of my board—was needed in the Family, and I must return to the mill. It was a severe disappointment to me, though I did not say so at home."

Segment 3

Lucy Leaves the Mill

When she got a little older, Lucy went to night school. Later, she left the mill and even got a chance to go to college. She became a teacher, and she also wrote eight books. Her best-known book tells about growing up and working in the mills. It is called *A New England Girlhood*. She wrote it in just a few years before she died, but it is still being read today (Gunning, 2006c).

Key Understandings
- Lucy Larcom was a kindly girl who made sacrifices to help her family.
- In the past some children in the United States had to work long hours to help out their families.

Preparation Write the title on the board, "Mill Child." Ask: What do you think this article might tell? What is a mill? Look at the illustration. What do they seem to be doing? The machines are spinning cotton into thread. Notice the round devices on top of the spinning-frame. They hold the thread that is being spun and are known as bobbins. What questions do you have about this article? What would you like to find out?

Segment 1. After-Reading Discussion

What is this first part of the selection telling you? What did you find out about Lucy? What do her actions tells us about her? From her actions, what kind of a person does she seem to be? What did you learn about mills in the 1800s? What do you think the second part of the article will tell you? What do you think Lucy's disappointment might be?

Segment 2. After-Reading Discussion

- What was Lucy's disappointment? What else did you learn about Lucy? Why do you think Lucy didn't say anything about her disappointment? What do you think this next section will tell you? What do you think Lucy might do after she leaves the mill?

Segment 3. Summary After-Reading Discussion

- What did you learn about Lucy's life after she left the mill? Based on what you have read, what conclusion can you draw about Lucy? What effect did working in the mill have on Lucy? Did it make her life better or worse?
- Does Lucy's story remind you of other stories that you have read about? Does Lucy remind you of anyone you know or have read about or seen on TV or in the movies?
- Based on information in the article, what conclusions can you draw about life in the middle 1800s? Do you think that children in poor countries are helping out their families the way Lucy did? What do you think about children being asked to go to work to help out their families? What connection can you make between children working in the mills and what's happening in other parts of the world?
- Was there anything in the article that wasn't clear? Were there any words that you didn't understand? Is there anything in the article that you still have a question about?

Literature Discussion Groups

Because literary pieces are open to interpretation, literature lends itself to discussion. Literature circles and similar discussion groups provide opportunities for students to discuss their reading in much the same way that you and a group of friends converse about a book that you have read. Students share favorite passages and compare interpretations. They also disagree with each other on occasion but do so agreeably. Groups might be teacher-directed or student-directed or some combination of the two. However, literature discussion groups are also based on the principles of accountable talk and use some of the same prompts and procedures as were used in Reading Seminar.

Selecting Books   The whole class might read books assigned by the teacher or students might be given some choice in the books to be read. Having a choice fosters motivation and ownership. Students might select from five or more books. The teacher provides an overview of each one, and time for students to browse the books. Students then list their top three choices. Based on students' selections, four or five groups of five to six students are formed (Bjorklund, Handler, Mitten & Stockwell, 1998). The teacher forms groups that are heterogeneous but might match below-average readers with books that they can handle or provide them with recordings of the books or other needed assistance.

Setting Ground Rules   Fruitful discussions depend on ground rules that foster both openness and respect for the views of others. Involve students in the process of creating ground rules. You might begin by talking about some excellent group discussions in which you have been involved and the elements that made them good discussions. Elicit a series of guidelines for an effective, respectful discussion. These might include such elements as

- One person speaks at a time.
- Everyone has the opportunity to speak.
- Use respectful talk.
- Challenge ideas but not people.
- Ask questions or disagree in a polite way.

Students might be given model phrases, such as "I disagree with that idea" rather than "I disagree with you" so that the disagreement is not personalized. Model the ground rules, and have students practice them. At the conclusion of discussions, talk over how well the ground rules worked. Provide corrective instruction and practice as needed. Review the ground rules and make changes as needed.

Initial Meetings   In their initial meeting students might discuss why they chose their book. This gives the students a chance to get to know each other as readers and also provides some insight into the perspectives of others (International Reading Association, 2005). Students might also decide how to handle the reading: how much they will read each night, if they are reading the text at home, and what nights they will read. As with other discussion groups, students are taught how to hold discussions. It takes about five meetings before students are able to function effectively (Almasi, O'Flahavan & Arya, 2001).

Reading the Text   Students might respond to prompts as they read: What is your opinion of the main character's actions? What do her actions reveal about her? Was there anything in this part of the novel that confused you? Or they might fulfill roles in much the same way that a cooperative learning group operates. Key roles include the discussion leader, summarizer, literacy reporter, illustrator, word chief, and connector (Daniels, 2002). The discussion leader develops questions for the group and leads the discussion. The summarizer summarizes the selection. The literacy reporter locates and might also explain colorful language. The reporter can read the passages out loud, ask the group to read them silently and discuss them, or, with other members of the group, dramatize them. An illustrator depicts a key part of the selection with a drawing or graphic organizer. The word chief locates difficult words or expressions from the selection, looks them up in the dictionary, and writes down their definitions. At the circle meeting, the word chief points out and discusses the words with the group. The connector finds links between the book and other books the group has read or with real events, problems, or situations. The connector describes the connection and discusses it with the group. Students periodically switch roles so that each member of the group experiences all the roles. As students grow more experienced, role sheets can be phased out. (See pages 135–138 for examples of role sheets designed for use with reciprocal teaching. These might be used as is or adapted for use with literature circles.)

In Book Club Plus, which is a type of literature circle (Raphael, Florio-Ruane, George, Hasty & Highfield, 2004), students record their responses in reading logs. The teacher might provide prompts and in some instances might provide activities in which students apply a skill, such as summarizing, comparing or contrasting, or drawing inferences. Entries in the reading log form the basis for the Book Club sharing. After the sharing, students note in their logs how the sharing might have changed their thinking or their understanding of their reading. Responses can take the form of drawings or graphic organizers.

Fostering Higher-Level Discussions

In order to most effectively foster the growth of higher-level thinking skills, it is essential that the students be taught to ask and discuss higher-level questions. They need to implement the principles of accountable talk. The following moves help create higher-level discussions (see Table 9.1):

- Stating
- Explaining
- Extending
- Supporting
- Clarifying
- Agreeing
- Disagreeing
- Seeking other viewpoints

Table 9.1 ● Major Discussion Moves

Discussion Moves	Description	Example
Stating	Stating idea or opinion	This is what I think happened that day.
Explaining	Explaining a statement	Here is what I meant when I said that Alex made a mistake.
Supporting/ Substantiating	Providing details or examples to prove or back up an assertion	Here is why I believe the main character was a genius.
Extending/ Following/Expanding	Seeks elaboration	Tell me more about that.
Clarifying	Asking to have a confusing point clarified	What do you mean? Can you say more about that? I'm not sure what you mean here. (If a response is not clear, you as the teacher might restate what you believe the student said and then ask if your restatement is correct: "You seem to be saying that having a job gave Maria a sense of independence, which helped her speak out against injustice.")
Modifying	Changing an idea	When I think about his other actions, now I'm not so sure that he was really a kind person.
Eliciting	Seeks elaboration or support	What were you thinking about when you read that part? Can you tell us more about that? What passages in the story led you to that conclusion?
Agreeing	Expresses agreement with a position & often explains why	I agree with you Anna because ___.
Disagreeing	Expresses disagreement with a position & often explains why	I understand what you are saying about the father, but I think the father was wrong to get rid of the dog.
Building	Builds on what others say	I'd like to add to what Monique said about Amelia Earhart's courage.
Questioning*	Seeks input from the group	Does anyone have a different idea? What do you think about the way Juan acted?
Restating/Revoicing*	Restates response for clarity	You seem to be saying that low wages contributed to the Great Depression.

Continued

Discussion Moves	Description	Example
Challenging*	Asks to consider an opposing fact or other position	Some people would say . . . How would you answer them?
Annotating*	Supplies missing information	The author doesn't tell us _____.
Marking*	Highlights important information	This is a key point.
Affirming/ Encouraging*	Points out what a participant is doing that is effective	Tania, I like the way you backed up your conclusions with lots of facts from the article.
Initiating/Opening*	Opens discussion	What is the author trying to say here?
Inviting*	Invites others to respond	Josh, what do you have to say about Franklin? Do you think he acted responsibly?
Monitoring*	Facilitates discussion	Let's hold our responses until we hear what Milano has to say.
Summarizing*	Highlights main points	From what we have discussed what seem to be the main causes of the problem?
Modeling*	Demonstrates a discussion technique, reasoning, or reading strategy	Sometimes I find myself thinking about what I want to say rather then listening to the person speaking. Here is what I do . . .
Debriefing/Reflecting*	Assesses quality and impact of a discussion.	Did the discussion change your views? We seemed to be getting off topic. What might we do to stay on topic?
Wait Time	Provides time for student to respond	After asking a question and after a student has responded, wait 3 to 5 seconds.

*The moves marked with an asterisk are mostly teacher probes and prompts but might sometimes be used by students. Conversely, the teacher might use some of the moves that students typically use. A number of the moves are adapted from Questioning the Author (Beck & McKeown, 2002) and from Pearson, Cervetti, Jaynes & Flanders (2003).

Initially, you might have students start out using the following phrases and add others as they increase their discussion skills.

Stating: "Here is what I think about the dog."
Supporting: "Here is why I think the dog was well trained."
Agreeing: "I agree with Jason. I believe the dog was well trained. And here is why I believe that."
Disagreeing: "I understand what you are saying, but I have a different idea."

After learning to use these basic discussion moves, students can be taught more advanced ones:

Seeking elaboration: "Can you tell us more about that?"
Clarifying: "I'm not sure I understand. Can you explain what you mean?"
Supporting: "What makes you say that? What in the story supports that?"
Seeking other viewpoints: "Does anybody have a different idea?"

Model how you might use the discussion moves. Also demonstrate a discussion. You might have colleagues come in and hold a discussion as students observe. Or you might have taped discussions from previous years. Students can practice their discussion moves in pairs as well as in whole-class discussions. Students should also be taught to talk to each other rather than to you and to look at each other, and call on each other by name. One of the most difficult tasks they will need to learn is to listen to each other. Just as with adults, children tend to formulate their responses in their minds while others are speaking rather than listening to everything that the others are saying.

Community Share

In community share, whole-class discussions are held. These discussions occur both before students read and discuss, and after they read and discuss. Before-reading discussions can be used to go over discussion procedures, introduce a needed skill, build background, or discuss the program in general. In after-discussion sharing, students might talk about what their groups read and discussed. Community share might include debriefing.

Debriefing

The debriefing includes eliciting an overview of the group's interpretation and an assessment of how the session went (O'Flahavan, 1994). Suggestions for improving the discussion and interpretation are recorded. Based on observation and the debriefing, the teacher notes needs and plans instruction. During debriefings, the teacher and the class discuss the previous sessions so that they can note areas that need improving and apply those to the upcoming session. Students might discuss problems with staying on the topic and plan ways of sticking to the topic. The group might complete a rubric as in Table 9.2 to assess the effectiveness of their discussions. As part of the debriefing, students might assess the effectiveness of the discussion by responding to questions such as these: "Did the discussion change your views about the text in any way? Did the discussion change your views about _____ in any way?"

Table 9.2 ● Rubric for Discussion Group

	Always	Usually	Sometimes	Never
We stuck to the topic.				
We listened carefully.				
We were polite.				
We supported our answers.				
Everyone participated.				
Things we did well				
Things we could do better				

You have the option of leading the discussion groups or letting them lead themselves. If the discussions are teacher-led, gradually turn more responsibility over to students. If the discussion groups are student-led, spend some time in the beginning as an active member of the group modeling discussion techniques and questioning behaviors. Maintain supervision and plan lessons based on your observations. Lessons might be devoted to improving discussion techniques or building higher-level reading strategies.

Writing

Most discussion groups discuss selections but don't write about them. Along with being taught how to participate in higher-level discussions, students also need to be taught how to respond in writing to higher-level questions. One discussion approach that does include instruction in writing is Junior Great Books. Of nine discussion approaches examined by researchers (Murphy & Edwards, 2005), Junior Great Books was the most effective for developing a combination of text-explicit comprehension, text-implicit comprehension, and critical-thinking/reasoning.

Demonstrating the Power of Discussion

To show the power of discussion, have students read a challenging poem or story, with a series of questions in mind. They might be looking for techniques that the author used to develop characters or themes, or they might be looking for examples of figurative language. After they have completed their readings and written their responses, have small groups of students compare their findings.

After students have discussed their findings, ask students to raise their hands if they heard anything in their small-group discussions that they hadn't thought of when working alone. In a whole-class discussion, have group leaders summarize their group's findings. Again ask students if they heard any ideas that they hadn't thought of when working alone or in small groups. Discuss the power of discussions to add to our thinking. As an alternative, have students rate their understanding on a 1–10 scale after an individual reading, after a small-group discussion, and after a whole-class discussion. Have students note whether or not their ratings increased. Discuss the importance and impact of discussion (Gallagher, 2005).

Small-group discussion approaches work well for ELL. ELL do better in small groups. Students who know more English help those who don't know as much. Students who are silent in large groups talk in small groups. Allowing students to use their first language also helps. However, students should also be encouraged to articulate their own responses. They shouldn't be too reliant on others to carry the discussion. Formulating their own responses helps them to develop needed English-language responses.

The Role of Strategy Instruction

Although discussion approaches can be highly effective, they should not be used to the exclusion of strategy instruction. The best results are obtained when strategy and discussion approaches are synthesized (Berne & Clark, 2006).

Using Discussions to Gain Insight into Cognitive Processes

A careful analysis of students' discussion responses coupled with conducting informal think-alouds are a highly effective means of gaining insight into students' comprehension skills on an ongoing basis. Much of the insight I gained into students' comprehension process was obtained as we discussed stories and articles in small-group and even whole-class discussions. Using prompts and probes such as the following, I was able to get a sense of the cognitive processes students were using and provide on-the-spot and long-term guidance.

- Can you tell me more?
- Can you explain what you mean?
- Let's go back to the story and see if we can find the answer.

- What might you do to help you answer that question? Can you go back over the story?
- What led you to that conclusion?
- What did the author say that leads you to say that?
- Was any part of the story confusing? If so, what part?
- What do you do when you run into a confusing part?

Probes and prompts should be tailored to fit the questions being asked and the students' needs.

Study Group Questions

- What elements of Accountable Talk do I already use in my classroom?
- What changes would I need to implement Accountable Talk more fully?
- What are the challenges of implementing Accountable Talk? How might I overcome these?
- How might I implement and/or adapt Reading Seminar?
- How might I start a literature discussion group?
- How might I include strategy instruction in my discussion groups?

Using Writing to Improve Higher-Level Literacy Skills

Writing is a powerful aid to thinking. As writing expert William Zinsser notes,

> Writing organizes and clarifies our thoughts. . . . Putting an idea into written words is like defrosting the windshield: The idea so vague out there in the murk, slowly begins to gather itself into a sensible shape (Zinsser, 1988, p. 16).

The Michigan Department of Education (Blakeslee, 1997) had this to say about the importance of writing in fostering reasoning:

> When held to high expectations for clarity in writing, students have to think deeply about the terms they choose to express their thoughts, as well as the logic of their arguments. Writing gives all students a chance to think about questions posed in class, rather than just listening to others' descriptions and explanations, providing a valuable forum for expression for those students who are reluctant to join into class discussions.

Not All Writing Is Equal

However, when it comes to cognitive development, not all writing is equal. Based on their study of writing, Langer and Applebee (1987) concluded that through writing, students gain new knowledge, review, reflect on, and extend ideas. However, the level and extent of the benefit depend on the level and extent of the writing.

Simply locating and recording information, as in taking notes from text, was of limited benefit. Writing that required reflection was of much more benefit. The most beneficial writing tasks were those that required comparing, contrasting, concluding, and evaluating. Writing that required students to organize or manipulate ideas resulted in deeper understanding and learning than writing that merely involved a retelling.

Writing Requires Instruction

In writing students don't make progress until they are challenged to compose more complex forms and are given instruction in how to do so. Students need careful guidance, direct instruction, and experience writing in a variety of modes. They need to be challenged to attempt new genres and new techniques. If writing is to be a vehicle for developing higher-level thinking skills, students need to engage in the kind of writing that demands them to think deeply about their topic. As in other areas of literacy, a carefully planned systematic program that builds on students' interests works best.

The key deficiency in students' writing is their failure to provide text-based elaboration. They claim that a character is selfish without providing examples from the text. They state that two countries are similar, but don't note the similarities. They write that they would have liked to have lived in another place or another time without explaining why. Fostering elaboration and other key writing skills requires highly effective instruction.

A writing strategy lesson has the following steps:

1. Identifying a strategy worth teaching.
2. Introducing the strategy by modeling it.
3. Helping students try the strategy out with teacher guidance.
4. Helping students work toward independent mastery of the strategy through repeated practice and reinforcement. (Collins, 1998, p. 65)

To determine a strategy worth teaching, think about the major writing tasks that students must perform and examine students' writing. Choose a strategy, such as providing text-based support for a claim, that is important to them in terms of their current development and future needs. The strategy can be introduced to a whole class, to a guided writing group, or even to an individual. After the strategy has been introduced, students should have a number of opportunities to apply it. Guide students as they adapt the strategy so that it functions as part of their writing repertoire. The writing strategy lesson consists of the following: minilesson, guided writing, writing time, conferences, and sharing.

Minilesson

In the minilesson you present a needed writing skill or concept. The minilesson lasts for only about ten minutes, so the skill should be one that is fairly easy to understand. The skill could be selecting topics, writing a lead, using varied verbs, or any one of a dozen easy-to-teach skills. Minilessons can also be used to explain workshop procedures. On occasion, minilessons can be expanded or conducted over a series of days if the skill is a complex one. However, don't make the instruction so lengthy that there is no time left for writing.

A minilesson has five elements: introduction, instruction, guided practice, independent practice, and application. There can also be a mid-workshop teaching point and share (Calkins & Pessah, 2003). In the introductory phase, you describe the skill and explain how it will help the students to become better writers. You also announce how the skill being taught fits into the overall program. You remind students of what they worked on yesterday and announce what they will be working on today. "Yesterday we talked about the importance of supporting the opinion you are expressing. Today we will be talking about using enough details so that your opinion has solid support." The strategy of using sufficient detail is modeled. For guided practice, the class adds details to a sketchy paragraph. In the application phase, you encourage students to apply the strategy that has been presented to today's writing. "Read over your pieces and see if you have given enough proof." Students might also exchange papers with a partner and read over each other's pieces to see if there are places where more proof might be added. In the mid-workshop teaching point, you might provide a brief reminder of the strategy or some advice that is based on what you have been observing as you move around the room or hold conferences. "As I looked over your papers, I see that you are adding details to prove the point you have made in your papers. Look at what you have added, and see if you have explained each point fully and clearly." In the share portion, students discuss how they applied the strategy. Incorporating all these elements keeps the focus on the strategy that has been taught and strengthens the impact of the instruction.

Guided Writing/Strategic Writing

While the rest of the class is writing, you can hold conferences with students on their writing or conduct guided writing lessons. During guided writing, students are taught writing strategies in small groups according to their stage of writing development and their needs. A guided writing lesson follows the same steps as a minilesson. To teach a writing strategy, provide examples of the target strategy and discuss the strategy with students and lead them to see how it will help their writing. Model the use of the strategy, showing, for instance, how you might use facts from a selection to support a claim. If possible, have students examine a piece that they are working on and apply the strategy to their work. If they don't have an appropriate piece, have them share with a partner how they might apply this strategy in their own writing (Calkins & Pessah, 2003). Provide guided practice and have students apply the skill by using it in their own writing, if possible. As they are writing, hold brief conferences in which you guide them as they apply the strategy. Revision and evaluation should focus on the element introduced. Review the skill in conferences and follow-up lessons until students have a firm grasp of it. Here is a sample strategic writing lesson. Notice that this lesson is more extensive than a minilesson and may take ten to twenty minutes to teach.

Writing Strategy: Supporting Claims with Details from a Text

Step 1. Introduction   Explain the importance of supporting claims with details. Make a connection between adding details and the writing work that students are now doing. "We worked on creating strong opening sentences. Today we will be looking at ways to support our opening sentences."

Step 2. Instruction   Have students read a model paragraph in which the writer has provided ample support for a claim or statement. Discuss with students what the writer did to make the piece convincing. List possible ways of providing support. Discuss the importance of providing support and how this might be done. Lead students to see that good writers use details and examples to support their ideas and opinions. Repeat this statement from time to time and remind students that this is an important rule of effective writing (Calkins & Pessah, 2003).

Show a paragraph, such as the following, that needs support. Do not use a student's paragraph, as this will embarrass the writer.

A Difficult Trip

The Pilgrims' trip to America was difficult. The Pilgrims were traveling on a small ship called the *Mayflower*. The Pilgrims ate the same food day after day. Storms belted the little ship.

Ask students whether the writer has provided sufficient support. Discuss the author's need to add more details. Discuss with students how you can make the piece more convincing by going back to the book and locating details that show how difficult the Pilgrims' voyage was. Add needed details and compare the revised paragraph with the original.

> The Pilgrims' trip to America was difficult. The Pilgrims were traveling on a small ship called the *Mayflower*. The *Mayflower* was built to carry 60 people, but there were 102 people aboard. The Pilgrims were crowded into a small, stuffy area below the main deck. The Pilgrims ate the same food day after day. They ate cheese, dried meat, fish, and hard chunks of bread known as "hard tack." Some of the food had worms crawling in it. There were no fresh vegetables or fresh fruit. But the worst part of the trip wasn't the crowded living area or the wormy food. It was the storms that belted the little ship. Giant waves tossed the *Mayflower* around like it was a toy boat. The Pilgrims wondered if they would ever make it to America,

Step 3. Guided Practice   Provide one or two sample paragraphs that are lacking in details. Working with students, add needed details.

Step 4. Independent Practice   Working individually or in pairs, students add details to strengthen weak paragraphs.

Step 5. Application   To make instruction both practical and effective, actively engage students in reflecting upon and applying skills and strategies that have been taught (Calkins & Pessah, 2003). Have students look at each other's drafts and see if there is a place where supporting details might be added. Encourage students to support claims or statements by adding needed details. During the ensuing workshop session, provide any needed assistance.

Step 6. Extension   As a follow-up, have volunteers show how they added details to provide support. In subsequent lessons, discuss the many ways in which claims or statements can be supported. Have students apply this skill in content area writing.

Step 7. Assessment and Review   In conferences and while looking over various drafts of students' writing, evaluate whether they are supporting their pieces. Provide additional instruction as needed.

Techniques for Fostering Application   In group instruction and in conferences, four approaches might be used to help students incorporate an effective strategy into their writing (Calkins & Pessah, 2003). These include:

Demonstration. The teacher shows a student how the strategy might be incorporated. "I can see, Deshawna, that you want the reader to discover that your grandmother was kind. You told the readers that your grandmother was kind. But how might you show the readers that your grandmother was kind? Can you think of any examples of your grandmother's kindness?"

Explicitly providing an example. Give the students an example from another piece of writing or an example from your experience. "You say here that your grandmother was the kindest person that you ever met. My grandmother was

kind, too. If I were writing about her, I would give examples. I would tell about the time when she gave her vacation money to a family so they wouldn't lose their home. Or the time she stayed up all night sewing my Halloween costume."
Guided practice. Through a series of prompts lead the students to see how the strategy might be applied. "You say here that your grandmother was the kindest person that you ever met. How might you convince the reader that your grandmother was kind? What might you tell the reader?"
Inquiry. Give the student a piece of writing that uses the strategy you are working on. Have the students look to see how the author used the strategy. "Let's look at this book, *Grandmother's Song* (Soros, 1998). What kind of person is the grandmother?" (The teacher leads the student to see that the grandmother is kind and loving.) How does the author, Barbara Soros, let you know what kind of a person the grandmother is? (The teacher leads the student to see that the author uses examples to show what kind of a person the grandmother is. Teacher and student conclude that the student could follow Barbara Soros's lead and use examples to show the kindness of the student's grandmother.)

To reinforce writing strategies, such as showing rather than just telling, demonstrate to students how you use the target strategy in your writing. To engender interest in the demonstration, use a technique without telling students what it is. Then invite pairs of students to tell a partner what you did. Discuss students' responses. By focusing students' attention on the technique and talking about the technique with partners and with the whole group or class, they might come to a better understanding of the technique and begin to use it in their writing (Calkins & Pessah, 2003).

Conferring

Since writing is highly individualistic, one-to-one conferences play a key role in writing instruction. Although conferences are brief—lasting 5 to 10 minutes, for the most part—they can be powerful. To get the most out of a conference, make a careful assessment of the student and where she is in her writing. Prior to the conference, review the student's writing folder and any notes you might have about the student. Begin the conference with an opening question that helps you discover where the student is now and what the student is working on. You might ask such questions as, "How is your writing going? What are you working on now?" You might comment on what the student is apparently doing now. "I see that you are adding examples to show what kind of a person your grandma is."

Determining Needs

Once you have a fairly good picture of the writer and where she is, note steps that might move her forward. Usually, there are a number of things that young writers might work on. Select the step that will take her the fartherest. Then decide what might be the best way to convey your teaching point. You might say, "I like the way you are telling about things your grandmother did. I have a suggestion. I believe your example would seem more real if you told what your grandmother said. If instead of saying she shouted at the dog, tell exactly what she shouted." Be sure to name the technique and encourage the student to continue to use it (Calkins, Hartman & White, 2003).

Kinds of Conferences

Depending on the needs of the writer, conferences take on different focuses. Some focus on content. In a content conference, you try to get the writer to say what he is going to write about. In a sense, this is an oral pretelling of the student's written piece. It elicits content from the student and is a kind of oral rehearsal for the writing that follows. Although there is some overlap, a process conference deals more directly with techniques. Using prompts and suggestions, the teacher leads the students to incorporate or apply an effective technique. The third kind of conference is a goals conference in which you talk to the writer about the kinds of things she has done in her writing and the kinds of things that she might work on in the future (Calkins, Hartman & White, 2003).

Essential Writing Strategies

There are dozens of writing strategies. Listed below are the ones that seem most essential for developing higher-level thinking skills. The strategies are listed in approximate order of difficulty. However, some strategies are taught at every level. For instance, writing an interesting lead would be a concern throughout the elementary and secondary school grades but would be a more complex undertaking in the upper grades than it would be in the lower ones.

- Writing clear, complete sentences.
- Writing a lead or beginning sentence. The lead or beginning sentence often gives the main idea of a piece and should grab the reader's interest and entice her or him to read the piece.
- Developing informational pieces. Informational pieces can be developed with details, including facts, opinions, examples, and descriptions. Failure to develop a topic is a major flaw in students' writing.

- Writing an effective ending. In general, an effective ending should provide a summary of the piece and/or restate the main point of the piece in such a way that it has an impact on the reader.
- Gathering appropriate and sufficient information for a piece. Writers do their best work when they are overflowing with information and can't wait to put it down on paper.
- Writing in a variety of forms: poems, stories, plays, letters, advertisements, announcements, expository pieces, newspaper articles, essays.
- Writing for a variety of purposes and audiences.
- Providing transitions so that one thought leads into another and the writing flows.
- Creating headings and subheadings for longer pieces.
- Eliminating details that detract from a piece.

Writing-Intensive Reading Comprehension

Writing and reading have a reciprocal relationship. Reading gives us information for our writing and also provides models for our writing. Writing, especially when composing informational texts, leads us to look more closely at the text and organize ideas. Typically, students write after they read. As an after-reading activity, writing becomes a way of responding and extending reading. However, writing can also be a during-reading tool for fostering comprehension while students are reading. J. L. Collins and his colleagues (2005) devised an approach in which student use thinksheets to promote a transaction between reading and writing in which the writing supports the reading and the reading supports the writing. Although thinksheets might appear to be worksheets, they actually provide a basis for interaction with the teacher. While students use their thinksheets to construct meaning as they read, the teacher holds on-the-spot conferences with the students and discusses their responses. Students' responses on the thinksheets become the basis for conversations about the students' reading and writing. Students also discuss their thinksheets in pairs and in small groups.

Workshop Approach

In a typical lesson, the teacher gives a minilesson related to the skill students are working on, assigns students to work on the first portion of the thinksheet, and confers with students as they work on the first portion of the thinksheets. After students have completed the first portion of their thinksheets, the teacher conducts another minilesson, which might be based on difficulties that students were having or might be a further application of the skill first taught. Students then go back to work on their thinksheets.

Targeted Reading

Using the text and the thinksheets is known as "targeted reading." In targeted reading students read a specific piece of text to obtain information in order to answer a question or complete a writing task. Students write in segments that last about five to ten minutes. The researchers discovered that tasks were needed that students could complete in a short amount of time. The brief writing periods allowed students to focus their attention without being overwhelmed. After completing two or three brief segments, students might then pull all that information together to complete a more extended response. For instance, in a selection about the blue whale, students might engage in an extended response that lasts for ten minutes or more.

The workshop is very much interactive. As Collins (2005) explained to students, "We are going to help each other. I'll help you and you help each other." Students were encouraged to work in pairs or small groups. The teacher also modeled how to respond to the questions and emphasized the importance of "getting ideas down."

Through writing, students and the teacher build understanding. They also become aware of where students need help. For instance, when asked to write a paragraph, one student confessed that, "I am not good at putting things into a paragraph." The teacher responded, "Make a list. Then I'll come by and show you how to put it into a paragraph. Do the best you can. Use information from the columns on page 1. If you put it down, we can help. That's the thing about writing; you have to put it down before we can help you."

"Getting it down" is an essential element. The teacher gets a better idea of where the student is having difficulty and so can provide assistance if the student has written something. The program requires that the teacher move around the room and provide individual assistance as students work on their thinksheets.

Breaking tasks down into smaller, more manageable parts helped students. However, they then had difficulty integrating the parts. A graphic organizer was added to the thinksheets to help students combine and integrate their responses from the three separate segments that they had worked on. In the redesigned think sheet, main ideas and supporting details are highlighted. The thinksheet states the main idea and asks readers to supply the supporting details. In three separate sections students record the supporting details. Students then use a graphic organizer to combine and integrate information from the three separate parts. In the last and most difficult step, students put all the information together to supply an extended response. However, the thinksheet is set up in such a way that students are guided to select and organize information rather than simply copying it. The directions ask students to look through their notes and/or find information in the article to answer questions about the article. An adapted thinksheet is presented in Table 10.1. In this thinksheet students are working on drawing conclusions. For more information about WIRC, go the program's website at www.gse.buffalo.edu/ePortfolio/view.aspx?u=wirc&pid=410. To make the task more manageable, students complete one segment at a time and then use the chart to put the information together. If students need more structure than has been provided, construct an organizer for them as in Table 10.2.

Two-Handed Reading

A key difference between typical worksheets and thinksheets can be seen in how they are filled out. Using worksheets, students read the text and then respond to the items on the worksheet. They do not refer to the text as they fill in the worksheets. In fact, the text might even be closed. Thinksheets are designed to be used as students are reading. Students were encouraged to do two-handed reading as they used their thinksheets. The thinksheets were laid out in such a way that the text and questions were aligned as in Table 10.1. They read with one hand and took notes with the other. This fostered the creation of text-based responses.

As a result of using the thinksheets, students have a better idea of what they are to do, and teachers become more aware of specific steps they can take to help the students. As students progress, the amount of assistance provided by the thinksheets is reduced. Students gradually become more independent.

An important component of the program is the use of discussion to foster comprehension. You might have students discuss the responses on their thinksheets and/or use one of the discussion approaches described previously: reciprocal teaching, Reading Seminar, or a literature discussion group.

Probable Passages

Probable Passages, which is similar to Predict-o-Gram, was also used in WIRC. A highly motivating and highly effective prereading strategy, Probable Passages activates background and fosters the use of predicting, detecting cause-effect and other relationships, and also promotes summarizing and group cooperation. To prepare a Probable Passages Thinksheet (Table 10.3), read and analyze the story. Select 15 to 20 key words. List the words on the chalkboard and have students place them into story categories: characters, setting, problem, solution, ending (Wood, 1984). Working in small groups, students discuss where the words should go and why. As

Table 10.1 ● Adapted Thinksheet: Making Inferences/Drawing Conclusions

How did Fizo save his owner?

_____

_____

What proof do you have that Fizo
was brave?

_____

_____

_____

How did Lulu save her owner?

_____

_____

What makes you think that Lulu was brave?

_____

_____

How did Fido save the Gumbley family?

_____

_____

What makes you think that Fido was brave?

_____

_____

Fizo

Sitting on the balcony of his home in Sydney, Australia, Fizo, a Silky Terrier, watched as his nine-year-old owner and three friends played below. Then Fizo spotted a large poisonous brown snake. The snake was getting ready to strike. Fizo leaped onto the snake's back and grabbed it with his jaws. The snake bit Fizo several times. But Fizo held on until the snake died. Fizo then passed out. Fizo was rushed to the vet. He was given antivenom. An antivenom is a medicine that fights poison. Fizo didn't wake up for three days. And it took him six months to re-cover fully. Fizo was given a medal for his bravery.

Lulu

Bear, a large pet dog, knew that there was something wrong with his owner. She had fallen and passed out. Bear barked and even smashed the bedroom window. But no one heard him. Lulu a pet pig saw that no one was coming to help. The trailer in which their owner lived had a pet door. A pet door is a special door cut out of the bottom of a regular door so that pets can go in and out of the house. Lulu shot through the pet door and out into the street. Then she lay on her back in the middle of the street and kicked her legs in the air. When a car stopped and the driver got out, Lulu started running back to the trailer. The driver followed her and discovered Lulu's owner. The driver called for an ambulance. Help was soon there. Later, doctors said that Lulu had saved her owner's life. Her owner would probably have died if help hadn't gotten there as quickly as it did. Lulu was rewarded with a very large jelly doughnut.

Fido

Dogs have saved their owners' lives. And even some cats have saved lives. But once a rat saved a family of three. A pet rat by the name of Fido was awakened at 2:00 in the morning by the smell of smoke. The rug in his owner's home had caught fire. Luckily, Fido's cage door had been left open. Fido jumped to the floor and ran to the door of his owner's bedroom. Inside Lisa Gumbley and her two daughters, nine-year-old Megan and three-year-old Shannon, were sleeping. The door was closed. Fido began scratching on the door. When no one came, he scratched harder. Finally, Megan heard the scratching. She figured that Fido had escaped from his cage. Megan picked up Fido and was taking him downstairs to put him back in his cage when she spotted flames. Still carrying Fido, she ran back upstairs and shouted to her mother and little sister. All three quickly ran out of the house. Their lives had been saved by an eight-month-old pet rat.

Continued

Comparison of the Three Pets

Write your answers in the blocks. Use information from your notes or the article.

Animal	Kind of Animal	Who They Saved	How They Saved Their Owners	Danger Pets Were In
Fizo				
Lulu				
Fido				

they discuss the placement of words, they naturally predict what will happen, make inferences, establish possible cause-effect relationships, and clarify the meanings of unfamiliar words or at least become aware of which words are unfamiliar so they can pay special attention to those as they read the selection (Beers, 2003).

After placing their words, students create a story based on the placement of the words. You can have students fill in a frame such as the one below or you can have

Table 10.2 ● Constructing a Response

After reading about these three animals, what conclusion can you draw about them? Write your conclusion. Use information from your notes, the graphic organizer, or the article to support your conclusion.

Hint: Write a beginning sentence that announces your conclusion.	_____
Hint: Give three examples to support your topic sentence.	1. _____ 2. _____ 3. _____
Hint: Write a closing sentence.	_____

Which animal do you think was the bravest? Use information from your notes and the chart to support your judgment.

Hint: Write a sentence that states which animal you believe was the bravest.	
Hint: Tell why you think the animal you chose as the bravest.	
Hint: Write a closing sentence.	

Source: From *Read, Reason, Respond: Boosting Literacy.* Unionville, CT: Galvin Publications. Reprinted by permission.

Table 10.3 ● Adapted Thinksheet for Probable Passages

Title _____ Date _____

Setting	Characters	Problem	Solution	Ending	Unknown Words

then create a brief summary of the story. The summary can be completed as a whole-class cooperative story, by pairs, small groups, or individuals.

Story Summary

The setting of the story is _____.
The main character is_____.
A problem arises when _____.
Then _____.
After that, _____.
The problem is solved when_____.
When the story ends_____.

> After completing the summary, students read the story. After reading the story, they compare their version with the original story.

Results   Writing Intensive Reading Comprehension (WIRC) produced dramatic gains. In terms of quantity, students tripled the number of words they used to respond to brief constructed response items and doubled the number of words used to answer extended response questions (Lee, 2005). Quality gains were equally outstanding. The proportion of students scoring at the Below Basic level dropped from 71.4% on Theme 1 to 12.5% on Theme 5. The proportion reaching the proficiency level increased from 14.3% in Theme 1 to 62.5% on Theme 5. The overall effect size for reading was 1.29. This means that a student reading at the 16th percentile would move up to the 60th percentile.

Dialogue Journals

Dialogue journals also boost comprehension. Dialogue journals are written conversations between student and teacher. The students write an entry about a chapter, story, or article they have read, or a topic. The entry could be the students' independent observations, or they could be in response to a prompt. Dissatisfied because individual conferences with students did not allow a depth of discussion of their self-selected reading, Atwell (1987) initiated dialogue journals. Writing provided students the opportunity to reflect on their reading and gain a deeper understanding of what they had read. Atwell collected and responded to the students' entries. In her responses, she was able to provide explanations or pose questions that lifted students' thinking to higher levels. Through her responses, she was also modeling ways of talking about writing. In their journals students could also raise questions. As one student commented, "The worksheets make you answer questions, but the dialogue journal makes me ask the questions, and then the teacher helps me think about possible answers" (Staton, 1984). Dialogue journals are a powerful tool for building higher-level thinking skills and also for getting to know students better.

As a practical matter, because responding to each student's journal daily could be burdensome, you might want to have one-fifth of the class turn in their journals each day. That way you respond each day to just a few students, but you see each student's journal once a week.

Double-Entry Journals Double-entry journals also foster higher-level thinking and responding. Double-entry journals have two columns. In the first column, the students record information or a quote from the text. In the second column, the students reflect on or pose questions about the material in the first column. Students might select passages to respond to that are surprising or puzzling or particularly appealing. Or they might select passages in response to a teacher prompt: "Which passages did you find to be especially frightening?" In an adaptation of double-entry journals, one teacher had students note in the first column specific passages that reminded them of something in their lives. In the second column, they described the personal connection that they were able to make (Dennis-Shaw, 2006).

In their journals, occasionally students might be asked to provide examples of times when they have used newly introduced strategies. In the second column, they can reflect on the effectiveness of the strategy or any personal reactions they have to using the strategy. Prompts that you provide might reflect the strategy that you are working on. When you are exploring inferring character traits, the prompt might ask students to note passages that show what kind of a person the main character is.

Using Varied Writing Modes and Structures

In order to foster higher-level literacy, your writing program should include developing students' ability to use a variety of writing modes and structures. Students need to be able to tell a story, describe people and places, explain a process or procedure, compare and contrast, and persuade. They need to be able to formulate a topic sentence and support it with facts, examples, and reasons. Instruction should be intensive and thorough. In many programs, especially those in the primary and middle grades, narration predominates as students recount a frightening experience, a favorite vacation, or a day when everything went wrong. While it is important that students write about personal experiences, it is also important that they develop a full set of writing tools.

One way of structuring your writing program would be to complement instruction in a particular strategy with the kind of writing that embodies that strategy as shown in Table 10.4. For instance, when students are learning to identify or construct main ideas, in their writing they could be learning how to construct and support topic sentences. When learning to compare and contrast, they can learn to write pieces in which they note similarities and differences.

Need for Extensive Writing

According to the National Commission on Writing (College Entrance Examination Board, 2003), elementary schools devote three hours or less each week to writing. Writing time can be increased by having students write in all subject area classes and by writing at home. In its plea for more emphasis on writing, the Commission commented,

Table 10.4 ● Joining Reading and Writing Strategies

Cognitive Skill/Strategy	Implementation in Writing
Main Idea/Supporting Details	Writing topic sentences. Supporting topic sentences with facts, examples, and reasons. Describing people, places, and events.
Summarizing/Constructing Lesson or Theme	Writing a summary. Describing lesson learned or theme.
Inferring/Concluding/Predicting	Drawing conclusions and supporting them. Writing cause/effect pieces.
Imaging	Imaging and describing persons and scenes.
Comparing/Contrasting	Comparing and contrasting people, places, events.
Connecting	Making connections by comparing characters with real or fictitious people or comparing fictitious events with real ones.
Evaluating/Critiquing	Expressing and supporting opinions. Writing persuasive pieces. Expressing literary judgments.

If students are to make knowledge their own, they must struggle with the details, wrestle with the facts, and rework raw information and dimly understood concepts into language they can communicate to someone else. In short, if students are to learn, they must write (p. 9).

Indeed one of the characteristics of successful schools is the prevalence of writing. This is especially true of 90/90/90 schools. In 90/90/90 schools, 90 percent or more of the students are eligible for free and reduced-price lunch and are members of ethnic minority groups, but 90 percent of students meet academic standards in reading or another area (Reeves, 2000). An essential element in the curriculum in 90/90/90 schools is the role of expository writing. Students are required to produce an acceptable piece of nonfiction writing on a periodic basis. For elementary schools, this is once a month. For secondary schools it is once a quarter. After being taught the necessary skills, students compose an informational piece. The pieces must include information that students do not already know so that the project builds background knowledge while building writing and reasoning skills. A key to the effectiveness of the writing program is the use of a common rubric.

Use of a Common Rubric

Writing is a whole-school activity and is assessed using a common rubric. The rubric provides clear standards for writing and for assessing (Reeves, 2003). The rubric is geared to students' grade level and English proficiency. A five-sentence paragraph might be designated as meeting proficiency for a young English learner, whereas an older native speaker might be required to a submit a three-page piece. The principal and teachers meet regularly to discuss and share students' writing. This promotes a common understanding of the writing standards and a more uniform application of the rubric. It also fosters a sense of ownership so that all staff members feel responsible for the students' writing. Students are held accountable. They are required to revise and edit as much as necessary in order to produce an acceptable piece. Writing assignments are not treated as work samples to be graded but as opportunities to build essential skills.

Another characteristic of 90/90/90 schools is an emphasis on written responses in performance assessments. The emphasis on written responses has a bonus benefit. "First, students process information in a much clearer way when they are required to write an answer. They 'write to think' and, thus, gain the opportunity to clarify their own thought processes. Second, teachers have the opportunity to gain rich and complex diagnostic information about why students respond to an academic challenge the way that they do" (Reeves, 2003, p. 190). By assessing students' written responses, teachers were better able to determine which concepts and skills students grasped and which they had difficulty with (Gunning, 2006a).

Study Group Questions

- How might I use writing to improve my students' higher-level thinking skills?
- To what extent do students' writing activities help build higher-level thinking skills?
- What are my students' major needs in the area of writing?
- What are my plans for building needed writing skills?
- Which of the suggestions made in this chapter might I implement?
- How might I make use of and/or adapt thinksheets?

chapter 11

Preparing Students for High-Stakes Tests

The best preparation for today's challenging high-stakes tests is a program that emphasizes higher-level literacy skills of the type explored in previous chapters. The best possible way to prepare students for all of life's demands, including high-stakes tests, is to provide them with materials that are challenging but that are on their level, with instruction that includes building background and strategies, and a program that monitors progress and provides corrective instruction as needed. Students need to do lots of reading and writing and talking both under your guidance and independently. Based on her examination of higher achieving schools, Langer (1999) concluded that preparation for high-stakes tests is most effective when it is embedded in the curriculum and not a separate course. When approached as a separate course, test prep programs tend to focus on the mechanics of responding rather than on the underlying skills and understandings that need developing. Students complete test-like tasks but are not typically provided with the deep systematic instruction they need. Often, the programs are one-size-fits-all, so that the best students are reading materials that are too easy, and the low-achieving students are reading materials that are too hard, and instruction is not geared to students' needs. Perhaps the most serious shortcoming of test prep programs is that they take time away from the reading of and responding to authentic, enriched reading. However, some preparation for tests is needed, especially if they contain unfamiliar formats or seek responses that are on a higher level than students are used to constructing. A planned program of test preparation would include the following steps.

Planned Program of Test Preparation

Step 1   Analyze the demands of tests that your students are required to take and compare the demands of the tests with the skills and strategies that are taught. Add skills if necessary. Integrate the teaching of needed skills into your curriculum.

Step 2   Analyze students' performance on the kinds of tests they will be required to take. See Chapter 2 for a review of those techniques.

Step 3   Plan a program based on students' current status and needs.

Step 4   Taking high-stakes tests is an essential skill for today's students and so should be taught. As with any other essential skill, discuss with students the importance of being able to respond to test questions. Share experiences that you have had and explain how you learned to take tests. Discuss any concerns that they might have.

Step 5   Model how you would go about responding to a test question. Select a relatively easy test question. Show how you would read the directions, read the selection, and read the test question. Using a think-aloud procedure, explain what is going on in your mind as you respond.

Step 6   Create a rubric for assessing your responses to a practice test question. Using the rubric, involve the class in assessing the response,

Step 7   As a group, have the class cooperatively respond to simulated test questions. Use the rubric as a guide. Start off with an easy-to-read passage so that below-level readers will be able to handle it, and the emphasis will be on understanding the passage rather than on decoding hard words.

Step 8   Provide guided practice as students respond to similar test questions. Initially, give extra assistance or scaffolding by building cognitive bridges as explained below.

Step 9   Have students take a practice test. Using a rubric, analyze responses and provide additional instruction as needed. Provide individual guidance to students who do not "pass" the test. If possible, provide sufficient guidance and practice so that they do pass a retest. The practice test and any other materials that you use must not be any higher than the students' instructional level. This means that you will need to obtain easier materials for your below-level readers.

Step 10   Have students apply their skills by taking a real test. Although the test might be used to obtain a grade, also use it as a learning experience. Provide corrective instruction to students so that they improve sufficiently to achieve a passing grade or better. Adopt a mastery approach. Look at tests as a means of providing information on which to base instruction rather than as a device for grading. Reteach those skills that students had difficulty with until they have mastered them to the point where they can pass the test.

On a regular basis, perhaps once a week, provide instruction in responding to test-type tasks. Tie this instruction in with your overall literacy program. If you are emphasizing summarizing, introduce a question that involves summarizing. If you are focusing on developing characters, pose a question that asks students to cite examples to show what kind of a person the main character was. Don't attempt to cover all response types in single year. The most ambitious program could probably cover one a month, but five to eight in a year would probably be a more realistic goal (Gunning, 2006a).

Building Cognitive Bridges

To help students formulate responses to high-level questions, build cognitive bridges (Guthrie, 2003). A cognitive bridge can take the form of a model answer, a graphic organizer, an answer organizer, or a frame. Some of these cognitive bridges have appeared in previous chapters. If at all possible, use a well-written response from one of your students (it could be from past years) as a model response. Highlight the key elements that make this a model response. A graphic organizer uses a semantic map or other appropriate visual to diagram the response. An answer organizer supplies a series of specific directions (Boyles, 2002): "Write the topic sentences first. To write the topic sentence reword the question. Write two examples to support the topic sentences. Write a concluding sentence." (See Figure 11.1 for a sample answer organizer.) If an answer organizer doesn't provide enough assistance, try an answer frame. Answer frames provide maximum assistance. To construct an answer frame, you fill in a portion of the answer. Place blank lines to indicate the unfinished portion of the response. Students complete the response by writing in the blanks. (A number of answer frames have appeared in previous chapters. See pages 71 and 171 for examples of answer frames.) Answer frames help students who would not be able to complete the task without a high level of support (Boyles, 2002). As students learn how to compose responses, answer frames should be reduced and gradually eliminated. Initially, answer frames might have just a few short blanks. Gradually the blanks can become more numerous and longer.

Boyles (2002) estimates that students should successfully complete five scaffolded exercises before attempting to compose responses without assistance. In his research with struggling readers, Guthrie (2003) found that it took nine days of instruction before they could summarize just one page. However, their success in learning the skill highlights the effectiveness of supplying added instruction when needed.

Figure 11.1 ● Answer Organizer

Imagine that you are living with the people of Mesa Verde during the 1200s when they left the mesa. Some of your friends and neighbors do not want to leave the area. Based on information in the article, what would you tell these people to convince them to leave?

To answer the question above, follow these steps:

1. Write a topic sentence that tells the people it is important that they leave.
2. Go back over the article and select reasons why the people should leave. List at least three reasons.
3. Put each reason in a sentence. Use the words *First, Second,* and *Third* to number the reasons.
4. Write a closing sentence that strongly states how important it is to leave.
5. Read over your answer. Make sure it is clear and has three or more reasons.
1. If students need more specific guidance, you might break down the organizer even more as in this example.

Write a topic sentence that tells the people it is important that they leave.

_____

_____

2. Write a sentence that gives a reason why the people should leave. The reason should be from the article. Begin the sentence with the word *First*.

_____

_____

3. Write a second sentence that gives a reason why the people should leave. The second reason should be from the article. Begin the sentence with the word *Second*.

_____

_____

4. Write a third sentence that gives a reason why the people should leave. The third reason should be from the article. Begin with the word *Third*.

_____

_____

5. Write a closing sentence.

_____

_____

Source: National Center for Educational Statistics (2005).

As students develop a concept of what makes an acceptable response, create a rubric with them. Have them use the rubric to judge their own writing. They might also use it as a basis for making suggestions to their partners, if they have a peer editor or writing partner. To help students become aware of what goes into an effective answer, have them judge sample pieces with their rubrics. However, don't use students' writing for this. That could be demoralizing.

Students' Performance on Higher-Level Tests

As discussed in Chapter 1, while working as a consultant in an urban public school, I came face to face with the difficulties students encountered when taking higher-level tests. Based on my observations, discussions with students and teachers, and an analysis of test results, I came to the conclusion that with a nickel's worth of help most students could dramatically improve their performance. My analysis of more than 100 released constructed response items from NAEP for the years 1994 to 2005 (National Center for Educational Statistics, 2005), from several sets of students papers from the schools where I consulted, and the results of released items from state tests lend further support to my belief (Gunning, 2005b). Like the second grader I described earlier in the text, many of the students have their answers in their heads. They just need to be shown how to formulate their responses.

A second group appear to be shallow comprehenders and/or responders. They have adequate decoding skills and have a literal understanding of the selection. However, their understanding lacks depth and organization. They need instruction that shows them how to dig into a story or article and also how to organize their responses. They can think deeply and organize their responses when guided to do so but don't do so as a matter of habit.

A third group has the necessary decoding skills, but lacks adequate comprehension, even on a literal level. These students are concrete thinkers. They need to have their thinking skills developed and basic comprehension skills built. They need added instruction and added practice. As Nuthall (1996) comments, "If the appropriate number of learning experiences occur, without significant gaps between them, learning occurs regardless of the learning ability of students" (p. 33). A fourth group of students have weak decoding skills and/or are reading significantly below grade level. They need a program that accelerates their overall reading ability so that they are reading on or close to grade level.

In this chapter, procedures are explored that will help students acquire the responding skills they need to cope with high-level literacy tests. The procedures are based on the kinds of difficulties students experience as they take higher-level tests (see Table 11.1). A key source of information on students' performance on high-level tests is the NAEP. In testing circles the NAEP is known as the "gold standard." As Salinger, Kamil, Kapinus, and Afflerbach (2005) explain, "NAEP rigorously measures what students learn, while steering clear of curricular trends or identifiable instructional programs. NAEP assesses comprehension of fairly long, intact passages similar to what students encounter in their school and out-of-school reading" (pp. 334–335). NAEP periodically releases sample items from

Table 11.1 ● Major Question Types and Response Difficulties

Question Type	Example	Response Difficulties
Locate/Recall		
Details	What are two things about arctic wolves that could be learned from reading this article?	Insufficient details. Not text based.
Main idea	What could be another title for this story?	Title too general. Circular reasoning. Lack of support.
Lesson/theme	What important lesson did the pine tree learn?	Too narrow. Insufficient support.
Summary	Write a brief summary of the article.	Failure to include all of the main ideas.
Integrate/Interpret		
Infer/conclude	Why would a student have more difficulty if she lost hearing in the left ear than in right ear?	Based on experience, not text. Incorrect. Failure to consider all information. Circular reasoning.
Inferring character traits	What kind of a person was the main character?	Superficial trait. Lack of support.
Inferring word meaning	In paragraph 2, the word extinguished means ____.	Failure to consider context.
Supporting conclusion	What makes you think older children missed a lot of school? Use information from the story to support your answer.	Insufficient details. Not text based.
Predict	What do you predict will happen next?	Trivial prediction. Not based on passage.
Compare/Contrast	Describe one way in which wombats and koalas are similar and one way in which they are different.	Failure to make comparisons or to support or explain.
Connect	Choose someone you know who is like the rat or the beetle. Explain how that person or character is like the rat or the beetle.	Failure to make a connection. Failure to show connection or use text-based information.
Critique and Evaluate		
Judging effectiveness of literary techniques	Do you think this story was exciting? Use an example from the story to explain why or why not.	Unsupported opinion. Opinion not related to story.
Judging fairness of text	Explain how you can tell that this passage is biased.	Lack of support. Lack of knowledge of techniques for slanting text.

past tests. Accompanying those released items are statistics noting how many students answered the item successfully, either, fully or partially. Included for constructed responses are sample student answers, a rubric for scoring each item, and an explanation of the rationale for scoring each item (National Center for Educational Statistics, 2005). Through analyzing the responses to more than 100 questions, it was possible to see what students could do well and what they had difficulty with. Suggested techniques for assisting students are based, in large part, on this analysis as well as personal and professional experiences, including tryouts with groups of students. Suggested techniques incorporate the general principles of providing cognitive bridges.

Questions on the Locate and Recall Level

Writing Text-Based Responses

The following responses illustrate a key failing in students' responding. After reading about life in colonial America during the winter, students were asked the following question: Pretend that you are an early American colonist. Describe at least three activities you might do during a cold winter evening. Be specific. Use details from the article to help you write your description.

Neither of the following responses to the above NAEP question received credit. Can you tell why?

> Response 1: Three activities that I might do in the winter go sled riding with a wooden sled. I might have a campfire with friends. I might build a snowman.
> Response 2: I would stay in the house when I would get cold. I would make angels in the snow. Shovel the driveway.

Although both students listed activities that might be engaged in during a cold winter evening, they were based solely on each writer's experiences. As the scorer commented, "These responses provide winter activities; however, none of these activities are text-based examples of what colonists might have done on a cold winter evening." The writers neglected to use details from the article. Basing responses on one's own experiences rather than the text is a common failing among student writers. To help students overcome that deficiency, encourage them to read all parts of the question. Also discuss ways in which they might use information from the text. Show students how to break the question down into its parts.

- Pretend that you are an early American colonist.

- Describe at least three activities you might do during a cold winter evening.
- Be specific.
- Use details from the article to help you write your description.

The first writer did the first three. She even mentioned using a wooden sled, which would have been the kind used in colonial times. However, she failed to use details from the article. She failed to incorporate the gist of the story, which focused on ways in which colonists kept warm in the winter. To help students write text-based responses, emphasize the need to get information from the text. This can be done in a number of ways. Model how you respond to a question that is seeking a text-based response. Show students how you would skim back over the text to find the appropriate details. Discuss how you would use details from that passage in your response. After writing your response, show how you would go back to the question and reread it and then check your answer to make sure that you did indeed answer the question that was posed. Explain to students that sometimes as you search for an answer or think how you are going to write your answer, you lose sight of the question, so it's helpful to go back and see what the question is actually asking. The second response also failed to include text-based details and also by mentioning "shoveling the driveway" apparently lost sight of the fact that the passage refers to colonial times.

Application

Here are some lessons that you might use to develop the ability to provide text-based responses.

With the class, analyze effective responses. Help students to see what goes into an effective response. Compose a rubric for an effective response. Also create an answer organizer and a graphic organizer. Have students help you decide what kind of graphic organizer might be best.

In order to keep the demands of the test question firmly in mind, encourage students to rewrite the question as a topic sentence. This means that the question "Pretend that you are an early American colonist. Describe at least three activities you might do during a cold winter evening. Be specific. Use details from the article to help you write your description" would become: "If I were an early American colonist, here are three specific activities that I would do on a cold winter evening." Of course, writing a topic sentence that incorporates most of the question doesn't guarantee that students' responses will be text-based, but, at least, it's a start. For the next step, have students go back to the text and underline, highlight, or mark with stick-on notes three activities. This is a crucial step

and should be emphasized and checked. Next have students record the three activities, preferably in paraphrased form. Then have students write a closing sentence that summarizes the response. As a final step, students should go back over
their response and make sure that it has three activities. They also need to make
sure that the three activities are ones that were mentioned in the article. Students
should check for clarity and correctness of writing. An answer organizer might
look like this.

Answer Organizer

To answer the question above, follow these steps:

1. Write a topic sentence that tells that if you were living in Colonial times,
   there are three things that you would do on a cold evening.
2. Go back over the article and find the things that people did on cold
   nights. Pick three things.
3. Put each thing that you would do in a sentence. Use the words *first*, *second*, and *third* to number the things that you would do.
4. Write a closing sentence that sums up the paragraph.
5. Read over your answer. Make sure it is clear and has three activities.
   Make sure the activities are mentioned in the article.

Teaching Activity

As a teaching activity, have students read the following article. Complete the response as a group with students. Guide them as they compose a topic sentence and
add three supporting details and a closing.

Elevator Poet

In the late 1800s African-Americans often had a difficult time finding goods
jobs. Paul Dunbar got a job as an elevator operator. In those days, elevators
were not automatic. They had to be run by trained operators. The job didn't
pay much, but when there was no one who wanted to ride the elevator, Paul
wrote poems. He became known as the "elevator poet." In 1892 a book of his
poems was published. Paul sold the book for a dollar to people who rode his
elevator. As word got around about the "elevator poet," Paul began getting invi-
tations from libraries to read his poems. After his second book of poems came
out, he was beginning to become famous. Some of the country's best-known
poets praised Paul's poems. In 1897, he was invited to England to read his
poems. Now he was beginning to become famous around the world.

How did people feel about Paul Dunbar's poetry? Give three examples that show what people thought of Paul Dunbar's poetry (Gunning, 2006d).

_____

_____

_____

_____

_____

To reinforce the concept of providing text-based support, develop a checklist with students that includes the key elements of an acceptable response. Adapt the checklist so that it fits your students. As students encounter other kinds of questions, adapt the checklist so that it fits these questions.

Provide added selections for guided and independent practice. Also gradually work up to longer pieces.

Including Sufficient Details, Reasons, or Examples

Another basic shortcoming of test takers is failure to include sufficient support for their responses. Note the following question from NAEP: What are two things about Shannon Lucid that could be learned from reading this passage? This should be an easy answer. The test passage is full of information about Shannon Lucid. However, only 52 percent of students received full credit for their responses. A key deficiency in students' responses was failure to provide sufficient information, supplying just one detail when two were called for. This same pattern was seen in a number of responses to other questions. Apparently students were losing credit simply because they failed to follow directions. To provide practice, again have students incorporate the question into the topic sentence. You might also provide a frame as in the following example.

Here are two things I learned about Shannon Lucid. The first thing I learned is

_____

The second thing I learned is

_____

_____ .

Provide practice with questions that ask for two or more details or examples. Have students develop and use a checklist to guide and check their responses.

Justifying a Title (Main Idea)

One of the most difficult NAEP questions asked students to justify a title: Do you think "A Brick to Cuddle Up To" is a good title for this article? Using information from the article, tell why or why not. Only 37 percent of students answered it correctly. Another 32 percent got partial credit. Answering the question requires that students know what the function of a good title is. They must realize that a good title states the main idea of the article. They then must decide whether the title of the article really does state the main idea. In other words, they must derive the main idea of the article. To get full credit, students must support their judgment by explaining the relationship between the main idea and the article. And they must provide support by explaining why the information in the article does or does not support the main idea. Here is a response that got full credit: "Yes I do think it is a good title. It is a good title because the article tells about how colonists kept warm in the winter and how they used heated bricks to keep warm."

In a response that earned partial credit, the writer provides a general reason but doesn't explain how the title relates to the article: "I think it is a good title because that's what the paragraph is about." The writer is just a sentence away from getting full credit. All he need do is to prove that the title is telling what the paragraph is all about by providing a detail or two that explain how colonists used heated bricks to warm their beds.

The major obstacle to correctly answering this type of question is that students seem to fail to understand the two-part process needed to answer questions that require not just the answer but also some sort of explanation or other support. Actually, students are being asked to do three things: decide whether the title is a good one, tell why or why not, and use information from the article to support their judgment. To emphasize the necessity to provide support, you might use an answer organizer that highlights the key elements of a response as in the following:

Topic sentence: tells whether you think the title is a good one.

_____

_____

_____

Why sentences: information from the article tells why the title is a good one or why it is not a good title.

_____

_____

_____

If students can write on the test page, have them underline or highlight information from the text to support their response. If they can't write on the test, they might use stick-on notes to indicate suitable information. Adapt the checklist in Figure 11.2 (see page 196) and have students use it to guide and check their responses.

Questions on the Integrate/Interpret Level

Explaining Why

The previous question about Shannon Lucid is one of the easiest. It simply asks students to tell two things about Shannon Lucid that could be learned from the passage. This following question asks for one thing that Shannon Lucid did to help her become an astronaut: Choose one thing Shannon Lucid did that helped her become an astronaut. Explain why it helped her. However, the second part of the question, which asks students to explain why the element chosen helped Lucid, posed problems. Only 18 percent of students earned full credit for this response. Some 41 percent received partial credit because of a failure to include the why part of the question. Typical partial credit responses include the following:

> One thing that helped Lucid to become an astronaut was she read about rockets and things like that.
>
> She never gave up and that gave her confidence.

The first response fails to tell how reading about rockets helped Shannon. In the second sample, the response fails to explain how having confidence helped her. In the selection a number of other helpful factors are described: Lucid's interest in Goddard, her dreaming of exploring space, her adventurous spirit, her pilot's license, and degrees in science. However, the article does not specifically explain how these factors helped her. Students must infer that and then explain their inference. For this kind of question, students pick out one thing that helped Lucid figure out how that helped her become an astronaut, and explain in writing how that helped. To help students respond correctly to why questions, you might try a combined answer organizer and frame similar to the following:

Answer Organizer/Frame

Topic sentence: One thing that helped Shannon Lucid become an astronaut is

_____.

Explaining why the thing I have chosen helped: This helped Shannon become an astronaut because _____.

Teaching/Practice Paragraphs   Provide guidance as students use a frame and answer organizer to respond to the questions that go along with the following passages.

Ears

Although our ears look the same, they handle sounds in different ways. Although both our ears can hear, the right ear is better at hearing people speak. The left ear is better at listening to music. Children who have lost hearing in the right ear have more trouble in school than children who have lost hearing in their left ear. Unless you are in music class, the right ear is better for learning than the left ear.

Why would a student who has lost hearing in her right ear have more difficulty in school than a student who has lost hearing in her left ear? (Gunning, 2006d)

Frame

Topic sentence: A student who has lost hearing in her right ear might have more difficulty in school than a student who has lost hearing in her left ear.

Why (because) sentence: The student will have more difficulty because

_____.

_____.

Manatees in Danger

Manatees are in danger. Manatees are mammals so they must breathe air. They can only stay under water for two or three minutes. Manatees are also slow swimmers. Because they are slow swimmers and must pop up to the surface every few minutes and live in shallow waterways, they have frequent accidents with boats. They also get tangled up in fishing and crabbing lines. In fact, people seem to be their main enemy.
Why are manatees in danger? Give two reasons. (Gunning, 2006d)

Answer Organizer

Topic sentence: _____
Reason one: _____
Reason two: _____

Putting Pieces of Information Together

Drawing inferences requires additional rethinking on the students' part. However, inferences vary in difficulty. An easy inference is this one in which students must simply put two pieces of information together as in the question: Why has Australia set up animal reserves to protect the wombat? The test article about wombats states: "As more and more people move into territories in which wombats live, they destroy the wombat's burrows and food supplies. In some areas where the wombat was once plentiful, it is now almost extinct. Animal reserves have been set up recently to protect the wombat." Nearly one-third of students lost credit because they failed to supply a reason for their response or the reason was not from the passage. Although all the necessary information for making the inference is contained in the passage, the answer is not directly stated in the passage. Readers must make the inference that the wombat is now extinct in some areas because its burrows and food supplies have been destroyed. And that is why reserves have been set up. Again, for this kind of question students should begin by composing a topic sentence that rewords the question. Compose a checklist (see Figure 11.2 on page 196) and have students use it to guide and check their responses.

Answer Organizer

Topic sentence: Tell what Australia has done to protect the wombat.

_____

_____

Supporting sentences: Tell why Australia had to take action to protect the wombat.

_____

_____

_____

_____

Providing Support

In item after item, students lost credit or received no credit at all because they failed to provide support for their responses. In fact, failure to provide support was the number one shortcoming in students' responses. This failure is exemplified in the following item:

After reading this article, would you have liked to have lived during colonial times? What information in the article makes you think this?

Only 20 percent of students received full credit. Most of the others failed to provide support. To answer this question, students needed to:

- Decide whether they would have wanted to live in colonial times.
- State their opinion.
- Use information from the article to support their opinion. The information needed to be appropriate and substantive.
- Show a connection between their opinion and information in the article. Students would need to use a connector such as *because*.

Many students made the mistake of failing to provide specific support. They made a general statement such as "No, I wouldn't like to live in colonial times because it sounds like it's very hard to live in the winter." The student has given a reason but has not supported it with information from the article. The student earned partial credit for demonstrating that he understood that the winters were hard, but he provided no specifics. The student needed to tell why. This reflects a common flaw in students' writing, a failure to elaborate. To overcome that shortcoming, have them complete answer organizers in which they are led to elaborate.

After reading the article, would you have liked to have lived in colonial times? What information in the article makes you think this?

Answer Organizer

1. Write a sentence that tells whether or not you would have wanted to live in colonial times.

   _____

   _____

2. Write a sentence that gives information from the article that explains why you would or would not have liked to have lived in colonial times.

   _____

   _____

3. Write a second sentence that gives information from the article that explains why you would or would not have liked to have lived in colonial times.

   _____

   _____

4. Write a closing sentence.

   _____

   _____

To provide practice with elaboration, have students complete the following or similar passages:

I like basketball. It's easy to play. Basketball is easy to play because

_____.

I like summer because I have a lot of fun during this season. Some of the fun
things that I do are _____.

Opinion/Proof Graphic Organizer   Perhaps because of its wording, students found
the following opinion question easier to answer: Do you think it would be fun to
catch blue crabs? Using information from the passage, explain why or why not.

Some 62 percent of students responded correctly. However, most of the 38 percent who did not receive credit failed to tell why or why not. To provide practice in
answering opinion questions, have students complete opinion-proof activities in
which they express their opinions in the left column and provide proof in the right-
hand column (Santa, Havens & Maycumber, 1996).

Opinion	Proof

Teaching/Practice Passages   Provide preparation and guidance as students respond
to the opinion questions for the following passages. Adapt the checklist in Figure
11.2 and have students use it to guide and check their responses.

Parachutes for Planes

You are flying high above the mountains in a small plane. Suddenly, your plane
goes into a spin. You pull hard on the controls. Nothing happens. The plane is spinning faster now, and it's falling. You reach toward a red handle and pull it. You say to
yourself, "I hope this works." You hear a popping sound as a small rocket shoots out
of a hatch on the plane. The rocket shoots toward the rear of the plane. It is pulling a
large parachute. You watch as the parachute opens up. The plane floats to the
ground. There is a soft bump as the plane touches down. You climb out of the plane
and say to yourself, "I'm glad my plane had a parachute."

Although parachutes for planes might sound like a dream for the future, they
aren't. Parachutes have been made that can be used to bring small planes to earth
when they get into trouble. One pilot Albert Kolk had his grandson and two friends

in his plane when it spun out of control "like a dog chasing its tail." Kolk yelled at the boys to fasten their seat belts and yanked the parachute handle. When the parachute opened his feeling of fear changed to a "peaceful, wonderful feeling." The parachutes have already saved the lives of close to 200 people.

Cost of Parachutes

The parachutes cost from $2,000 to $16,000, depending on the size of the plane. That might sound like a high price, until you have to use one. So far the parachutes have only been used on small planes. Small planes only weigh about 2,000 to 4,000 pounds and only go about 175 miles an hour. Now the company that makes the parachutes is working on parachutes that could be used on small jets. The parachutes would have control devices, so that the pilot could guide the plane as it floated to earth (Gunning, 2000d).

Do you think having parachutes for planes is a good idea? Why or why not? Use information from the article to support your opinion.

_____

_____

_____

Grease Mobiles

Instead of filling up at a gas station, some car drivers stop by restaurants. They run their cars on the oil that is used to cook french fries and other foods. The car owners have diesel engines. Diesel engines run on diesel fuel, but they can also run on vegetable oil. Before a car can run on vegetable oil, it must have a special kit. The kit has a tank for holding the vegetable oil. It also needs a filter so any dirt in the oil is removed.

There are some problems with using vegetable oil. It gets hard when it is cold. So people running their cars on vegetable oil need a special heater to keep the oil warm. They also need to use regular diesel fuel to start their cars. Once the car has warmed up, they can then switch to vegetable oil.

Unused vegetable oil can be used to run diesel engines, but unused vegetable oil costs as much or more than diesel fuel. Used vegetable oil is free. In fact, restaurants are happy to give it away. If they don't give it away, restaurant owners have to pay to have it taken away. Using vegetable oil saves money for car owners and restaurant owners, too (Gunning, 2006d).

Is running a car on vegetable oil a good idea? Why, or why not? Use information from the story to support your opinion.

_____

_____

_____

_____

To reinforce the concept of making a judgment and providing text-based support, adapt the checklist in Figure 11.2 and have students use it to guide and check their responses.

Questions about Character Traits

Asking about character traits is a popular discussion and test question as in this question from NAEP: What do Turtle's actions at Spider's house tell you about Turtle? Only 41 percent of students responded correctly. Most of the others described Turtle's actions at the house, but did not infer what his actions said about him. To help students supply adequate explanations, you might use the following or a similar answer organizer.

Answer Organizer for Explaining Character Traits

Topic sentence describing actions:

_____

_____

Sentences telling what actions show about the character:

_____

_____

Comparing/Contrasting   On assessments students are frequently asked to compare and contrast. This requires the ability to see similarities and differences. Compare/contrast questions vary in difficulty. Questions that ask for either similarities or differences are easier than questions that ask for both. Questions that specify how many similarities and differences are being asked for are easier than those that are more open-ended. The following question is relatively easy because it is asking for one similarity and one difference from a selection that specifically states similarities and differences: Describe one way in which wombats and koalas are similar and one way in which they are different.

Despite being a fairly straightforward question, only slightly more than half the students were able to answer it correctly. Many provided only a similarity or only a difference. And some did not provide accurate information. To cope with the problem of supplying erroneous information, have students go back over the selection and reread the similarities and differences and, if possible, mark the similarities or differences with a highlighter or stick-on note.

Explain and encourage the use of the language used to indicate similarities and the language used to denote differences:

Similarities: *similar, same, alike, both*
Differences: *different, but, however, although*

To provide practice in expressing similarities and differences, have students complete the following or similar frame sentences that are expressing likenesses:

Both _____ and _____ are (or have) _____ .

> Both African and Asian elephants are _____
>
> Wombats and kolas are similar because they both _____

The following frames might be used to express differences:

> _____ is (has), but _____ is (has) _____ .
>
> Although both African and Asian elephants have large ears, the ears of the African elephant are _____ .
>
> Koalas live in _____ but wombats make their homes
>
> _____ .

When given a comparison/contrast question that was more open-ended and asked for examples, students were even less successful: "Tell how Elisa and Cory are alike and different. Use examples from the story to explain your opinion." Just about a third of students were able to provide a full-credit response. Many did not provide examples or did not provide sufficient examples. Many also gave superficial differences and similarities. There is an extra step in this kind of question. In addition to stating that there is a similarity and a difference, the difference and the similarity must be described or given a label. And the example for the similarity and the difference must be included. For this type of question, students might use the following answer organizer.

> Topic sentence stating that there is a similarity: _____
>
> Telling what the similarity is: _____
>
> Support: Give example(s) _____
>
> Topic sentence stating that there is a difference: _____
>
> Telling what the difference is: _____
>
> Support: Give example(s) _____

Teaching/Practice Passages

Famous Students

The other students in Dayton High School in Dayton, Ohio, had no way of knowing it, but one day, three of their students would become famous throughout the world. Paul Dunbar would go on to become a famous poet. Orville and his brother Wilbur would invent the airplane. Orville was in Paul's class. Wilbur, who was older than Orville, was two years ahead of Orville and Paul. All three boys were hard workers.

Paul started a newspaper while he was still in school. The Wright brothers repaired bikes and started a printing business. They printed Paul's newspaper.

In some ways Paul was very different from the Wright brothers. Paul liked to work with words. His mother had learned poetry when she was a slave. She worked in the home of her owners, who often read poetry to their children. Paul's mother listened in. From the time he was a baby, Paul's mother recited poems and sang songs to him. Paul wrote his first poem at the age of six. And he continued to write poems for the rest of his life. Wilbur and Orville liked to work with machines. They opened a bicycle shop, but became interested in flying. For much of their lives they worked with flying machines (Gunning, 2006d).

Besides going to the same high school how were the Wright brothers and Paul Dunbar similar? Give examples.

The Wright brothers were similar in at least one way. They both were
_____. Paul Dunbar _____.
The Wright brothers _____.
In later years all three boys became _____.
The Wright brothers _____.
Paul Dunbar _____.
How were the Wright brothers and Paul Dunbar different? Give examples.
The Wright brothers were different from Paul Dunbar. Paul Dunbar liked to

_____.
He _____.
The Wright brothers liked to _____.
They _____.

Dugongs and Manatees

Have you are heard of an animal called the dugong? Dugongs are large sea animals. They can grow to be 10 feet long (3 meters) and weigh up to 800 pounds (363 kilograms). Dugongs are sometimes known as "sea cows." Like cows they spend much of their time eating grass. Only the grass they eat is under the sea.

Dugongs are mammals. This means that they need to breathe air. They can only stay under water for a few minutes. Dugongs like to live in warm, shallow water where sea grasses grow. Most dugongs live in the waters around Australia. Dugongs have poor eyesight but keen hearing. They find grasses with their whiskers. Whiskers cover their upper lip and their large snout. The whiskers are feelers that tell the dugongs what is being touched.

Dugongs take a long time to grow up. Some animals grow up in a few months. But dugongs take 16 or more years before they are ready to have babies. But that's okay. Dugongs live for 70 years or more. They are one of the longest-living mammals on earth. They live just about as long as people.

Manatees are cousins to dugongs. Like dugongs, manatees are mammals so they must breathe air. They can only stay under water for two or three minutes. Manatees are also large sea creatures. They can be 12 feet long and weigh 1,500 pounds or more. Like dugongs, they eat sea plants. They feed on the plants that grow at the bottom of streams, rivers, and canals. They use their front flippers to push themselves along the bottom of the waterway. Manatees eat a lot. They eat up to 200 pounds of plants a day.

Manatees grow up a little faster than dugongs and don't live quite as long. They only live for about 60 years. (Gunning, 2006d)

Describe ways in which dugongs and manatees are similar and ways in which they are different. Give examples from the article.

_____

_____

_____

Adapt the checklist in Figure 11.2. Emphasize the need to select important differences and similarities. Have students use the checklist to guide and check their responses.

The most difficult comparison/contrast question was a connection question in which students had to use both textual and background knowledge as in the following item: "Some of the ways colonists kept warm during the winter were different from the ways that people keep warm today. Tell about two of these differences." More than 80 percent of the students failed to get full credit. Students failed to provide two differences, talked about only heat in colonial days or heat today, or failed to make a connection between colonial times and today. Help students break down questions of this type into the kinds of operations required:

- Tell how colonists kept warm
- Tell how we keep warm
- Point out the differences

Figure 11.2 ● Checklist for Using Support from the Article

- Did I rewrite the question as a topic sentence? _____
- Did I include details that support the topic sentence? _____
- Did my support come from the article? _____
- Did I give enough support? _____

Here is a frame for this kind of question.

> The colonists kept warm by _____ and
> by _____.
> Today we have different ways to keep warm. Today we keep warm by
>
> _____
> _____.
> The colonists kept warm mainly by _____, but
> we keep warm mainly by _____.

Connection Questions

In connection questions students are asked to describe a connection to a person, event, or experience as in the NAEP item: "Choose someone you know, have read about, or have seen in a movie or television show who is like the rat or the beetle. Explain how that person or character is like the rat or the beetle." Just over a third of the students got full credit for this item. Students failed to tell why the two characters were alike or didn't link the outside character to Rat or Beetle, or the similarity was a trivial one.

Answer Organizer/Frame for Connection Questions

> _____ is like _____. Here is why. They both
> _____ and they
> both _____.

Adapt the checklist in Figure 11.2 and have students use it to guide and check their responses.

Connection questions require using outside information along with text information. However, the process starts with text-based information. For example, if a student is asked to make a connection between a character he read about and a real person or fictional character, the student should decide which character he is going to focus on and which trait or traits he is going to write about. He then needs to identify a person or character who shares similar traits. The traits should be significant. Age or size or gender would not normally be significant. Honesty, sense of adventure, generosity, or ambition would be. The writer then has to show a connection between the two. In their responses, students must include

- Text character
- Traits of text character with supporting examples
- Real, TV, or fiction character with traits similar to those of text character
- Traits of real, TV, or fiction character with supporting examples
- Connection between the two

Although the traits might be the same, the ways those traits are manifest will be different so the supporting examples will be different.

Questions on the Critique/Evaluate Level

Critique and Evaluate requires taking a critical look at the text and evaluating the fairness of the author's message or the literary quality of a selection. As with other areas, students lost credit or received no credit because they failed to explain responses or provide needed support. However, questions in this area often required some knowledge of literary techniques. For instance, students had difficulty explaining the meaning of symbols or figurative language or had difficulty explaining how the language of a poem differed from ordinary language. An area of particular difficulty was identifying and/or explaining themes.

Theme/Lesson Learned   "What is one lesson that could be learned from reading this passage? Use information from the passage to support your answer." This is a type of question that is frequently asked. A lesson is similar to a theme. However, instead of asking for the overall idea that the author intended to convey, it answers the question: What is the author trying to teach here? To get the lesson, the students need to think carefully about the entire selection. That makes this a difficult question. Often the key to the lesson is noting how the characters changed or acted during the selection. Students lost credit on this question on the NAEP because they gave information about the story, but didn't draw a lesson from it. Or, conversely, they stated a lesson, but the lesson was not related to the story. To answer this question, students need to think carefully about the story and the lesson the author was trying to convey. They should be looking at the main characters and how they may have changed or what might have happened to them. Students need to ask: "What is the author trying to teach here? What lesson can I draw from this story?" Then students need to back up their statement of the lesson with details from the story. Model the process, but emphasize that a story can be interpreted in different ways. Show how the details in the story—the actions of the character, for instance—led you to infer a lesson. In some instances the lesson is stated. But students still need to show how they would use details from the story to support their choice of lessons.

At higher levels, students might be asked to state the theme of a selection rather than the lesson learned. Eighth graders were asked to state the theme of "Thank You, Ma'm" by Langston Hughes, which is the story of a would-be mugger who ends up being befriended by his victim. Students were given leeway to construct a number of themes. However, they had to construct a theme that embodied the overall impact of the selection. Some students noted minor lessons instead of themes. They needed to think more deeply about the selection. A number of students failed to support their themes with details from the story. Many of the students who lost credit constructed plausible themes but failed to provide support for them. However, a number of students failed to get credit because they summarized the story or listed key story events but did not state a theme.

Analyzing Responses to Multiple-Choice Items

This chapter has focused on skills needed to respond to open-ended questions. However, responses to multiple-choice items can be used to gain insight into the strategies and processes students are using to answer questions and to plan instruction that will help students use more effective response strategies. When answering multiple-choice questions, students often make one of four kinds of errors: answer grabbing, text matching, not looking back, and related (Kelleher & Larson, 2006).

- Answer grabbing. The student simply chooses an answer that is appealing. The answer has no support in the text. The students might have just skimmed the passage or might not have even read it or might not have read it with comprehension.
- Text matching. The student choses an option based on remembering seeing some of the words in the passage that are similar to the words in the answer option.
- Not looking back. The student failed to look back to the target passage even when directed to do so. The student answers on the basis of background knowledge or personal opinion instead of looking back.
- Related. The student read the passage with comprehension and put some thought into each response. The student selected an answer that was plausible but was not the best answer. The student did not compare possible answers to see which one was best.

Students typically use a combination of strategies. Students might not look back to clarify an answer and might engage in some answer grabbing because of poor comprehension. Weaker readers tend to use answer grabbing. Stronger readers tend to make related errors.

Instead of focusing just on the total score, analyze incorrect responses to see what kinds of choices students were making and what these choices indicate about the strategies they were most likely using. You might also ask students how they go about answering multiple-choice questions. Ask them what led them to select a particular answer. Based on your analysis of errors, you can then discuss with students what they are doing to answer test questions. You can discuss with

• ....

200

answer-grabbing students why it is important to read the selection carefully and think about what the selection said. You can tell students who are failing to look back that it is important to go back to the selection to locate information. You can model with students who are choosing related options how to consider all answer choices to find the one that is best. With instruction students' responding improves (Kelleher & Larson, 2006). They get more answers correct, and their incorrect answers move from the answer grabbing or text matching categories to the related category.

Providing Ongoing, Embedded Practice

Preparing students to take higher-level tests is an ongoing endeavor that should be a part of the regular curriculum. The idea is not to teach to the test but to teach with the test in mind (Farr, 2004) by engaging in the following:

- Embed key skills in your everyday activities. As you discuss stories, talk over character traits, lessons learned, and themes. Have students make comparisons and make connections. In addition to oral responses, have students compose written responses. They might respond to their reading in response journals. In your tests, include items similar to those contained on the assessment that students will be taking.
- Provide systematic instruction in needed response skills. Once a week or once every two weeks, provide instruction and practice in the types of response skills that students need most.
- Play you be the scorer. Have students judge sample responses. You can use the sample pieces discussed here. There are a number of other samples on the NAEP site at http://nces.ed.gov/nationsreportcard/itmrls/.
  In fact there are 202 sample questions. However, these include multiple-choice as well as constructed-response items. Texas even has an interactive test that students can take and score themselves: www.tea.state.tx.us/student .assessment/resources/online/2004/grade3/read.htm.

However, as a practical matter, obtain samples of the kinds of tests that your students will be taking and sample responses. If rubrics are not provided, develop them with students.

Study Group Questions

- How do I prepare students for high-stakes tests?
- Is my program embedded, separate, or a combination?
- Which skills do I emphasize?
- Are there any essential skills that are not included in my program?
- How might I prepare students for high-stakes tests but still teach in an authentic way?
- What kinds of cognitive bridges might I build?
- Which of my students are not adequately prepared for the high-stakes tests they are required to take? How might I help those who are not prepared?

Developing a Whole School Program

Despite being housed in a building that is more than 100 years old and is situated in one of the poorest neighborhoods in one of the poorest cites (Hartford, Connecticut), Henry C. Dwight Elementary School does an exemplary job of educating its students. In addition to strong leadership, a dedicated staff, a program that fosters wide reading of high-quality texts, Dwight has a carefully planned program that prepares students for one of the nation's most challenging high-stakes tests. The school has a yearly plan that specifies what themes and skills and strategies will be emphasized each week. (Some skills may be emphasized for several weeks.) This emphasis is tied in to both the state curriculum framework and the state mastery tests. The emphasis might be on summarizing or inferring. During the time period in which the emphasis is on summarizing, every teacher, including content area teachers, stresses summarizing. The skills goal for that time period is posted in each room. Teachers are supplied with a description of the goal as well as questions, graphic organizers, and activities that might be used to teach and reinforce the skill. In each classroom, teachers posted samples of students' summaries under the heading: "We Can Summarize." Both students and staff were well aware of the skill being emphasized. (Actually a skill such as summarizing needs a number of weeks.)

When character study was being emphasized, students posted their responses under the heading: "We Can Infer Character Traits." In addition to being taught how to infer character traits, students discussed character traits in their literature circles. Accountable talk was very much a part of their discussions. Students also responded to prompts in their journals: "What makes the character unique? Is the character like you? How did the character change?" In addition to teacher-provided prompts, students were encouraged on two days out of five to respond to their own prompts. To increase the use of text-based responses, students were given stick-on notes to attach to appropriate passages. When they composed their responses, they used their stick-on notes as a base. In discussions, students were asked again and again to find evidence to prove or clarify a point.

In 2001 Dwight had the lowest achievement of all the schools in Hartford and was one of the lowest achieving schools in the state. Four years later, Dwight had the highest achievement in Hartford and ranked in the top 10 percent in the state. In 2005 Dwight was named as a blue ribbon No Child Left Behind School. Schools such as Dwight prove that children in the lowest achieving schools can be taught high-level literacy skills. The staff had a bundle of potential excuses: old building, high rate of poverty, population of children drawn from 21 different counties, history of failure. Instead of using excuses, they did what needed to be done and proved once again that if you teach students they will learn. And if you teach them on a high level, they will learn on a high level.

Components of a Program for Developing High-Level Literacy

There are many lessons to be learned from Dwight and other schools that have succeeded in developing higher-level literacy skills. As exemplified by Dwight, key components of a higher-level literacy program would be goals or standards that incorporate high-level reading and writing and to which the whole faulty subscribes, a rich curriculum that features extensive reading and writing, ongoing assessment that uses data as a basis for planning, instructional techniques and approaches that include the fostering of accountable talk in whole-class and small-group discussions, extra support for students who need it, an array of high-quality materials, ongoing staff development, supportive parents and community, and a dedicated staff that has a common vision and has a basic belief in students' ability to achieve higher-level literacy.

Staff Development

A key component in the implementation of a program of higher-level literacy is on-going professional development. The most effective professional development is based on student data. Data provides evidence of a need for change and also shows where change should occur. In addition, data from ongoing monitoring of students guides the professional development efforts (Joyce & Calhoun, 1996). It shows whether professional development is being successful or whether additional changes are needed. For faculty who have doubts about students' ability to achieve on high levels, data that shows improvement is very encouraging.

Professional development should include application and follow-up (Showers, Murphy & Joyce, 1996). Even when providing a theoretical base for instructional techniques, multiple demonstrations of techniques, and the opportunity to practice them in a workshop setting, only 10 percent of teachers actually implemented the techniques. However, when these elements were accompanied by extensive support, nearly 90 percent of the teachers implemented the techniques.

Teachers were urged to try out the techniques in their classrooms on a long-term basis and to continue using them regularly. Study groups were formed so that teachers could discuss their efforts, observe each other, and coach each other in the use of the techniques. The researchers found that it takes 20 to 30 trials before new techniques are integrated into teachers' repertoire of teaching tools. Ultimately, the implementation of the new techniques resulted in improved student performance. In one middle school, the average achievement test scores jumped from the twenty-fifth to the forty-second percentile.

Professional development needs to be ongoing. Study groups are especially good for looking into new approaches or techniques for teaching higher-level thinking skills. These can be held monthly or more frequently. Grade-level meetings are especially good for tracking students' progress. Grade-level meetings should be held weekly or biweekly. At these meetings discuss students' progress on higher-level literacy tasks. Having data is essential. Once teachers have the data, they can track progress and alter instruction when necessary.

In one study the achievement of students whose teachers attended grade-level meetings was compared with students whose teachers did not attend. Students of attending teachers moved from the thirtieth to the seventieth percentile. Students of nonattenders did not change their percentile rank (Knox, 2002).

Building Ladders for the Short Kids

Marie Clay (2004), the world-famous force behind Reading Recovery, reminds teachers that we need to "Build ladders for the short kids." The short kids are those who need a bit of scaffolding to reach the standards we set for the average student. The first rung on the ladder for the short kids is to assess students to see what level they are on and to gain some insight into their ability to apply key strategies. Other rungs include giving them material on their level, gearing instruction that builds on what they know but fills in the missing gaps, starting with brief, easy selections and moving gradually into longer, more complex selections. The next rung is to provide systematic instruction in key strategies and to make a special effort to build the necessary prerequisite skills. Other rungs include monitoring progress and adjusting instruction as needed, providing extensive practice and reinforcement, and reviewing periodically.

To foster thinking skills, Graham Nuthall (1999), who engaged in a long-term, extensive series of studies of teaching and learning in the classroom, emphasizes providing instruction and appropriate practice activities in order to develop higher-level thinking skills.

> Tasks need to be set up that model and give students practice in activities that involve making connections between related pieces of information and identifying implications and potential differences and contradictions. As students practice these activities and become experts in the habits of mind involved in the activities, these habits become internalized and an unconscious but automatic part of the way their minds deal with new experiences. (p. 337)

This principle applies to all students, including the short kids. Restricting the intellectual complexity of tasks (as is usual for students in low-track classes) results in progressive lowering of scores on test of academic aptitude (Oakes, Gamoran & Page, 1992). The short kids might need added teaching sessions. As Nuthall (1996) comments, "If the appropriate number of learning experiences occur, without significant gaps between them, learning occurs regardless of the learning ability of students" (p. 33).

Freidman (2005) advises having a well-planned system of assessment and corrective instruction. Most assessment systems are long on assessment and short on corrective instruction. Freidman suggests having corrective materials ready before you test students. Let students know that you will provide them with assistance if they need it. If students get answers incorrect, find out why and reteach. As Freidman notes, "The biggest difference in students' ability is not whether they can learn material but how much instruction they need to master it" (p. 86). The most effective corrective instruction is one on one because it addresses the student's specific needs. However, if the resources aren't available, you might try providing instruction for small groups of students who have similar needs.

Freidman also suggests emphasizing teaching evaluation rather than teacher evaluation. In other words, evaluate the results of the teaching rather than the style of the teaching. We can't do much about our traits. Introverts can't make themselves into extraverts, but we can improve our teaching techniques and the results of our teaching.

Helping Good Decoders Who Are Poor Comprehenders

Approximately 10 to 15 percent of students are good decoders but poor comprehenders (Dymock, 1998; Yuill & Oakhill, 1991). In her study of good decoders who were poor comprehenders, Dymock (1998) found that these students had difficulty with listening as well as reading comprehension. The results suggested that these students had limited vocabularies and background knowledge, and struggled with some syntactic structures. Students who are good decoders but poor comprehenders are often overlooked in the early grades, where the emphasis is on decoding and low-level comprehension. This is unfortunate because the research suggests that these students would benefit from a program of language and vocabulary development. If more emphasis is placed on comprehension in the early grades, students who are having difficulty with comprehension would be identified earlier.

For many underachieving students, decoding is not the issue, even in the early grades. Decoding skills are relatively easy to teach, and most students learn them quite well. Based on a one-to-one assessment of all the students in grades one through three in an urban public school, I found that most of the students had adequate decoding skills, but vocabulary and comprehension scores were lower than expected. However, although there was a systematic program for developing decoding skills, there was none for developing language and vocabulary. Decoding skills were taught each day. Vocabulary skills were only taught when new words were being introduced in preparation for the reading of a new selection. Little time was spent on developing language or higher-level thinking skills.

Helping English Language Learners

English language learners do less well on reading tests than do native speakers of English, and that gap increases as students move through the grades. Experts on second language learning recommend that teachers take the following steps to assist English language learners (Gersten & Baker, 2000):

- Build and use vocabulary as a curricular anchor. Vocabulary is the key to progress for ELL. Before students read a selection, preteach key vocabulary.

Select words that are important to an understanding of the selection but which will also occur again and again in the future. Cover 6 or 7 words in depth rather than trying to cover 15 or 20 words.

- Use visuals to reinforce concepts and vocabulary. Whenever possible, use visuals to illustrate new vocabulary and new concepts. However, don't restrict the use of visuals to pictures. Jot down on the board key words for a new concept or topic. Make generous use of graphic organizers. Involve students in the creation of graphic organizers.

- Implement cooperative learning and peer-tutoring strategies. Reluctant to answer in a whole group, the ELL become more active in a small group or when working with a partner. Peer tutoring works well with ELL. Encourage ELL to be active participants. Formulating responses stretches their development of English.

- Use native language strategically. If possible, use students' native language to explain complex concepts or procedures that they are having a difficult time grasping. Also allow students to respond to higher-level questions first in their native language and then in English.

For ELL stress language development, especially the language needed to cope with academic tasks. Along with teaching higher-level skills and strategies to ELL, teach the language that is used to understand and implement those skills and strategies. You need to be aware that you are teaching language in addition to content.

Steps for Constructing a Higher-Level Literacy Program

- Set higher-level standards (goals). The first step for constructing a program of higher literacy is to adopt higher-level literacy standards or goals. These should be aligned with state and local standards and with the standards assessed on the tests that your students will be taking. You will most likely need to go beyond the standards that are assessed and you might need to add to the standards published by the state and your local system.

- Assess your students. Find out what level your students are on and how well they can respond to higher-level questions. Along with other assessments, you may use the Survey of Higher-Level Reading and Responding Skills located in Appendix B. Also decide on the devices you will use to assess your students' achievement. Standards or goals and assessment should be aligned.

- Create a culture of understanding. Emphasize the importance of constructing meaning and taking corrective steps or seeking help when meaning is lacking.

- Create an environment in which every student is a high-level thinker. In your heart of hearts, you might not believe that all students are capable of achieving higher-level literacy. However, if you act as though you do, your beliefs will change. If you give all students wait time, helpful prompts, systematic instruction, materials on their level, and extra help when they need it, they will achieve at high levels. Some will just take longer to get there and will need more help than others.
- Make sure that every student becomes an expert in some area.
- Build language and thinking skills in all areas, including the content areas.
- Systematically teach higher-level reading and responding skills in depth. Remember that it takes four to six weeks to learn a new strategy. Although strategies might be taught in isolation, students should be taught to use them in integrated fashion.
- Have students use graphic organizers as a way of organizing their thinking.
- Read high-quality selections to students and encourage to them read high-quality materials. Plan challenging reading and writing tasks.
- Foster wide reading.
- Develop students' ability to engage in accountable talk. Set up discussion groups.
- Monitor students' progress. Use the results to reteach and replan.
- Involve the home and community. Encourage parents to talk to their children and engage them in discussions about books and current happenings. Maybe you can get a parent or community volunteer who is trained in Junior Great Books to conduct a book discussion group.

Making an All-Out Effort

In a sense, fostering higher-level thinking should permeate all of the school's activities. It isn't just for reading and writing during the language arts period. Fostering higher-level thinking begins with the belief that even the youngest students as well as those who struggle are capable of high-level reading and writing. Extra help is provided for students who need it. From day one, understanding is stressed in and out of the classroom. Students are taught to seek understanding. They are taught the tools for seeking help when understanding is lacking. Seeking help is not seen as a sign of weakness but as the mark of an effective learner. Students are led to think deeply about their reading and writing. They learn from others and others learn from them. They learn to ask questions and to support responses in all content areas. They learn to value knowledge along with inquiry. An impossible dream? If it can happen in one of the poorest schools in one of the poorest cities, it can happen anywhere.

Study Group Questions

- What are the components of a program for developing high-level literacy?
- What do I need to do to develop a program of higher-level literacy in my classroom?
- How might a whole school program for fostering higher-level skills be developed?
- What are the steps that might be taken to implement a program of higher-level skills?

Reciprocal Teaching Lesson: Student Copy of Selection

Potatoes for Breakfast, Lunch, and Supper

Do you like potatoes? Would you like to eat potatoes at every meal? Years ago, in Ireland, many of the people ate potatoes for breakfast, lunch, and supper. Each person ate between seven and fifteen pounds of potatoes a day. The Irish ate baked potatoes, fried potatoes, mashed potatoes, boiled potatoes, and roasted potatoes. They ate potato soup, potato pancakes, and potato cakes.

Why did the Irish eat so many potatoes? They were very poor. Most families had tiny bits of land on which to grow their food. They grew potatoes because it was possible to grow a lot of potatoes on a small piece of land. Storing potatoes was easy. They were kept in pits in the ground and were dug up when needed.

A Kindly People

Although the Irish were poor, they were a kindly people. Even though they barely had enough to eat, they would feed anyone who came to their door. If a stranger came to dinner unexpectedly, they figured they could put another potato in the pot or cut a potato in half to share with the stranger. They had a saying about feeding others: "We've an extra potato right hot on the fire, for one who travels through wet bog and mire."

The Great Hunger

A great hunger came to the Irish people in 1845. Their potato crop was hit by a plant disease known as a blight. Potatoes began rotting in the field. Not having enough to eat, more than a million men, women, and children died of starvation. Millions more sailed for the United States, Canada, or Australia. The blight wasn't over until 1850. Before the blight, Ireland had 9 million people. After the blight, there were just 5 million left.

Survey of Higher-Level Reading and Responding Skills

The Survey of Higher-Level Reading and Responding Skills consists of two informational passages, one on a third-grade level and one on a fourth-fifth grade level. Each passage is accompanied by eight multiple-choice and three open-ended questions. The items assess comprehension of main ideas, details, inferences, and the ability to summarize a passage and support responses. Students should take the test on the appropriate level. Students reading on a third-grade level should take Level C: "Arctic Fox." Students reading on a fourth- or fifth-grade level should take Level D–E: "Crumb Rubber." Students should not be given test selections that are beyond their level, but may take portions that are below their level. Students reading above a fifth-grade level may also take Level D–E. Even though Level D–E is below the students' reading level, it will still show how well students respond to higher-level multiple-choice and constructed response items. However, also assess and observe students as they work in materials on their level to see how well they handle more challenging materials.

● ....

212

To administer the test, explain its purpose to students. Tell them it will help you to see what kinds of questions they can answer with no difficulty and what kinds of questions they have difficulty with. By seeing what they can do well and what is hard for students, you can plan lessons that will help them to become better readers and writers.

The test is not timed, but students should be able to complete it in about 30 to 45 minutes. Allow students to write on the test materials. They might also underline, highlight, or make notes.

As students are taking the test, observe them carefully. Look for signs that students are having difficulty. Use open-ended probes to shed light on the nature of their difficulty. Ask such questions as

- How is it going?
- You seem to be having difficulty? Is there anything that I can help you with?
- Is there anything that you don't understand?
- Is something confusing you?
- What is this question asking you? How do you plan to answer this question?
- Read this paragraph to me. What is the paragraph saying?

Questions of this type will help you locate the source of students' difficulty. They will also reveal students who know the answer and can respond orally but have difficulty composing written responses.

Analyzing Test Results

Arctic Fox

Questions 1, 2, and 3 are assessing the ability to comprehend key details. The answers to Questions 1 and 2 are directly started in the article. The answer to Question 3 requires the student to reason that the fox will feel cold because 50 degrees below zero is below the cut-off point of 40 degrees below zero. Questions 4 through 5 are main idea multiple-choice questions. Questions 6, 7, and 8 are inferential/conclusion questions. Questions 7 and 8 require the students to use context to infer the meanings of words. Questions 9, 10, and 11 are open-ended questions designed to assess the ability to locate and comprehend directly stated details, support a main idea, and support a conclusion. To use the results of this assessment to plan instruction, note the following:

- Answering any two of Questions 1, 2, and 3 suggests adequate literal comprehension.

- Answering Questions 4 and 5 suggests adequate comprehension of main ideas.
- Answering any two of Questions 6, 7, and 8 suggests adequate inferential comprehension.
- Answering Questions 9, 10, 11 with a score of 3 or more for each suggests proficient comprehension of details, main idea and summarizing, and supporting conclusions. It also suggests adequate responding skills.

If students do poorly overall, check to make sure that they are on the appropriate level and use lookbacks. Students reading on a lower level than grade three would have difficulty with the selection. If students can answer the literal questions but have difficult with main idea, summarizing, or inferential questions, they may need instruction with deriving main ideas, summarizing, or drawing and supporting conclusions. If they are able to answer the main idea or inferential multiple-choice questions but have difficulty with the open-ended items, they might have difficulty constructing a response. Each open-ended item is accompanied by a rubric. Use the rubrics to determine specific strengths and weaknesses.

Crumb Rubber

Questions 1 and 2 are assessing the ability to comprehend key details. The answers to Questions 1 and 2 are directly started in the article. Questions 3 and 4 are main idea multiple-choice questions. Questions 5 through 8 are inferential/conclusion questions. Questions 7 and 8 require the students to use context to infer the meanings of words. Questions 9, 10, and 11 are open-ended questions designed to assess the ability to support a main idea, summarize, and draw and support a conclusion. To use the results of this assessment to plan instruction, note the following:

- Answering Questions 1 and 2 suggests adequate literal comprehension.
- Answering Questions 3 and 4 suggests adequate comprehension of main ideas.
- Answering any three of Questions 5, 6, 7, and 8 suggests adequate inferential comprehension.
- Answering Questions 9, 10, 11 with a score of 3 for each suggests proficient comprehension of details, main idea and summarizing, and drawing and supporting conclusions. It also suggests adequate responding skills.

If students do poorly overall, check to make sure that they are on the appropriate level and use lookbacks. Retest with the Arctic Fox selection. If students can answer the literal questions but have difficulty with main idea, summarizing, or inferential questions, they may need instruction with deriving main ideas, summarizing, or drawing and supporting conclusions. If they are able to answer the main idea or inferential multiple-choice questions but have difficulty with the open-ended items, they might have difficulty constructing a response. Use the rubrics to determine specific strengths and weaknesses.

Answer Key

The Arctic Fox

1. d	4. b	7. c
2. b	5. d	8. d
3. d	6. a	

9. See rubric.
10. See rubric.
11. See rubric.

Crumb Rubber

1. d	4. b	7. d
2. c	5. d	8. a
3. c	6. d	

9. See rubric.
10. See rubric.
11. See rubric.

Rubrics

Rubric for Arctic Fox

9. Why doesn't the arctic fox mind snow or cold? Support your answer with details from the article. (directly stated details)

Score	0	1	2	3	4
	Details are not supplied or are not accurate or are not from the article.	Only one detail is supplied and is not explained.	Only one detail is supplied and is explained. **or** Two details are supplied but not explained.	Two details are supplied but are only partly explained.	Two details are supplied and explained.

Continued

Score	0	1	2	3	4
Sample Responses		The arctic fox has a thick coat. **or** The artic fox has pads on its feet.	The arctic fox has a warm fur coat that keeps it warm. **or** The arctic fox has furry feet that keep it warm. **or** The arctic fox has a thick fur coat and furry feet.	The arctic fox has a thick fur coat. The thick fur coat keeps it warm. And it has furry feet.	The arctic fox has a thick fur coat and furry feet. The thick fur coat and furry feet keep it warm.

10. Explain why changing the color of its coat helps the arctic fox. Support your answer with information from the article. (summarizing)

Score	0	1	2	3	4
	Answer is too vague or inaccurate	Main idea is hinted at but not fully stated. **or** There are one or two details but no main idea.	Main idea is stated but not supported.	Main idea is stated and partly supported.	Main idea is stated and fully supported.
Sample Responses		The arctic fox changes its coat in summer and winter. **or** The artic fox has a white coat in the winter.	The arctic fox changes its coat to match its surroundings.	The arctic fox changes its coat to match its surroundings. It has a white coat in the winter and a brown coat in the summer.	The arctic fox changes its coat to match its surroundings. It has a white coat in the winter and a brown coat in the summer, so its enemies and the animals it hunts for food have a hard time seeing it.

11. How do you know that the arctic fox is a clever animal? Support your answer with details from the article. (supporting a conclusion)

Score	0	1	2	3	4
	Response is inaccurate or does not provide relevant information.	Conclusion is stated but is only vaguely supported.	Conclusion is stated but is only supported with one detail.	Conclusion is stated but is only supported with two details, or details are not fully explained.	Main idea is stated along with all the key details. Summary is brief and clearly written.
Sample Responses		The arctic fox is clever. It can live in a cold place.	The arctic fox is clever. It can catch animals that are crawling under the snow.	The arctic fox is clever. It can catch animals that are crawling under the snow. And it gets food by following other animals and stealing food from them.	The arctic fox is clever. It can catch animals that are crawling under the snow. It sails on chunks of ice looking for food. And it gets food by following other animals and stealing food from them. It also stores food in its den.

Rubric for Crumb Rubber

9. Why are old tires dangerous to our health? Support your answer with information from the article. (directly stated details)

Score	0	1	2	3	4
	Answer is too vague or inaccurate.	Only one detail is supplied and is not explained.	Only one supporting detail is given and explained.	Two details are supplied but are not fully explained.	Main idea is stated and fully supported.

Score	0	1	2	3	4
Sample Responses		Rats make their nests in old tires. **or** Water collects in old tires. **or** Water in old tires provides an excellent place for mosquitoes to live.	Rats make their nests in old tires and spread disease. **or** Mosquitoes make their homes in old tires. Mosquitoes spread disease.	Rats live in old tires and spread disease. Mosquitoes live and breed in the water in old tires.	Rats and mosquitoes live in old tires and spread disease.

10. Write a brief summary of the section of the article entitled "The Many Uses of Crumb Rubber." (summarizing)

Score	0	1	2	3	4
	Summary is inaccurate or does not provide relevant information.	Summary idea is stated but no supporting details. **or** There are one or two details but no main idea.	Main idea is stated but has just one supporting detail. Summary may be hard to follow.	Main idea is stated but has just two details. Summary might be too lengthy and a little vague in parts.	Main idea is stated along with all the key details. Summary is brief and clearly written.
Sample Responses		Crumb rubber has a lot of uses. **or** Crumb rubber is used on playgrounds.	Crumb rubber has a lot of uses. Crumb rubber is used on playgrounds.	Crumb rubber has a lot of uses. Crumb rubber is used on playgrounds and to make a lot of other stuff.	Crumb rubber has a lot of uses. Crumb rubber is used on playgrounds and to make roads. It is also used to make a number of other products such as car bumpers, mats, and bins.

Rubrics

11. What makes you think that it is difficult to make crumb rubber? Support your answer with details from the article. (supporting a conclusion)

Score	0	1	2	3	4
	Response is in-accurate or does not pro-vide relevant information.	Conclusion is stated but is not supported.	Conclusion is stated but is only supported with one detail or is vaguely supported.	Conclusion is stated but is only supported with two de-tails, or details are not fully explained.	Main idea is stated along with all the key details. Summary is brief and clearly written.
Sample Responses		Crumb rubber is difficult to make.	Crumb rubber is difficult to make. It has to be cut up into small pieces.	Crumb rubber is difficult to make. It has to be cut up into small pieces and steel pieces have to be taken out of it.	Crumb rubber is difficult to make. It has to be cut up into small pieces and frozen so that steel pieces and nylon threads can be re-moved.

Read, Reason, Respond, and Reflect

Survey of Higher-Level Reading and Responding Skills

Read the article and answer the questions that follow.

The Arctic Fox

1. If you saw an arctic fox in the summer and then saw that same fox in the winter, you might not know that it was the same fox. In the summer, the arctic fox has a brownish gray coat. Its coat matches the color of the forest where it lives. That makes it harder for its enemies to see it. It also makes it harder for the animals that the arctic fox is hunting for food to see it. In the winter, the arctic fox's coat turns white. The arctic fox lives in cold places where there is plenty of snow. With its white coat, the arctic fox is hard to see when there is snow on the ground.

2. The arctic fox does not mind snow. Its white fur coat is very thick. It keeps the arctic fox warm. The arctic fox even has furry feet. The fur on the pads of its feet keeps its feet warm even when it is very cold. The artic fox doesn't feel the cold until the temperature drops to 40 degrees below zero.

3. Arctic foxes don't hibernate or sleep through the winter. But many of the animals that it would hunt for food are hibernating. The arctic fox might have to do a lot of extra hunting in order to find food. The arctic fox will hop on a floating chunk of ice and sail along on it to search for food. Arctic foxes also steal other animals' food when they get the chance. Arctic foxes often follow polar bears. When the polar bear catches food, the arctic fox steals some.

4. The arctic fox has a sharp sense of hearing. It can hear animals crawling under the snow. When it hears animals crawling under the snow, it jumps on the snow so that it can break through the snow's crust. Then it grabs the animal that was trying to run under the snow.

5. During the summer, the arctic fox <u>stores</u> food. It hides the food in its den or under rocks. Then it has food for the winter in case it needs it. The arctic fox is able to <u>survive</u> long, cold winters.

Circle the letter of the correct answer.

1. According to paragraph 3, what is the main reason why it is harder for the arctic fox to find food in the wintertime?
   a. It is very cold during the winter in the arctic.
   b. The leaves have fallen from the trees.
   c. It is harder to sneak up on animals when there is snow on the ground.
   d. Many animals that it might hunt for food are hibernating or sleeping in their dens.

2. According to paragraph 4, how does the arctic fox find small animals that are under the snow?
   a. It digs tunnels.
   b. It listens for animals running under the snow.
   c. It looks carefully for signs of tunnels built by small animals.
   d. It hides near the dens of small animals.

3. According to paragraph 2, when will the arctic fox have cold feet?
   a. when the ice begins to freeze
   b. when it is zero degrees
   c. when it is 20 degrees below zero
   d. when it is 50 degrees below zero

4. Paragraph 1 is mainly about
   a. where the arctic fox lives.
   b. the changing of coats by the arctic fox.
   c. what the arctic fox's summer coat looks like.
   d. when the arctic fox grows a white coat.

5. Paragraph 2 is mainly about
   a. what the arctic fox looks like.
   b. where the arctic fox spends its winter.
   c. why the arctic fox lives in a cold place.
   d. how the arctic fox keeps warm in the winter time.

6. From paragraph 3, you can conclude that
   a. the arctic fox must try harder to get food in the wintertime.
   b. the arctic fox sneaks up on hibernating animals.
   c. the arctic fox shares its leftover food.
   d. the arctic fox eats very little during the wintertime.

7. In paragraph 5, the word <u>stores</u> means _____.
   a. eats very slowly
   b. takes from others
   c. puts away for use later
   d. sells to others

8. In paragraph 5, the word <u>survive</u> means _____.
   a. stay outside when it is cold
   b. take a long rest
   c. sleep through the winter
   d. stay alive

9. Why doesn't the arctic fox mind snow or cold? Support your answer with details from the article.

_____

_____

_____

_____

10. Explain why changing the color of its coat helps the arctic fox. Support your answer with information from the article.

_____

_____

_____

_____

11. How do you know that the arctic fox is a clever animal? Support your answer with details from the article.

_____

_____

_____

_____

Read, Reason, Respond, and Reflect

Survey of Higher-Level Reading and Responding Skills

Read the article and answer the questions that follow.

Old Tires

1. Each year, we throw away about one tire for each man, woman, and child living in our country. That comes out to approximately 300 million scrap tires each year. And that number is increasing. Right now there are about two billion scrap tires in the United States.

2. Scrap tires are an eyesore. Millions of scrap tires have been thrown away in fields, empty lots, and even in streams and ponds. Besides being an eyesore, old tires can be dangerous to our health. <u>Discarded</u> tires provide an excellent place for rats to build a nest and raise a family. Water that collects in old tires provides an excellent place for mosquitoes to live and breed. Both rats and mosquitoes can cause disease.

3. In some areas old tires have been collected in dumps. A single scrap tire dump might have a million tires or more. If they catch on fire, these tire dumps send thick smoke billowing into the air. Tires are made mainly of rubber, but oil and chemicals are also used along with rubber to manufacture them. The smoke from burning tires contains chemicals that are poured into the air. Water is used to put out the fires. Unfortunately, the water used to <u>extinguish</u> the fires carries oil and chemicals from the burned tires to nearby streams and pollutes them. That is the bad news about old tires. The good news is that old tires can be put to new uses.

4. Discarded tires can be used to make crumb rubber. Crumb rubber is made by grinding up tires into small pieces.

The Many Uses of Crumb Rubber

5. You might have played on crumb rubber. Crumb rubber can be used to make a soft covering for playgrounds. The crumb rubber covering is six inches thick, so children have a soft landing when they fall. Many playgrounds have surfaces that are made of wood chips, sand, dirt, or asphalt. Asphalt is the black covering that is used to make roads, driveways, parking lots, and the covering for some playgrounds. Crumb rubber is softer than asphalt or dirt. It is even softer than sand or wood chips.

6. Besides being used to construct playground surfaces, crumb rubber can be used to make bumpers and mats for cars. It can be used to manufacture

tiles for floors and bins and buckets. Crumb rubber can be used to make roofs for houses. When mixed with asphalt, crumb rubber is even used to repair old roads and to construct new roads. Roads made from crumb rubber last longer.

Advantages of Crumb Rubber

7. In some ways crumb rubber is superior to other materials. Crumb rubber doesn't rot or get eaten by termites the way wood does. Crumb rubber doesn't smell bad, and it doesn't crack the way some plastics do. Crumb rubber also lasts for a long time. Best of all, making crumb rubber is a good way to get rid of old tires.

Making Crumb Rubber

8. The first step in making crumb rubber is cutting the tire into small pieces. Tires have steel wires and threads inside to make them stronger. The steel wires and threads have to be removed. To get rid of the steel wires and the threads, the tires are frozen at temperatures of 300 degrees below zero. At that temperature, the tires are like glass. Giant hammers break the tires apart into bits of rubber, loose threads, and bits of metal. Powerful magnets are used to extract the bits of steel. Screens and vacuums are used to remove the threads. At last all that is left are small pieces of rubber known as crumbs. The crumbs are then ready to be used in playgrounds or to make new products.

Circle the letter of the correct answer.

1. According to paragraph 6, what happens when roads are made of crumb rubber and asphalt?
   a. The roads are cheaper to make.
   b. The roads are softer.
   c. The roads looks better.
   d. The roads don't wear out as fast.

2. Why are the cut-up tires being used to make crumb rubber frozen at such a low temperature?
   a. This keeps the cut-up tires from catching fire.
   b. This makes the cut-up tires stronger.
   c. This makes it easier to break the cut-up tires into parts.
   d. This makes it easier to add different colors to the cut-up tires.

Read, Reason, Respond, and Reflect

•	....

224

3. Paragraph 3 is mainly about
   a. where old tires can be found.
   b. how do fires in tire dumps get started?
   c. the harmful effects of tires in tire dumps.
   d. why there are so many old tires.

4. Paragraph 5 is mainly about
   a. the many ways in which crumb rubber is used.
   b. why crumb rubber is good for playgrounds.
   c. why kids can get hurt on playgrounds.
   d. the kinds of materials used on playgrounds.

5. The reader can conclude from paragraph 5 that
   a. most playgrounds are now made from crumb rubber.
   b. crumb rubber playgrounds cost more than other playgrounds.
   c. crumb rubber playgrounds are easier to make than other playgrounds.
   d. crumb rubber can help keep kids from being hurt.

6. The reader can conclude from paragraph 7 that crumb rubber
   a. has more uses than wood.
   b. cost more than wood.
   c. looks better than wood.
   d. will probably last longer than wood.

7. In paragraph 2, the word <u>discarded</u> means _____.
   a. very large
   b. taking up space
   c. not costing much
   d. thrown away

8. In paragraph 3, the word <u>extinguished</u> means _____.
   a. put out something that is burning
   b. go away from or disappear
   c. make a mess of something
   d. place in large piles

9. Why are old tires dangerous to our health? Support your answer with information from the article.

   _____

   _____

_____

_____

_____

10. Write a brief summary of the section of the article entitled "The Many Uses of Crumb Rubber."

_____

_____

_____

_____

_____

_____

11. What makes you think that it is difficult to make crumb rubber? Use details from the article to support your answer.

_____

_____

_____

_____

_____

_____

Source: From _Read, Reason, Respond: Boosting Literacy_. Unionville, CT: Galvin Publications. Reprinted by permission.

references

Professional Books

Afflerbach, P. (1990). The influence of prior knowledge on expert readers' main idea construction strategies. *Reading Research Quarterly*, 25, 31–46.

Afflerbach, P. P., & Johnston, P. H. (1986). What do expert readers do when the main idea is not explicit? In J. F. Baumann (Ed.), *Teaching main idea comprehension* (pp. 49–72). Newark, DE: International Reading Association.

Allington, R. L., Johnston, P. H., & Day, J. P. (2002). Exemplary fourth-grade teachers. *Language Arts, 79*, 462–466.

Almasi, J. F., O'Flahavan, J. F., & Arya, P. (2001). A comparative analysis of student and teacher development in more and less proficient discussions of literature. *Reading Research Quarterly*, 36, 96–120.

Anderson, R. C. (1990, May). *Microanalysis of classroom reading instruction*. Paper presented at the Annual Conference on Reading Research, Atlanta, GA.

Anderson, V., & Roit, M. (1993). Planning and implementing collaborative strategy instruction for delayed readers in grades 6–10. *The Elementary School Journal, 94*, 121–137.

Applegate, A. (2004). *Expanding thoughtful literacy in young children: Techniques for developing questions to promote critical response*. Paper presented at the annual meeting of the International Reading Association, Reno.

Applegate, M., Quinn, K., & Applegate, A. J. (2006). Profiles in comprehension. *The Reading Teacher*, 60, 48–57.

Atwell, N. (1987). *In the middle*. Portsmouth, NH: Boynton/Cook.

Baumann, J. F. (1986). The direct instruction of main idea comprehension ability. In J. F. Baumann (Ed.), *Teaching main idea comprehension* (pp. 133–178). Newark, DE: International Reading Association.

Baumann, J. F., Seifert-Kessel, N., & Jones, L. A. (1992). Effect of think-aloud instruction on elementary students' comprehension monitoring abilities. *Journal of Reading Behavior*, 24, 143–172.

Bean, T. W. (2003). *Using young-adult literature to enhance comprehension in the content areas*. Naperville, IL: Learning Points Association. Available online at www.learningpt.org/pdfs/literacy/young.pdf.

Beck, I. L., & McKeown, M. G. (2002). Questioning the author: Making sense of social studies. *Reading and Writing in the Content Areas, 60*(3), 44–47.

Beck, I. L., Omanson, R. C., & McKeown, M. G. (1982). An instructional redesign of reading lessons: Effects on comprehension. *Reading Research Quarterly, 17*, 462–481.

Beers, K. (2003). *When kids can't read, What teachers can do, A guide for teachers 6–12*. Portsmouth, NH: Heinemann.

Benson, V., & Cummins, C. (2002). *The power of retelling, Developmental steps for building comprehension*. Bothell, WA: Wright Group/McGraw-Hill.

Benson-Castagna, V. (2005). *Reciprocal teaching, A workshop*. Houston, TX: Author.

Bereiter, C., & Scardamalia, M. (1982). From conversation to composition: The role of instruction in a developmental process. In R. Glass (Ed.), *Advances in instructional psychology*, volume 2 (pp. 1–64). Hillsdale, NJ: Lawrence Erlbaum.

Berliner, D. (1984). The half-full glass: A review of research on teaching. In P. Hosford (Ed.), *Using what we know about teaching*. Alexandria, Va.: Association for Supervision and Curriculum Development.

Berne, J. I., & Clark, K. F. (2006, May). *Strategic literary discussion: Teachers and students test new ground for comprehension strategy use*. Paper presented at the International Reading Association Convention, Chicago.

Beyer, B. (2001). Putting it all together to improve student thinking. In A. L. Costa (Ed.), *Developing minds, A resource book for teaching thinking* (3rd ed.) (pp. 417–424). Alexandria, VA: Association for Supervision and Curriculum Development.

Beyer, B. (2001). What research says about teaching thinking skills. In A. L. Costa (Ed.). *Developing minds, A resource book for teaching thinking* (3rd ed.) (pp. 275–282). Alexandria, VA: Association for Supervision and Curriculum Development.

Biemiller, A., & Meichenbaum, D. (1992). The nature and nurture of the self-directed learner. *Educational Leadership, 50*(2), 75–80.

Bjorklund, B., Handler, N., Mitten, J., & Stockwell, G. (1998). *Literature circles: A tool for developing students as critical readers, writers, and thinkers*. Paper presented at the 47th Annual Conference of the Connecticut Reading Association, Waterbury, CT.

Blachowicz, C. L. Z. (1986). Making connections: Alternatives to the vocabulary notebook. *Journal of Reading, 29*, 643–649.

Blakeslee, T. (1997). *Writing in science*. Ann Arbor: Michigan Department of Education.

Boyles, N. (2004). *Constructing meaning*. Gainesville, FL: Maupin House.

Boyles, N. (2002). *Teaching written response to text: Constructing quality answers to open-ended comprehension questions*. Gainesville, FL: Maupin House.

Brown, A. L., & Campione, J. C. (1996). Psychological theory and the design of innovative learning environments: On procedures, principles, and systems. In L. Schauble & R. Glaser (Eds.), *Innovations in learning: New environments for education* (pp. 289–325). Mahwah, NJ: Erlbaum.

Buddy, C. (2005). Proficient readers and writers determine what is important in text. Available online at www.madison.k12.wi.us/tnl/langarts/pdf/determine.

Calder, L., & Carlson, S. (2002). *Using "think alouds" to evaluate deep understanding*. Policy Center on the First year of College. Available online at www.brevard.edu/fyc/listserv/remarks/calderandcarlson.htm.

Caldwell, J. H., Huitt, W. G., & Graeber, A. O. (1982). Time spent in learning: Implications from research. *Elementary School Journal, 82*, 471–480.

Caldwell, J., & Leslie, L. (2002). *Does proficiency in middle school reading assure proficiency in high school reading: The possible role of think alouds*. Available online at www.soe.uwm.edu/fileBroker.php/3555/caldwell.doc.

Calkins, L. 2001. *The Art of Teaching Reading*. New York: Longman.

Calkins, L., Hartman, A., & White, Z. (2003). *The conferring handbook, Units of study for primary writing: A yearlong program*. Portsmouth, NH: Heinemann.

Calkins, L., & Mermelstein, L. (2003). *Nonfiction writing: Procedures and reports, Units of study for primary writing: A yearlong program*. Portsmouth, NH: Heinemann.

Calkins, L., & Pessah, L. 2003. *Launching the writing workshop, Units of study for primary writing: A yearlong program*. Portsmouth, NH: Heinemann.

Caruso, C. (1997). Before you cite a site. *Educational Leadership, 55*(3), 24–25.

Christenbury, L., & Kelly, P. (1983). *Questioning: A path to critical thinking*. Urbana, IL: National Council of Teachers of English.

Ciardiello, A. (1998). "Did you ask a good question today?" Alternative cognitive and metacognitive strategies. *Journal of Adolescent & Adult Literacy, 42*, 210–219.

Clay, M. M. (2003, December). *Simply by sailing in a new direction*. Paper presented at the National Reading Conference, Scottsdale, AZ.

College Entrance Examination Board (2003). *The neglected "R," The need for a writing revolution, Report of the National Commission on Writing in America's Schools and Colleges*. Princeton, NJ: Author. Available online at www.writingcommission.org.

Collins, J. L. (2006, April). *The many faces of strategy instruction*. Paper presented at the annual meeting of the American Educational Research Association, San Francisco. Available online at www.gse.buffalo.edu/ePortfolio/view.aspx?u=wirc&pid=407.

Collins J. L. (2005, December). *Writing to enhance comprehension in low-performing urban elementary schools*. Paper presented at the National Reading Conference, Miami. Available online at www.gse.buffalo.edu/ePortfolio/view.aspx?u=wirc&pid=407.

Collins, J. L. (1998). *Strategies for struggling writers*. New York: Guilford Press.

Collins, K. (2005, November). *Growing readers*. Paper presented at the annual meeting of the Connecticut Reading Conference.

Collins, K. (2004). *Growing readers, Units of study in the primary classroom*. Portland, ME: Stenhouse.

Costa, A. L., & Marzano, R. (2001). Teaching the language of thinking. In A. L. Costa (Ed.). *Developing minds, A resource book for teaching thinking* (3rd ed.) (pp. 379–383). Alexandria, VA: Association for Supervision and Curriculum Development.

Chinn, C. A., Anderson, R. C., & Waggoner, M. A. (2001). Patterns of discourse in two kinds of literature discussion. *Reading Research Quarterly, 36*, 378–411

Cummins, C. (2005). *Internalization and transfer of comprehension processes: Integrated strategies using the GO-Chart! Impact on instruction, learning, and motivation*. Paper presented at the National Reading Conference, Miami.

Cunningham, A., & Stanovich, K. (1998). What reading does for the mind. *American Educator*, Spring/Summer, *22*, 8–15.

Daane, M. C., Campbell, J. R., Grigg, W. S., Goodman, M. J., and Oranje, A. (2005). *Fourth-Grade Students Reading Aloud: NAEP 2002 Special Study of Oral*

Reading (NCES 2006-469). U.S. Department of Education, Institute of Education Sciences, National Center for Education Statistics. Washington, DC: Government Printing Office.

Daniels, H. (2002). *Literature circles, Voice and choice in book clubs and reading groups* (2nd ed.). Portland, ME: Stenhouse.

Dennis-Shaw. S. (2006). *Guided comprehension: Making connections using a double-entry journal.* Read• Write• Think. Available online at www.readwritethink .org/lessons/lesson_view.asp?id=228.

Dewitz, P., Carr, E. M., & Patberg, J. P. (1987). Effects of inference training on comprehension and comprehension monitoring. *Reading Research Quarterly, 22,* 99–121.

Dillon, J. T. (1983). *Teaching and the art of questioning.* Bloomington, IN: Phi Delta Kappa.

Duffy, G. G., & Roehler, L. R. (1987). Improving reading instruction through the use of responsive elaboration. *The Reading Teacher, 40,* 514–520.

Dymock, S. (2005). Teaching tips: Teaching expository text structure awareness. *The Reading Teacher, 59,* 177–181.

Ellis, E. (2004). *About graphic organizers: Q&A: What's the big deal with graphic organizers?* Masterminds Publishing. Available online at http://graphicorganizers .com/about.html.

Farr, W. (2004). *Putting it all together: A reading anthology, guided reading and reader's workshop.* Paper presented at the annual meeting of the Connecticut Reading Association, Cromwell.

Fountas, I. C., & and Pinnell, G. S. (2001a). *Guiding readers and writers grades 3–6.* Portsmouth, NH: Heinemann.

Fountas, I. C., & Pinnell, G. S. (2001b). *Using guided reading to strengthen students' reading skills at the developing level grades 1–3.* Portsmouth, NH: Heinemann.

Fredericks, A. D. (1986). Mental imagery activities to improve comprehension. *The Reading Teacher, 40,* 78–81.

Freidman, M.I, (2005). *No school left behind, How to increase student achievement.* Columbia, SC: The Institute for Evidence-Based Decision-Making in Education, Inc.

Gallagher, K. (2005). *Deeper reading, Comprehending challenging texts, 4–12.* Portland, ME: Stenhouse.

Gaskins, I. (2005). *Success with struggling readers, The Benchmark School approach.* New York: Guilford Press.

Gambrell, L. B. (1980). Think time: Implications for reading instruction. *The Reading Teacher, 34,* 143–146.

Gersten, R., & Baker, S. (2000). *Practices for English-language learners. An overview of instructional practices for English-language learners: Prominent themes and future directions* [Topical Summary]. Denver, CO: National Institute for Urban School Improvement (ERIC Document Reproduction Service No. ED 445 176).

Good, T. L., & Brophy, J. E. (1994). *Looking in classrooms.* New York: HarperCollins.

Great Books Foundation (1999). *An introduction to shared inquiry, A handbook for Junior Great Books leaders* (4th ed.). Chicago, IL: Author.

Gunning, T. (2008). *Creating literacy instruction for all students* (6th ed.). Boston: Allyn and Bacon.

Gunning, T. (2006a). *Assessing and correcting reading and writing difficulties* (3rd ed.). Boston: Allyn and Bacon.

Gunning, T. (2006b, December). *An analysis of student performance on basic and higher-level comprehension questions: An exploratory study.* Paper presented at the National Reading Conference, Los Angeles.

Gunning, T. (2006c). *Closing the literacy gap.* Boston: Allyn and Bacon.

Gunning, T. (2006d). *Read, Reason, Respond: Boosting Literacy.* Unionville, CT: Galvin Publications.

Gunning, T. (2005a). *Creating literacy instruction for all students* (5th ed.). Boston: Allyn and Bacon.

Gunning, T. (2005b, November). *Assessing the comprehension processes of good decoding but poor comprehending students.* Paper presented at the National Reading Conference, Miami.

Gunning, T. (2003). *Building literacy in the content areas.* Boston: Allyn and Bacon.

Guthrie, J. T. (2004, May). *Classroom practices promoting engagement and achievement in comprehension.* Keynote Presentation at Reading Research 2004, Reno, NV.

Hansen, J., & Pearson, P. D. (1982). *Improving the inferential comprehension of good and poor fourth-grade readers* (Report No. CSR-TR-235). Urbana: University of Illinois, Center for the Study of Reading (ERIC Document Reproduction No. ED 215–312).

Harris, K. R., & Graham, S. (1996). *Making the writing process work: Strategies for composition and self-regulation.* Cambridge, MA: Brookline.

Harste, J. C., Short, K. G., & Burke, C. (1988). *Creating classrooms for authors: The reading-writing connection.* Portsmouth, NH: Heinemann.

Hyerle, D. (2004). Thinking maps as a transformational language for learning. In D. Hyerle (Ed.) *Student success with thinking maps* (pp. 1–16). Thousand Oaks, CA: Corwin Press.

Hyerle, D. (2001). Visual tools for mapping minds, In A. L. Costa (Ed.). *Developing minds, A resource book for teaching thinking* (3rd ed.) (pp. 401–407). Alexandria, VA: Association for Supervision and Curriculum Development.

Hyman, R. T. (1978). *Strategic questioning.* Englewood Cliffs, NJ: Prentice-Hall.

International Reading Association. (2005). *Literature discussion groups in the intermediate grades.* Newark, DE: Author.

International Reading Association. (2006). *Literacy demands in the workplace.* Newark, DE: Author.

Joyce, B, & Calhoun, E. (1996). School renewal: An inquiry, not a prescription. In B. Joyce and E. Calhoun (Eds.), *Learning experiences in school renewal: An exploration of five successful programs* (pp. 175–190). Eugene, OR: ERIC Clearinghouse on Educational Management, (ERIC Document Reproduction Service No. ED 401 600).

Joyce, B., & Showers, B. (2002). *Student achievement through staff development.* Alexandria, Va: Association for Supervision and Curriculum Development.

Keene, E. O., & Zimmermann, S. (1997). *Mosaic of thought: Teaching reading comprehension in a reader's workshop.* Portsmouth, NH: Heinemann.

Kelleher, M. E., & Larson, A. F. (2006, November). *Using error identification to improve reading instruction.* Paper presented at the Connecticut Reading Association Conference, Cheshire, CT.

Kendall, J., & Khuon, O. (2006). *Making sense: Integrated reading and writing lessons for English language learners.* Portland, ME: Stenhouse.

Kibby, M. W, & Wieland, K. (2004). *How readers think during vocabulary acquisition: Findings from the verbal protocols of good readers when encountering unknown words in context with applications to instruction.* Paper presented at the International Reading Association Convention, Reno.

Kies, D. (2005). *The hypertext books: Underlying assumptions.* Available online at http://papyr.com/hypertextbooks/comp2/assume.htm.

Knox, C. M. (2002). *Accelerated literacy for English language learners (ELLs): A field-tested, research-based model of training and learning.* Paper presented at the annual conference of the International Reading Association, San Francisco.

Krehbiel, C. (2005). *Examining student work: Protocol for improving reading instruction.* Digital Workshop, U.S. Department of Education. Available online at www.paec.org/teacher2teacher/overview9.html.

Lake, J. H. (1973). The influence of wait time on the verbal dimensions of student inquiry behavior. *Dissertations Abstracts International, 34,* 6476A (University Microfilms NO. 74-08866).

Langer, J. A. (1999). *Beating the odds: Teaching middle and high school students to read and write well.* Albany, NY: National Research Center on English Learning and Achievement. (ERIC Document Reproduction Service No. ED 435 993).

Langer, J. A. (1992). Rethinking literature instruction. In J. A. Langer (Ed.), *Literature instruction: Focus on student response* (pp. 35–53). Urbana, IL: National Council of Teachers of English.

Langer, J. A. (1990). Understanding literature. *Language Arts, 67,* 812–816.

Langer, J. A., & Applebee, A. N. (1987). *How writing shapes thinking.* Urbana, IL: National Council of Teachers of English.

Lee, J. (2005, December). *Assessing the effectiveness of writing intensive reading comprehension intervention.* Paper presented at the National Reading Conference, Miami.

Lukens, R. J. (1995). *A critical handbook of children's literature* (5th ed.). New York: HarperCollins.

Lyman, F. (1981). The responsive classroom discussion. In A. S. Anderson (Ed.), *Mainstreaming Digest.* College Park: University of Maryland College of Education.

Madigan, T. (2005). *The development of interactive thinksheets to bring reading and writing together.* Paper presented at the National Reading Conference, Miami.

Manzo, A. V. (1969). The ReQuest procedure. *Journal of Reading, 13,* 123–126.

Manzo, A. V., Manzo, U. C., & Albee, J. J. (2004). *Reading assessment for diagnostic-prescriptive teaching.* Belmont, CA: Wadsworth/Thomson.

Marzano, R. J. (2004). *Building background knowledge for academic achievement.* Alexandria, Va: Association for Supervision and Curriculum Development.

Marzano, R. J., Gaddy, B. B., & Dean, C. (2000). *What works in classroom instruction.* Aurora, CO: Mid-Continent Research for Education and Learning.

McGinley, W. J., & Denner, P. R. (1987). Story impressions: A prereading/writing activity. *Journal of Reading, 31,* 248–253.

Meichenbaum, D., & Biemiller, A. (1998). *Nurturing*

independent learners: Helping students take charge of their learning. Cambridge, MA: Brookline Books.

Menke, P. J., & Pressley, M. (1994). Elaborative interrogation: Using "why" questions to enhance learning from text. *Journal of Reading, 37,* 642–645.

Moldofsky, P. B. (1983). Teaching students to determine the central story problem: A practical application of schema theory. *The Reading Teacher, 38,* 377–382.

Monti, D., & Cicchetti, G. (1993). *TARA: Think-aloud reading assessment.* Roslyn, NY: Berrent Publications.

Mullis, I. V. S., Martin, M. O., Gonzalez, E. J., & Kennedy, A. M. (2003). *PIRLS 2001 International report: IEA's study of reading literacy achievement in primary schools in 35 countries.* Chestnut Hill, MA: Boston College.

Murphy, P. K., & Edwards, M. E. (2004, April). *What the studies tell us: A meta-analysis of discussion approaches.* Paper presented at the meeting of American Educational Research Association, Montreal, Canada.

Myers. P. N. (2005–2006). The princess story teller: Clara Clarifier, Quincy Questioner, and the Wizard: Reciprocal teaching adapted for kindergarten students. *The Reading Teacher, 59,* 314–324.

Nation, P. (2001). *Learning vocabulary in another language.* Cambridge: Cambridge University Press.

National Assessment Governing Board (2005). *Reading framework for the 2009 National Assessment of Educational Progress.* Washington, DC: American Institutes for Research.

National Center for Educational Statistics (2005). *NAEP questions.* Available online at http://nces.ed.gov/nationsreportcard/reading/.

Nessel, D. (1987). The new face of comprehension instruction: A closer look at questions. *The Reading Teacher,* 40, 604–606.

New Literacies Research Team (2006). *Results summary report, Survey of internet usage and online reading, Research Report Nos. 1–6.* Storrs, CT: Neag School of Education, University of Connecticut. Available online at www.newliteracies.uconn.edu/pubs.html.

Norton, D. E. (1989). *Through the eyes of a child.* Columbus, OH: Merrill.

Nuthall, G. (1999). The way students learn: Acquiring knowledge from an integrated science and social studies unit. *The Elementary School Journal, 99,* 303–341.

Nuthall, G. (1996, December). *What role does ability play in classroom learning?* Paper presented at the meeting for the New Zealand Association for Research in

Education. Neslon, New Zealand. (Eric Document Reproduction Service No. ED 414042)

Oakes, J., Gamoran, A., & Page, R. (1992). Curriculum differentiation: Opportunities, outcomes and meanings. In P. Jackson (Ed.), *Handbook of research on curriculum* (pp. 570–608). New York: Macmillan.

Oczkus, L. (2005). *Reciprocal teaching strategies at work, Improving reading comprehension, grades 2–6* (videorecording). Newark, DE: International Reading Association.

Oczcus, L. (2003). *Reciprocal teaching at work: Strategies for improving reading comprehension.* Newark, DE: International Reading Association.

O'Flahavan, J. F. (1994). Teacher role options in peer discussions about literature. *The Reading Teacher,* 48, 354–356.

Olson, J. L. (1987). Drawing to write. *School Arts, 87*(1), 25–27.

Palincsar, A. S., & Brown, A. L. (1986). Interactive teaching to promote independent learning from text. *The Reading Teacher, 39,* 771–777.

Paul, R., & Elder, L. (2001). *Critical thinking: Tools for taking charge of your learning and your life.* New York: Prentice Hall.

Pearson, P. D., Cervetti, G., Jaynes, C., & Flanders, A. (2003). *Using research to guide professional development within the CIERA school change project: The case of comprehension instruction in Patterson Elementary School.* Ann Arbor, MI: CIERA.

Perie, M., Grigg, W., and Donahue, P. (2005). *The Nation's Report Card: Reading 2005* (NCES 2006-451). U.S. Department of Education, National Center for Education Statistics. Washington, DC: U.S. Government Printing Office.

Peterson, P. L., & Swing, S. R. (1982). Beyond time on task: Students' reports of their thought processes during class-room instruction. *Elementary School Journal, 82,* 481–491.

Piercey, T. D., & Hyerle, D. (2004). Maps for the road to reading comprehension. In D. Hyerle (Ed.), *Student success with thinking maps* (pp. 63–73). Thousand Oaks, CA: Corwin Press.

Portalupi, J., & Fletcher, R. (2004). *Teaching the qualities of writing.* Portsmouth, NH: Heinemann.

Presseisen, B. Z. (2001). Thinking skills: Meanings and models revisited. In A. L. Costa (Ed.), *Developing minds: A resource book for teaching thinking* (pp. 47–57). Alexandria, VA: Association for Supervision and Curriculum Development.

Pressley, M., Johnson, C. J., Symons, S., McGoldrick, J. A., & Kurita, J. A. (1989). Strategies that improve children's memory and comprehension of what is read. *Elementary School Journal, 89*, 3–32.

Princiotta, D., Flanagan, K. D., and Germino Hausken, E. (2006). *Fifth grade: Findings from the fifth-grade follow-up of the early childhood longitudinal study, kindergarten class of 1998–99 (ECLS-K)* (NCES 2006-038) U.S. Department of Education. Washington, DC: National Center for Education.

Rapaport, W. J. (2004, May). *What is "context" in contextual vocabulary acquisition? Lessons learned from artificial intelligence and verbal protocol of good readers when they encounter unknown words in context.* Paper presented at the International Reading Association Convention, Reno.

Raphael, T. E. (1986). Teaching question/answer relationships, revisited. *The Reading Teacher, 39*, 516–522.

Raphael, T. E. (1984). Teaching learners about sources of information for answering questions. *The Reading Teacher, 28,* 303–311.

Raphael, T. E., Florio-Ruane, S., George, A., Hasty, N. L., & Highfield, K. (2004). *Book club plus, A literacy framework for the primary grades.* Newark, DE: International Reading Association.

Reeves, D. (2003). *High performance in high poverty schools: 90/90/90 and beyond.* Center for Resource Assessment. Available online at www.makingstandardswork.com/ResourceCtr/fullindex.htm.

Reeves, D. 2000. *Accountability in action.* Denver, CO: Advanced Learning Press.

Resnick, L. B. (1999, June 16). Making America smarter. *Education Week on the Web, 18.* Available online at www.edweek.org/ew/vol-18/40resnick.h18.

Resnick, L. B., & Hall, M. W. (2001). *The principles of Learning: Study tools for educators.* [CD-ROM, version 2.0]. Pittsburgh, PA: University of Pittsburgh, Learning Research and Development Center, Institute for Learning. <www.instituteforlearning.org>.

Richards, J. C., & Gipe, J. P. (1993). Getting to know story characters: A strategy for young and at-risk readers. *The Reading Teacher, 47*, 78–79.

Rosenshine, B., & Meister, C. (1994). Reciprocal teaching: A review of the intervention studies. *Review of Educational Research, 64, 479–530.*

Rodriguez-Brown, F. V. Worthman, C., Burnison, J. C., & Cheung, A. (Eds.), *47th Yearbook of the National Reading Conference* (pp. 90–102). Chicago, IL: National Reading Conference.

Rosenshine, B., Meister, C., & Chapman, S. (1996). Teaching students to generate questions: A review of the intervention studies. *Review of Educational Research, 66*, 181–221.

Rowe, M. B. (1969). Science, silence, and sanctions. *Science for Children, 6*(6), 11–13.

Salinger, T., Kamil, M., Kapinus, B., & Afflerbach, P. (2005). Development of a new framework for the NAEP reading assessment. In B. Maloch, J. V. Hoffman, D. L. Schallert, C. M. Fairbanks, & J. Worthy (Eds.). *54th yearbook of the National Reading Conference* (pp. 334–338). Oak Creek, WI: National Reading Conference.

Santa, C. M., Havens, L. T., & Maycumber, E. M. (1996). *Creating independence through student-owned strategies* (2nd ed.). Dubuque, IA: Kendall/Hunt.

Showers, B., Murphy, C. & Joyce, B. (1996). The River City program: Staff development becomes school improvement. In B. Joyce & E. Calhoun (Eds.), *Learning experiences in school renewal: An exploration of five successful programs* (pp. 13–51). Eugene, OR: ERIC Clearinghouse on Educational Management. (ED 401 600).

Stahl, S. A., & Kapinus, B. A. (1991). Possible sentences: Predicting word meanings to teach content area vocabulary. *The Reading Teacher, 45,* 36–43.

Staton, J. (1984). Thinking together: Language interaction in children's reasoning. In C. Thaiss & C. Suhor (Eds.), *Speaking and writing, K–12: Classroom strategies and the new research.* Urbana, IL: National Council of Teachers of English.

Stauffer, M. H. (1999). *Online on literary elements.* University of South Florida. Available online at www.cas.usf.edu/lis/lis6585/class/litelem.html.

Stauffer, R. G. (1970). *Reading-thinking skills.* Paper presented at the annual reading conference at Temple University, Philadelphia.

Stauffer, R. G. (1969). *Directing reading maturity as a cognitive process.* New York: Harper & Row.

Sternberg, R. (1985). *Beyond IQ: A triarchic theory of human intelligence.* Cambridge, England: Cambridge University Press.

Sutherland, Z. (1997). *Children and books* (9th ed.). Glenview, IL: Scott Foresman.

Taba, H. (1965). The teaching of thinking. *Elementary English, 42,* 534–542.

Temple, C., Martinez, M., Yokota, J., & Naylor, A. (1998). *Children's books in children's hands: An introduction to their literature.* Boston: Allyn and Bacon.

Torgesen, J. K. (2004, May). *Adolescent literacy, reading comprehension, & the FCAT*. Paper presented at the CLAS Conference, Naples, FL. Available online at www.fcrr.org/science/sciencePresentationsTorgesen.htm.

Valencia, S. (2001). *Integrated theme tests, Levels 2.1–2.1*. Houghton Mifflin Reading. Boston: Houghton Mifflin, p. 10.

Vockell, E. (2004). *Educational psychology: A practical approach*. Available online at http://education.calumet.purdue.edu/Vockell/EdPsyBook/.

Vygotsky, L. S. (1981). The development of higher forms of attention in childhood. In J. V. Wertsch (Ed.), *The concept of activity in Soviet psychology*. Armonk, NY: Sharpe.

Westby, C. (1999). Assessing and facilitating text comprehension problems. In H. W. Catts & A. G. Kamhi (Eds.), *Language and reading disabilities* (pp. 154–223). Boston: Allyn and Bacon.

Whitley, S. (2005). *Memletics concept mapping course*. Memletics.com. Available online at www.memletics.com/.

Williams, D. (1999, December). Learning to teach better by examining student work. Chicago: *Catalyst*. Available online at www.catalyst-chicago.org/12-99/129main.htm.

Williams, J. P. (1986). Research and instructional development on main idea skills. In J. F. Baumann (Ed.), *Teaching main idea comprehension* (pp. 73–95). Newark, DE: International Reading Association.

Wilson, J. (1960). *Language and the pursuit of truth*. London: Cambridge University Press.

Wood, K. (1984). Probable passages: A writing strategy. *The Reading Teacher, 37*, 496–499.

Yopp, R. H., &, Yopp, H. K. (2000). *Literature-based reading activities* (3rd ed.). Boston: Allyn and Bacon.

Yuill, N., & Oakhill, J. (1991). *Children's problems in text comprehension: An experimental investigation* (Cambridge Monographs & Texts in Applied Psycholinguistics). New York: Cambridge University Press.

Zapatopia (2006). *The Pacific Northwest tree octopus*. Available online at http://zapatopi.net/treeoctopus/.

Zinsser, W. (1988). *Writing to learn*. New York: Harper & Row.

Trade Books

Allard, H. (1977). *Miss Nelson is missing*. Boston: Houghton Mifflin.

Bunting, E. (1997). *December*. San Diego, CA: Harcourt.

Carle, E. (1987). *Have you seen my cat?* New York: Scholastic.

Cisneros, S. (1991) "Eleven." In S. Cisneros, *Woman Hollering Creek and other stories*. New York: Random House.

Defoe, D. (1719, 1998). *Robinson Crusoe*. Mineola, NY: Dover.

Ginsburg, M. (1972). *The chick and the duckling*. New York: Simon & Schuster.

George, J. C. (1959). *My side of the mountain*. New York: Dutton.

Hall, K. (1995). *A bad, bad, day*. New York: Scholastic.

Hill, E. (1980). *Where's Spot?* New York: Putnam.

Lee, H. (1961). *To kill a mockingbird*. New York: HarperCollins.

Lionni, L. (1963). *Swimmy*. New York: Knopf.

Lowry, L. (2004). *Messenger*. Boston: Houghton Mifflin.

McGovern, A. (1968). *Stone soup*. New York: Scholastic.

Nodset, J. L. (1963). *Who took the farmer's hat?* New York: HarperCollins.

O'Brien, R. C. (1971). *Mrs. Frisby and the rats of NIMH*. New York: Aladdin.

Odell, S. (1960). *The island of the blue dolphins*. New York: Dell.

Paulsen, G. (1987). *Hatchet*. New York: Simon & Schuster,

Pomerantz, C. (1984). *Where's the bear?* New York: Greenwillow.

Soros, B. (1998). *Grandmother's song*. Cambridge, MA: Barefoot Books.

Soto, G. (1993). *Too many tamales*. New York: Putnam's.

Steig, W. (1988). *Brave Irene*. New York: Farrar, Straus, Giroux.

Stolz, M. (1992), *Stealing home*. New York: HarperCollins.

Ziefert, H. 1996). *The turnip*. New York: Penguin.

index